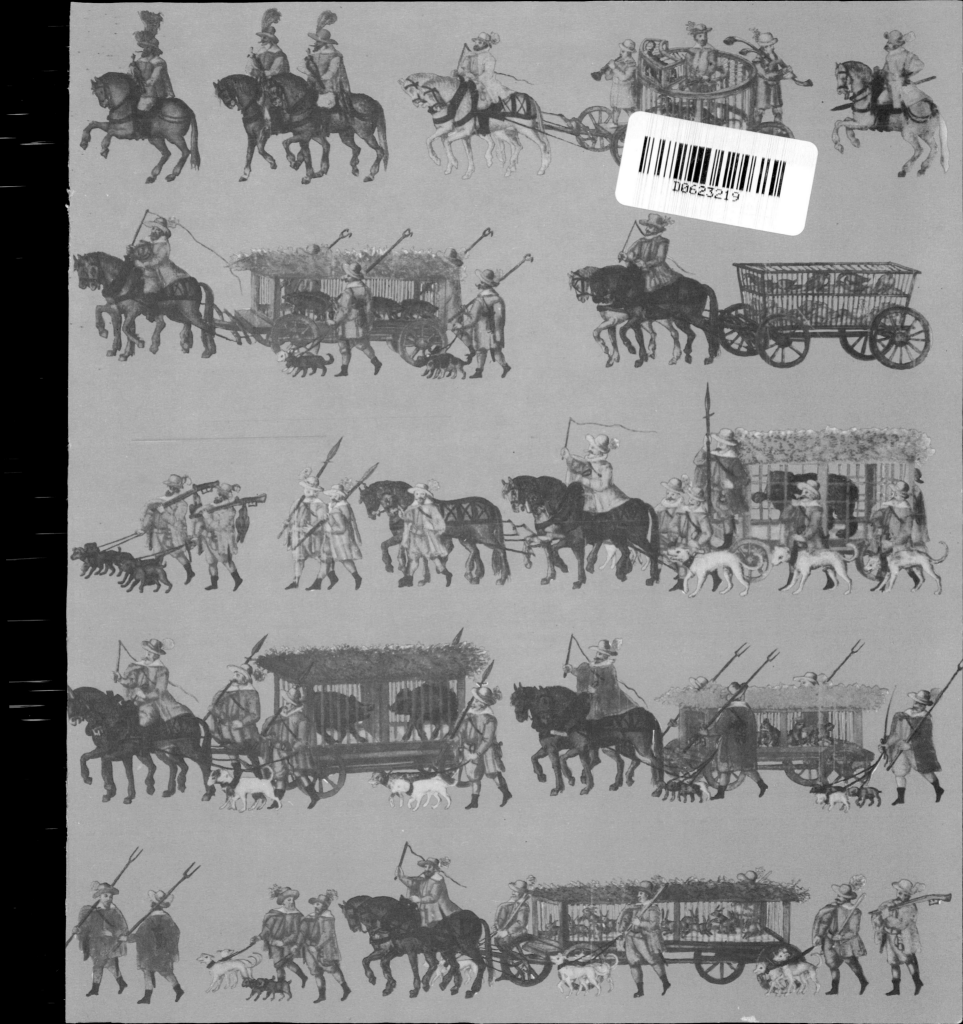

Erich Hobusch

Fair Game

A History of Hunting, Shooting and Animal Conservation

ARCO PUBLISHING, INC.
New York

English version by Ruth Michaelis-Jena
and Patrick Murray, M.B.E., F.S.A. (Scot)

Published 1980 by Arco Publishing, Inc.
219 Park Avenue South, New York, N.Y. 10003
Copyright © 1980 by Edition Leipzig
All rights reserved
Printed in the German Democratic Republic
Library of Congress Cataloging in Publication Data
Hobusch, Erich.
  Fair game.
  Bibliography: p. 273
  1. Hunting—History. 2. Wildlife conservation—
History. 3. Wildlife management—History. I. Title.
SK21.H6   333. 95'4   80–19008
ISBN 0–668–05101–9

Contents

Introduction

There are many accounts of hunting and shooting of all times and from many countries reports of hunting for the sole purpose of acquiring food and clothing in order to maintain at best a precarious existence, and, at the other end of the scale, accounts of lavishly organised hunts, magnificent trophies, expeditions and safaris full of adventure. We also learn about the extermination of whole species of animals, but equally of the protection and conservation of rare animals and plants.

Nowadays many a critical question is asked as to why people want to shoot and what their position is concerning wildlife in general and its conservation. Is a passion for hunting and shooting or the wish for relaxation and recreation sufficient justification for blood sports?

With many people the mere mention of shooting stirs a feeling of compassion with "the poor animals". This somewhat sentimental notion is the foundation of many of the nature conservation movements, originating in the nineteenth century. They demanded complete protection for all animals. Conservationists and people interested in blood sports have always passionately defended their own position and ethics, and both factions are united in condemning reckless shooting and demanding fair rules for hunting and shooting in order to secure the protection of game.

A true sportsman will honour tradition and fair rules, and acknowledge that these very rules help towards maintaining the balance of nature.

Yet, the controversy between the shooting lobby and that for complete conservation goes on and cannot apparently be solved. Questions arising can neither be answered by a song in praise of hunting and shooting nor by a romantic love for unspoilt nature. Hunting and shooting should, however, not be an egoistic pleasure indulged by a privileged minority who for enjoyment only is willing to upset nature's balance. Increasingly responsible sportsmen, scientists and nature lovers started to make their voices heard during the nineteenth century, demanding laws concerning hunting and shooting and scientifically founded nature conservation. The choice between blood sports and nature conservation is largely irrelevant today as both sides now join in protecting our natural resources.

Certainly nature should be protected for the good of mankind, and equally there should be hunting and shooting within a set of rules. Neither pleasure nor commercial considerations should allow one-sided interference with nature. Genuine protection exists in a balance dictated by common sense, taking into account aesthetic as well as commercial considerations. In that way hunting and shooting and conservation will join to create conditions for animals to survive in their natural habitat.

Even though the character of hunting and shooting is constantly changing with changing social conditions, the keeping of the ecological balance of nature and preservation of nature's riches for future generations must always remain of prime importance.

Interest in wildlife is now worldwide, including the concern for the protection of endangered species. National and international associations have drawn up many proclamations, and under the patronage of the United Nations and their special organisations important international agreements concerning man's natural environment have been reached. These agreements prohibit the dealing in 178 kinds of mammals, 113 different birds and 58 kinds of reptiles, amphibia and fish. Game has been hunted and coursed for thousands of years but it has only been properly protected for a few decades and thus saved from annihilation.

A seventeenth-century report states literally that the Lord High Master of the Chase for the Holy Roman Empire, the Most Serene Elector of Saxony, Burgrave of Magdeburg, Duke Johann Georg I had caught himself, shot or driven during his reign—from 1611 to 1655—116,906 game animals. His son, the Elector Johann Georg II of Saxony killed during his reign—from 1656 to 1680—the vast number of 111,141 animals which means an average of thirteen a day.

To kill at least thirteen animals a day over twenty years has nothing to do with noble sport. Reports like these have been repeated in social histories over the centuries. But on checking the original sources* it is easily discovered that hunting reports of the period accredited the absolute monarch alone with the whole bag of the

---

* "Vorzeichnis was Ihre Churf. Durchl. zu Sachsen in Viertzig Jahren von den 11. July Anno 1611 bis auff den 20. Dez. Anno 1650 an Hohen und Niedrigen Wildpret in Jagen, Pirschen, Streiffen und Hetzen geschossen, gefangen und gehetzt." MS. in the Landesbibliothek, Dresden, R 7 b, 373 B 1.

day, even though the mighty prince would only take part in a few hunts each year. It was to glorify the hunting success of his master for future generations that the chronicler counted all game killed at court hunts as killed by his monarch. So the legend grew of fabulous hunting success and the passion for hunting of whole generations of hunters, who, fascinated by the chase, achieved miraculous quarry.

If nowadays a good shot kills thirteen game animals at any time on his hunting ground, this very ground is considered a rich one. But does a big bag or enormous trophies really mean all that much to today's sportsman? Surely, he is more responsible and aware of the part his activities play in the general ecology of modern life. He does realise that sport is much more than mere shooting.

The present book sets out to investigate the effects that hunting and shooting have had on wildlife at different periods of man's history, and how it was responsible for the reduction or even annihilation of certain species under varying historical conditions.

It is impossible to go into all aspects of the history of field sports and the protection of wildlife. We shall, however, attempt to show through examples how different ways of hunting, shooting and trapping were used in different regions of the world. Methods of game conservation will also be discussed.

My special thanks are due to the forest supervisor Dr. R. Bösener (†), onetime Forestry Department Tharandt of the Technical University Dresden, for his valuable assistance in the interpretation of technical questions, also Dr. E. Schwartz, Eberswalde, Dr. R. Weinhold, Bereich Kulturgeschichte/Volkskunde am Zentralinstitut für Geschichte of the Academy of Sciences of the German Democratic Republic, and Dr. K. Sälzle, late Director of the Deutsches Jagdmuseum München for their much appreciated advice. Finally I wish to thank most warmly the members of Edition Leipzig as well as the scientific staff of various museums and photographic collections who have all supported me generously during my work on the text and illustrations of this book.

Berlin 1977   Erich Hobusch

1 Start of the hunt

2 Hunting Register 1611—1656 of the Elector Johann Georg I of Saxony.
Sächsische Landesbibliothek, Manuscript Collection, Dresden

3 Lucas Cranach the Elder: Stag hunt of the Elector Johann Friedrich of Saxony,
arranged for Emperor Charles V. 1544, Prado, Madrid

4 *A night's hunting at the Kama River in the Soviet Union*

5 *Herd of fallow deer in flight*

Game and the Hunt in Prehistoric Society

1   "Great Frieze" with hunters, cattle, stags and ibex (section). Rock painting from the Mesolithic Age. Alpera/Albacete, Eastern Spain

Famous Prehistoric Hunting Settlements

"Through thousands of years the ancestors of man lived solely by hunting and for hunting. Hunting secured their existence, supplying food and clothing. Primitive man's passion for hunting determined his relation to nature."

World Exhibition of Hunting and Shooting 1971,
Budapest — Man and Nature — Hunting all over the World.

Scientific research and excavations have provided much knowledge about hunting in prehistoric times. We can now reconstruct the various methods of trapping and hunting used by Neolithic man. Apart from the study of the actual hunting techniques and hunting weapons, several methods for the qualitative and quantitative analysis of bone material found, have been developed. With the help of the Carbon 14 method (measuring the decay of the radioactive carbon isotope in organic material) a relatively exact dating of finds has been made possible. Some 20,000 of the mammoth *(Elephas primigenius)* * were, for example, found in Europe, some 50,000 in Siberia and several thousands in Alaska and America.

In 1974 archaeologists in the German Democratic Republic made new and sensational discoveries concerning groups of Palaeolithic hunters who hunted big game some 350,000 years ago in Central Europe in the wooded steppes of the so–called Yarmouth–Interglacial period.

Commissioned by the Academy of Sciences of the German Democratic Republic, prehistorians from the Landesmuseum für Vorgeschichte in Halle/Saale uncovered in Bilzingsleben in Thuringia on the banks of the Wippra a hunting settlement of early Pleistocene man. During the excavation work in 1974 two parts of a skull

* Terms adopted are those of *Grzimeks Tierleben—Enzyklopädie des Tierreiches.* Zurich, 1967, Vol. 13.

(back of the head) and part of a pelvic bone of early man were found and preserved. Anthropologists ascribed these finds to a stage in the development of *Homo erectus*. This is the most northerly point so far for the discovery of remains of early man. Well known finds near Heidelberg (lower jaw found at Mauer in 1907), in Chou–K'ou–Tien and Lan–T'ien in China, Sangiran in Java, the Olduvai Gorge in East Africa and Ternifine in Algeria were supplemented in recent years by finds at Vértesszőllős in Hungary, where another hunting settlement of prehistoric man was excavated. Perhaps the oldest in Europe was found recently near Nice on the Côte d'Azur. At a depth of 15 metres a 400,000 years old settlement which possibly served for summer hunting and fishing, was laid bare in the dunes. Thanks to modern methods of excavation a complete reconstruction has become possible of the way of life of early Stone Age hunting groups. This means at one and the same time an exact analysis of the surroundings of these people. Even though reports of this particular excavation have not yet been published, the following picture may already be formed of the life and habitat of these hunters:

The Bilzingsleben camp settlement was found to be situated at the course of a small stream into a larger lake. Because of the existing layer of sand below the limestone (Travertine) the different periods of settlement could be exactly determined in the limestone, and the stores containing the hunters' quarry could be carefully excavated. This particular find showed a special "bone culture", with the hunters mainly using utensils made from bone, in contrast to the Later Stone Age settlements.

All bone utensils found at Bilzingsleben show clear traces of fashioning. Also early stone tools were discovered which are likely to have served for piercing hides. No clothing nor proofs of the use of fire were found so far in the course of the excavation.

The main quarry of these hunters was the Pleistocene wood elephant, about 5 metres tall. In Bilzingsleben a tusk 3.50 metres long and with a diameter at its base of 40 centimetres was excavated. The existence has been proved also of the rhinoceros of the forest and several kinds of deer, including the giant stag. Typical representatives of the fauna of the period in and near the water whose bones were excavated, are the beaver and several kinds of fish. Also bones of a much bigger variety of beaver than the present Castor beaver were found. As an exact scientific report of the finds is being prepared, a full list of animals hunted by Early Pleistocene man, should be available in the not too distant future. But even with the results of excavations available so far, a fairly clear picture emerges about the life style and hunting habits of *Homo sapiens fossilis*.

Next to fossilized bones, we now have another important source material for the study of the hunt in prehistoric times. This material is also the oldest authentic proof of man's artistic activity. The unique pictorial documents were created by Early Stone Age hunters more than 20,000 years ago, when they made drawings of the animals they hoped to capture in rocks and caves.

And what have we learnt from the discovery of these cave paintings which have been known to exist in Southwest Europe for the last hundred years?

It was the year 1868. In the bare, rocky, sun-drenched lands of Santillana del Mar, a little coastal town in the Northwest of Spain, one of the annual battues was taking place. A fox was being run. Suddenly the gamekeeper's dog had disappeared without a trace. During the search for it, a plaintive whimper was heard from the depth of a cave. Luckily the dog was rescued from the subterranean passage which led to a cave. Hollows and clefts are nothing extraordinary in the country by the Bay of Biscay, and the huntsmen took no further notice. Yet we owe the knowledge of one of the most beautiful and marvellous manifestations of Palaeolithic art to this chance happening.

Seven years later, in 1875, Don Marcellino de Sautuola undertook extensive research in the cave. He discovered several bones with strange drawings scratched on them. These fossilized bone engravings attracted much attention at the World Exhibition in Paris in 1878. Until then representations of the prehistoric hunt and animals of the period were practically unknown.

Fresh interest in these finds was kindled when a year later news came from the same cave. The twelve-year-old daughter of Don Marcellino, Maria, suddenly discovered on the low roof of the great hall of the cave a beautiful painting of animals, executed in bright red, brown and yellow shades. The little girl's surprised shouting: "Papa, mira, toros pintados!" became known all over the world. Indeed, Maria had discovered the first important prehistoric cave paintings, and the cave was called after the girl's exclamation "Altamira".

At the International Congress for Anthropology and Prehistoric Archaeology, in Lisbon in 1880 the first reproductions of these animal pictures were shown as lithographs. Experts from everywhere, however, considered them fakes made by a clever dilettante, and after that the cave paintings were again forgotten. It was not until 9 October 1902 that the professionals officially accepted the authenticity of the unique animal frieze of Altamira, recognising it as the most beautiful and interesting example of Palaeolithic cave painting.

Meantime more caves with a great number of rock paintings had been discovered. They all were without a doubt of prehistoric origin, and at last the Altamira paintings gained their proper place in the art works of the period, and made for a better understanding of hunters and hunting during the Palaeolithic Age.

The cave—280 metres long—consists of several great halls where more than 150 rock paintings in beautiful colours are preserved. For these paintings the artists used simple mineral colours such as ochre, red chalk, manganic earth and several iron oxide materials. The figures of animals were painted mostly in red, brown and black tones of varying shades.

The cave of Altamira alone accounts for seventeen different colours, but blue and green are completely absent. To light these dark caves, torches were used, also bowls filled with animal fat. The wick was most likely made from the intestines of animals. The multi-coloured frieze on the roof of the Gran Sala, "the Great Hall of the Beasts" at Altamira, is certainly one of the most impressive of all Palaeolithic paintings.

The main material for representation at that period are the hunted animals themselves. Hunting provided food, in fact all the basic needs of Palaeolithic man's existence. This need for obtaining quarry characterised prehistoric hunting and also inspired the artist.

We must then ask ourselves who were the painters of these animals and hunting scenes which were discovered in more than 120 caves in Northern Spain and Southern France?

The pictures are dated as belonging to a late culture of the Palaeolithic Age, and were most widely spread in the so-called Franco-Cantabrian circle. They are the works of groups of hunters, and reached a climax in prehistoric art during the Middle and Late Magdalenian period—the final Pleistocene culture. Tourists from all over the world now visit the caves in great numbers. In recent years Lascaux alone saw 100,000 visitors annually.

The best known and most impressive rock paintings are the following caves in the Southwest of Europe:—

Sketches of the best known drawings:	Name and place of cave: (country, district)	discovered in:		representing	techniques employed
	ALTAMIRA Santander Spain	1875/ 1879	cave, 280 m long, with famous ceiling paintings in the *Gran Sala*, the Hall of the Beasts.	more than 150 animals, mainly bison, stag and horse	figures: brown, black and ochre
	FONT–DE–GAUME Dordogne France	1901	long, narrow cave, 124 m long (size of figures up to 2.07 m). In the same rock as Les Combarelles.	more than 200 figures, among them 80 bison, 23 mammoths, 40 horses, 17 reindeer and 1 bear	painting in red, brown and black
	CASTILLO near Puente Viesgo Santander Spain	1903	cave, over 300 m long; with excavation layer 18-20 m deep, in the valley of Rio Pas.	mainly stag, bison, horse and more than 50 impressions of human hands.	red and brown figures of animals
	NIAUX Ariège France	1906	Well preserved paintings in the "Black Hall"; a cave some 1,400 m long.	more than 25 bison, 16 horses and 6 ibex	mainly black paintings; in the loamy soil engravings of bison and fish.
	LA PASIEGA near Puente Viesgo Santander, Spain	1911	Ramified cave close to El Castillo	226 coloured wall paintings, 86 engraved figures, wild horses, stags and cattle	paintings many times painted over, probably seven layers of painting, mainly red, yellow and black; well preserved.
	LASCAUX near Montignac Dordogne France	1940	The most important Palaeolithic cave; very well preserved paintings.	over 60 horses, 20 of cattle, many stags, 7 bison, 6 wild cats, 1 bear	mainly ochre, iron oxide and manganite
	LE PECH–MERLE Lot France	1922	The biggest of all caves, containing paintings. Main gallery— 120 × 18 m	mammoths, cattle and horses	mainly black figures of animals
	ROUFFIGNAG Dordogne France	1956		42 mammoths, 27 ibex, 14 bison, 17 horses, 11 rhinoceroses	partly engraved, partly black paint; excellent representation of rhinoceros and mammoth
	PINDAHL at Colombres–Pimiango Oviedo Spain	1908	Situated above a difficult cliff above the Bay of Biscay	wild horses, bison, elephants, sea fish and stags	important paintings and engravings in red
	LES–TROIS–FRERES cave Ariège France	1904		more than 600 engravings of animals, some only 10 cm large, mainly bison, reindeer and wild horses	technique related to engraving on ivory. Only "sorcerer" in colour—mask of a stag.

In the famous caves of the Franco–Cantabrian circle more than a thousand different paintings and engravings in the rock have been listed, all dealing mainly with animals. Nearly every animal species hunted at the time is portrayed: mammoth, woolly–haired rhinoceros, reindeer, bison, wild horse, cave–bear, wolf, ibex and antelope. There are also fish and birds among the many species shown. Some fur–bearing animals and small rodents are missing in the pictures although they are present in bone finds. More than twenty caves also show representations of man. One of the most important of these is the so–called sorcerer from the Trois Frère cave in the department of Ariège in the south of France.

Clothed in the skin of a wild horse, and wearing an animal head–mask, a long beard, the ears of a wolf and a stag's antlers, the sorcerer is supposed to cast a spell over the animals to be hunted. The wishful thinking of the Ice Age hunter is expressed in these ritual scenes of sympathetic magic. The roots of this thought go back to the time of groups of Palaeolithic hunters who through sympathetic magic, sacrifice, dance and magic formulae hoped to gain rich quarry. As the writer Brentjes (1968) put it: "With sympathetic magic hunting weapons are thrown at the rock paintings, and it was believed that these very weapons would kill the same animals during the actual hunt. But the magic would only work if the animals were represented as close to nature as possible and so these animal pictures often are extremely life–like."

Recently archaeologists from the Soviet Union discovered a hunting settlement in the Urals, in the caves of Shulgan Tash. There they found red–coloured drawings of eleven mammoths, one rhinoceros, three wild horses, a bison as well as the representation of a "bear–man". The age of these pictures is estimated at some 15,000 to 18,000 years.

In prehistoric hunting magic the representation of the animal on stones and rocks was not looked at as a work of art, rather was it considered a real thing. These magical religious rites and traditions remain alive with many peoples to the present day. Through the strong emotional effect of the ceremonies connected with the cult, the keenly desired wild game was to be turned into actual quarry by magic, and hunting grounds were always to be full of game. The relation of prehistoric man with the bear who inhabited the caves, is of special interest. In many caves of the Alps

2   Sorcerer and game animals from the Cave of Trois Frères, Southern France.

(Drachenloch, Wildmannlisloch, Drachenhöhle a.o.) late Palaeolithic hunters worshipped the bear "with extreme loving piety" as K. Sälzle stated in his work, *Tier und Mensch—Gottheit und Dämon* (1965). It was, however, not only the cave bear, the brown bear, the polar and the grizzly bear, too, were included in this cult. This primitive hunting cult of sacrifice is to be found mainly in the mythology of Palaeolithic Asia (particularly with Siberian and Sub–Arctic North American hunting tribes). With firmly laid down rites the slain bear was greatly worshipped. Once caught and ritually killed, the animal was treated as a guest, and the huntsman apologised for having had to kill it.

There are reports about the Koryaks stating that when the bear's meat was eaten at a banquet, the animal was still treated as a guest by putting its skin and head in a place of honour. "Sacrifices are made to the bear, the animal is addressed in speeches and the bear's blood is drunk, while the meat is distributed among the guests. The final act of the ceremony is the laying down of the bear's skull in a sacred place or the solemn burial of it, sometimes with the rest of the bear's bones. The Tungusians and Yakuts had a rule according to which no bone was to be broken while eating the bear's meat" (from: Sälzle).

These hunters believed that these acts of magic would bring the bear back to life and that the bear would continue to live in the shape of another young one. It was necessary therefore to be on good terms with the spirit of the bear killed which was at one and the same time the spirit of the forest.

It is told of the Chukchi of Alaska that they believed in "the souls of animals to be born again in other animals, as long as man treats his quarry properly. Then from the skull of the animal a new bear will be born, from which man will benefit."

The close relationship of Stone Age hunter with the animals around him, created a logical connection, influencing his thought and behaviour. Not only did the hunter represent in his paintings the typical and most marked behaviour patterns of the animals, he developed new methods of trapping and hunting them which presupposed logical thinking.

After early and only accidental successes in hunting, exact observation of the habits and behaviour of animals helped to accumulate knowledge on where to come across the game and how the animals would act at a given moment. Favourable places for observation were watering points and the usual trails taken by the game. Many excavations have proved that as early as the Late Palaeolithic Age methods of trapping were used which are basically still current in many parts of the world. Along with the making of pitfalls, the following can be traced to the Mesolithic Age: the harpoon trap, the spring trap, striking and deadfall traps, slings and hangman's traps. There were also traps fixed with a spear and leg traps. All these systems made possible a more rational pursuit of hunting. Success was more continuously attained, it was multiplied, and the hunter saved time. Through developing the mechanism of the trap—one of the first technical inventions in the history of mankind—the obtaining of food for groups of hunters and plant gatherers was much improved.

The leg trap belonged to one of the most interesting systems of trapping, and its use was widely spread in the Old World from Africa to the Karakorum mountains in India and the Amur river in the Northeast of Asia. The mastery of hunting with traps is a very important achievement of prehistory. The German ethnographer, Julius E. Lips, in his book, *The Origin of Things*, describes the invention, saying: "Man for the first time made a machine which worked in his absence, the intelligence of man created a robot which with mechanical precision took man's place. This magic tool was the animal trap. It took over from the thrown net, the club, the hand–thrown sling and the shot arrow. It had much better and more calculable results. By constructing an ingenious releasing mechanism, resting on the principle of the lever, the slightest touch will set a well–built trap into action." The principles of physics were thus applied very early, a long time before Archimedes was born.

The leg trap is used up to the present day by many Asiatic and African hunters as exhibits at the World Exhibition of Hunting and Shooting in Budapest in 1971 showed.

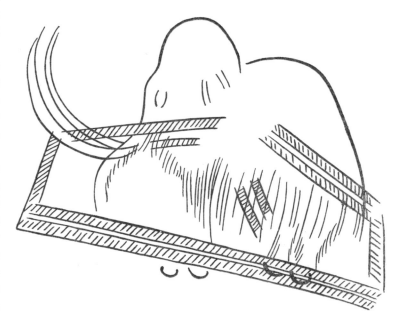

3 Mammoth in a pitfall. Cave of Font de Gaume, Dordogne, Southern France

The use of traps in hunting led to regular observation and regular hunting in regions rich in quarry, and in that way hunting settlements remained occupied for a longer space of time. In spite of all this, game was hardly reduced in prehistoric days, and numbers of animals were little effected. We owe the exact knowledge of different systems of traps again to pictorial representations in some caves. An interesting drawing in the cave of Font–de–Gaume shows a mammoth in a pitfall. Some scientists, however, believe this particular drawing to be a totem of a group of hunters. In contrast to the pitfall, the deadfall has a simple release mechanism—a central pole—which closes the trap on touch. This trap is specially useful for larger game, and was mainly operated on trails taken by large game.

Through a clever combination of pitfalls and setting traps on the main game trails along steep slopes, the Stone Age hunters obtained big bags. A Palaeolithic pitfall was discovered by chance in Le Moustier in the South of France. When planting a nut tree, an old woman came across a beaker made of flint. Prehistorians dated this as belonging to the Solutréan period of the Old Stone Age. On closer inspection of the place where the find was made near the river Vézère, several insignificant looking pits were discovered. Filled with debris and stones, they were up to 1.60 metres deep and at their upper edge 2.3 metres wide, and had been driven into the limestone. Then twenty–one further pitfalls were found, a well thought–out system of traps. Game had to take a trail across a small plateau some 10 metres above the course of the river to reach a watering place in the nearby valley. The pitfalls lay safely in this restricted trail. Most likely the plateau would be enclosed by palisades, so that animals were forced to walk across the pits, and fell into them. In a wild panic the remaining animals would rush down the closeby steep slope which again meant certain death.

The method of hunting by encircling herds of game, and the driving them over rocks or precipices, was deliberately used by the hunter of the Early Palaeolithic Age. By this large–scale hunting abundant supplies of food could be obtained, and man was free from the constant threat of hunger. Places have been discovered with the remains of thousands of hunted animals.

The best known of these is a field near the limestone rocks of Solutré, Dept. Sâone–et–Loire, in Southern France. Not far from the city of Lyons at the foot of the mountain range of Solutré the finds extend over 4,000 square metres at a depth of 10 metres dating from the Middle and Early Palaeolithic Age. In the layer discovered, belonging to the Aurignacian period of the Early Palaeolithic Age, there is a pile about 2.30 metres high of many bones of wild horses. A calculation of the fossil material showed an estimated number of 10,000 wild horses captured here. Hundreds of generations of wild horse hunters drove herds of horses into the river valley by making noise and kindling fires. Through carefully prepared palisades they then drove them onto the plateaus. In a panic the horses fled through the countryside, and when there was no escaping, the frightened animals jumped down the steep precipices, and became easy quarry for the hunters. The same hunting method of the battue was still being used with red deer in nineteenth–century Norway. Near the Hornelen mountains in Western Norway, where rocky cliffs plunge vertically into the sea, the peasants in the village of Vingen waited annually with impatience for the autumn trail of deer. They surrounded the moving herd, drove it towards the West across the mountain ridge and over steep cliffs, where the animals tumbled into the Nordfjord below.

Ten to twelve metres above the bay many rock paintings of stags from the Neolithic Age have been preserved. In a frieze, one kilometre long, more than four hundred stags are represented. They all move towards the sea. This very frieze is an important document in the history of hunting.

The following list gives a survey of excavated prehistoric settlements and details of the fossil bone material.

Palaeolithic hunting settlements

Dolni Vestonice (Moravia)	Czecho-slovakia	One of the biggest hunting settlements of the Palaeolithic Age. Mainly bones of mammoth. Here the oldest ceramic statues in the world were found.
Drachenloch near Vättis, High Alps, 2,445 m. above sea level	Switzer-land	500 to 1,000 cave–bears aged mainly between two and eight years.
Gourdan (Haute Garonne)	France	more than 3,000 reindeer
Ilskaya Krasnodar Territory	U.S.S.R.	more than 2,000 bison
Istallosköer (cave in the Bükk mountains)	Hungary	remains of 2,000 cave–bears, 80% of them young animals
Meiendorf Schleswig–Holstein	Federal Republic of Germany	settlement of reindeer hunters; 111 reindeer antlers, more than 1,000 reindeer.
Predmost (Moravia)	Czecho-slovakia	remains of more than 1,000 mammoth and more than 25,000 stone tools
Solutré (Southern France)	France	settlement of hunters of the wild horse; more than 10,000 wild horses
Stellmoor near Ahrensburg	Federal Republic of Germany	1,300 reindeer antlers; 40 axes made from antlers

Paintings and fossilized bone finds give a relatively reliable picture of the distribution of animals hunted.

It is remarkable, however, that paintings of the giant stag are rare in the caves of Eastern Spain and the South of France, even though these huge animals were common in the then steppes of these countrysides.

During the Ice Age the Franco–Cantabrian region remained largely free of ice. A park–like scene developed there with groups of trees and the typical fauna of the grassy steppe. The warmth–loving animals retreated to these areas from the advancing ice. They were then pursued by groups of Old Stone Age hunters who had their resting places here.

Next to the wood elephant *(Elephas antiquus)* with its mighty tusks was the slightly smaller elephant of the steppe *(Elephas trogontherii)* as well as several kinds of rhinoceros, all of these quarry of the Middle Ice Age hunter.

The stag of the steppe and the giant stag *(Megaloceros giganteus antecedens)* also belonged to the animals of the forests and steppes. As a typical animal of the forest, the early giant stag had a relatively short pair of antlers, spanning some 1.50 metres. The plate–like brow–tine was extremely flat, and the ice–tine was missing. With increasing deterioration of the climate and the advance of tundra landscape arctic forms of giant mammals, the woolly–haired rhinoceros *(Rhinoceros antiquitatis)*, the mammoth *(Elephas primigenius)* and later the reindeer *(Rangifer tarandus)* were added to the coveted quarry of the Ice Age hunter. In later milleniums, and with the ice receding, cold–loving animals migrated further north. In place of the Early Ice Age tundra a typical steppe vegetation re–developed in the warmer period between the second–last and last glacial periods in the Franco–Cantabrian area, with a fauna according to it.

The characteristic quarry of the hunters of this period were several species of wild horses, mainly small ones and also the tarpan, the wild horse of the Asiatic steppe, wild cattle *(Bison bonasus)* and aurochs *(Bos primigenius)*.

The cervina—the species of red deer—represented by the stag *(Cervus elaphus)* and the elk *(Alces alces)*, increased in the post–glacial period, also the true giant stag *(Megaloceros giganteus germanicus)*. With their enormous antlers, reaching a width of 3—4 metres, these fossilized stags were the most spectacular of their kind.

In 1971 at the World Exhibition of Hunting in Budapest, in the Hall of Honour, "Hunting all over the World", the antlers of a giant stag from Britain attracted much attention. The manager of the exhibition had to attach an additional label to the exhibit stating "fossil" to avoid further inquiries after the whereabouts of such enormous stags. And what do we actually know about these giants?

In the mid–nineteenth century in the peat bogs of Northern Ireland many finds were made of the bones of giant mammals. From there the antlers reached the most important museums of natural history everywhere. Next to these fairly well–preserved finds from Ireland—complete skeletons are a rarity even there—other finds of giant stags became known from Northern Europe, Siberia and recently also from China. These finds prove that the powerful animals were spread over the whole North of the globe as late as 10,000 years ago. About 8,000 B.C. the last giant stags became extinct. At the resting places of Early Ice Age hunters remains of the giant stag have been rarely found, their share is not even quite 2 per cent of the whole fossilized bone material.

Even though finds seem to indicate a wide spread of the giant stag in the post–glacial steppe, there are no authentic proofs about hunting the enormous animal. The majority of the skeleton remains at the settlements are of female or very young animals of the megaloceros. The giant stag was not easy quarry for the Mid–Ice Age hunter. Battues, usually so successful, could seldom be used with this lone giant. The method of straight attack with Ice Age thrust weapons appears not to have been very successful either, as easy flight for the animal in the very open countryside was a handicap to the hunter; attacking from a distance by throwing a javelin or a harpoon was the most likely method for limited success. The little success obtained was by chance hunting only, and in general the enormous animal must have been left alone.

The extinction of the giant stag is due purely to ecological factors. It is often said that the sabre–toothed tiger was the natural enemy of the giant stag. However, as the tiger was mainly an eater of carcasses, this animal could not have contributed much to the stag's extinction.

The reason for the decline of several species of Pleistocene animals was caused neither by hunting nor beasts of prey, nor was it due to the extraordinary size of the animals. It was rather caused by the highly specialised adaptation of the fauna to certain conditions of their surroundings. With the advance of post–glacial forests the giant stag with its enormous antlers did not find enough open steppe, and these changed conditions essentially contributed to its extinction. Next to the battue, hunting by javelin, bow and arrow spread in the late Palaeolothic Age.

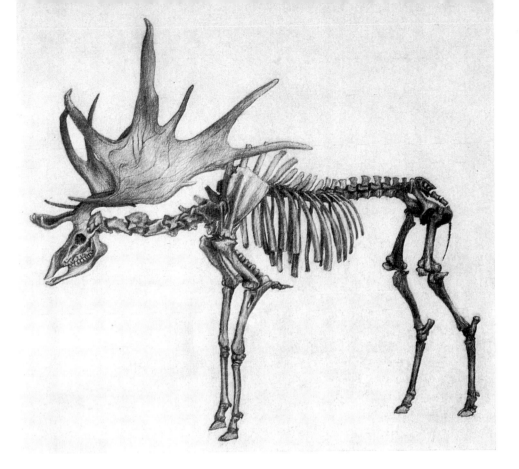

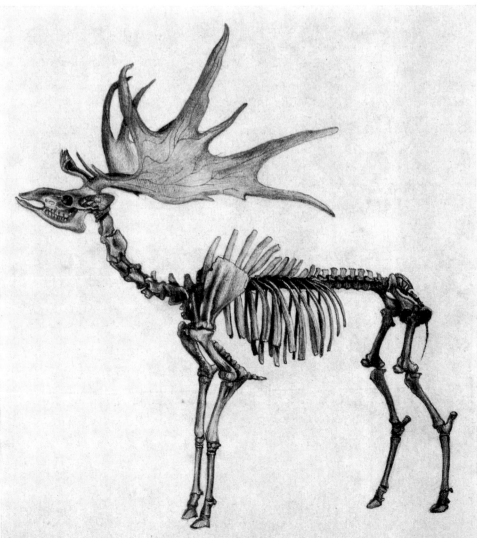

6   New reconstruction of an Irish giant stag (1959). Through reconstructing the spinal disks, the spine was lengthened by 106 mm., resulting in a completely different anatomy of the animal. Above: new reconstruction (Museum of Hamburg-Altona), below: old reconstruction.

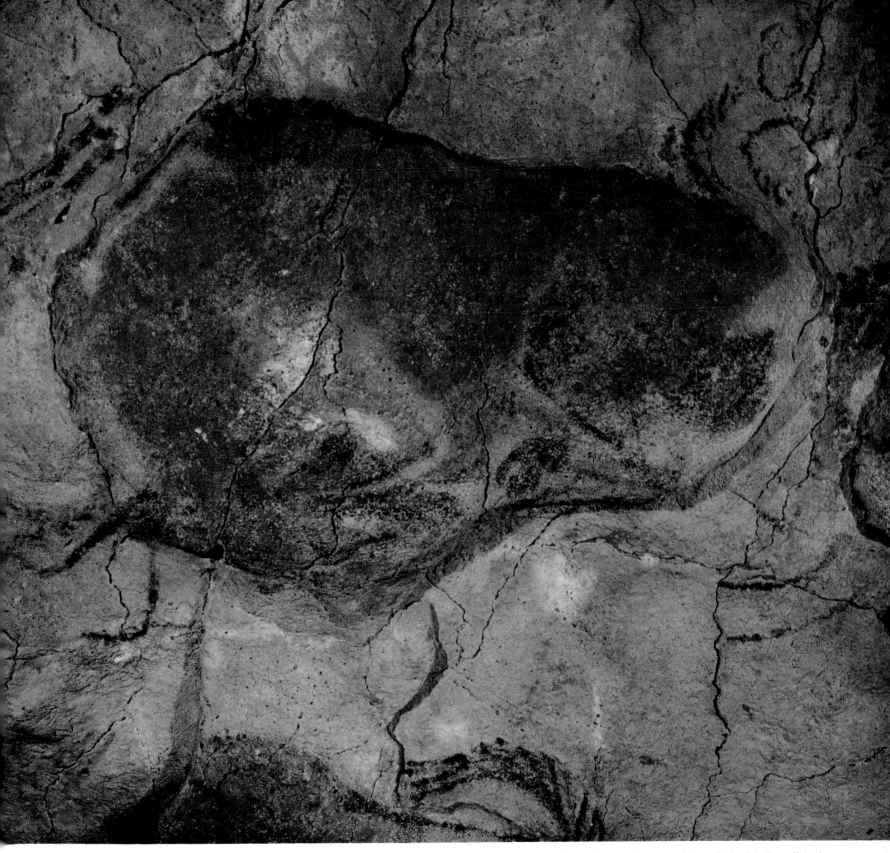

7   *Irish giant stag, with a span of antlers of 302 cm. Deutsches Jagdmuseum, Munich*

8   *Representation of bison. Rock painting in the "Great Hall of the Beasts" in the Cave of Altamira/Santander, Spain.*

9 *Deer antlers and the rib of a horse with drawings of bison, from the Pekárna Cave, Moravia. Moravian Museum, Brno (Czechoslovakia)*

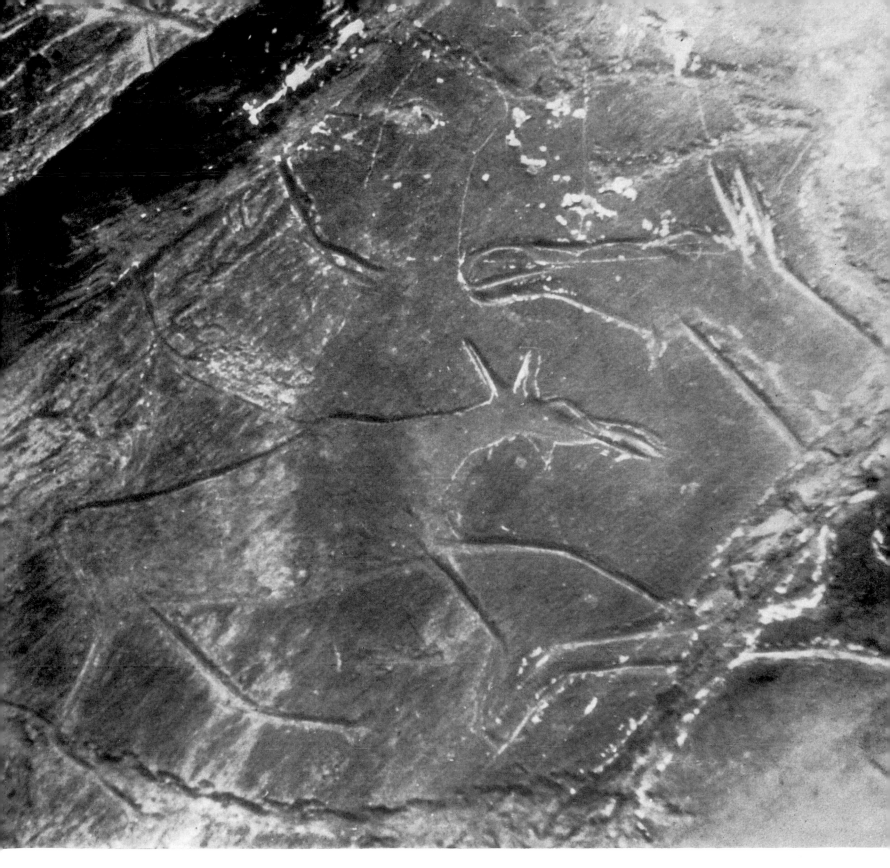

10   *Elks. Neolithic rock engravings on the river Tom in Siberia, U.S.S.R.*

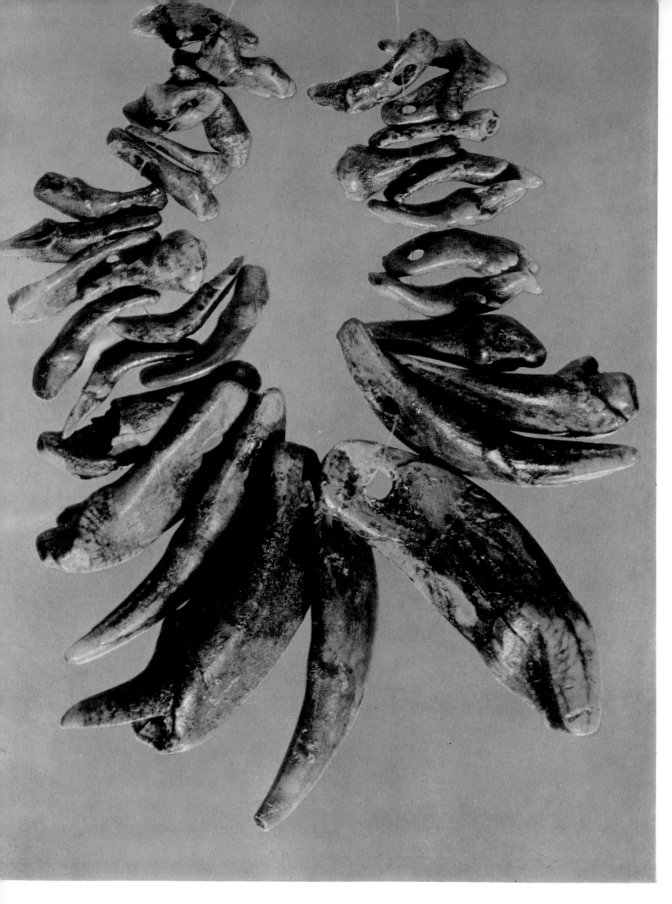

11   *Animal teeth as ornaments.*
Moravian Museum, Brno
(Czechoslovakia)

12   *Rock engravings of Bronze*
Age hunters near Tanum, Norway

13   Hunting antelopes. Rock painting of the Bushmen. Burley, South Africa

These new methods led to attacking from a distance, especially red deer and fowl. Recent research by the Russian anthropologist, M. M. Gerassimov, shows that prehistoric javelins were made from the tusks of the mammoth. For about three quarters of an hour these tusks, wrapped in skins, were put into the fire to make them soft and pliable. In that way hunting spears and javelins were easily made, as the ivory again became hard on cooling. For the first time the hunter conquered space and was able to kill birds on the wing. Many rock paintings of the Neolithic period, from different parts of the world, are pictorial documents of the hunt with bow and arrow. In Africa alone 2,000 finds were made during the last decades, with more than 100,000 imaginative rock and cave paintings, representing animals of the hunt. Rock painting in North Africa can be divided into four definite periods: –

Chronology:	Climate	Rock paintings, representing:	Period in the History of Art	Examples of paintings
8000—6000 B.C.	Tropical (the Sahara Desert was a steppe).	Big game of the tropics, primitive figures of animals and many "demon"–like figures.	"Period of the Buffalo" — Time of the Hunters —	
3500—2000 B.C.	Changeable tropical climate (dry periods, savannas)	Climax of North African rock paintings. Realistic representations of animals—large herds of wild game—first domesticated animals (cattle).	"Period of domestic Cattle" — Time of the Herdsmen—	
1500—200 B.C.	Dry climate with the formation of large desert–steppes (only mountain and oasis could be inhabited).	First representation of horse and cart (Biga). Big game disappears. The Sahara Desert becomes a divide between African and Mediterranean fauna.	"Period of the Horse"	
200 B.C. to the present	Desert climate (monsoon zones), large deserts of sand, stone and rubble.	Along the caravan routes simple, primitive representations of man and animal (mainly dromedaries).	"Period of the Camel"	

In contrast to the impressive cave paintings of the Old Stone Age the New Stone Age ones in Spain, Africa, North Europe and the Near East, the hunter is focussed in the very centre of attention, man chasing and killing wild animals.

The sharp contours and the colours true to nature have disappeared, to be replaced by monochrome, red or black figures, with excellent representation of the typical attributes and movements of the hunters and the animals.

For more than 50,000 years the hunters of Europe, Asia and Africa have drawn and painted their quarry on rocks and in caves, and have in that way created realistic documents to the state of hunting in prehistoric society.

Only with the transition from nomadic hunter to settled animal-breeding farmer, brought about by the domestication of certain wild animals, did a new epoch in the history of man come about, an epoch ruled by productive economy, with domesticated animals and cultivation of plants. This led to a complete change of the meaning of hunting and its purpose.

The following survey provides an idea of the great variety of realistic presentations of prehistoric hunting. It lists New Stone Age rock paintings of hunting scenes: –

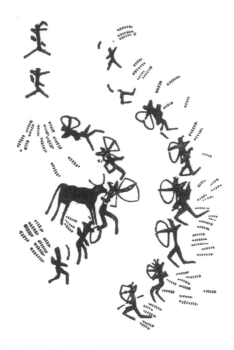

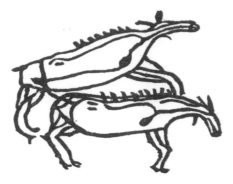

Fylke, Norway
Elks, copulating. Neolithic rock drawing in scratch technique. The heart of the animals is represented, too.

Gasulla Rift near Ares del Maestre, eastern province of Castellón, Spain
Representation in red, black and brown of a wild boar hunt in the Mesolithic period.

Kargur Taeh, Libya
Great number of rock paintings with hunting and war scenes.

Ti–N–Tazarift, Libya
These Neolithic rock paintings of the Sahara depict war and hunting scenes with bow and arrow and throwing sticks.

Vallorta Rift near Albocácer, province of Castellón, Spain
Mesolithic representation of a stag hunt.

Western Siberia, U.S.S.R.
Neolithic rock drawing in scratch technique representing an elk from the River Tom.

Fynkanvatn near Meløy (Northland), Norway
Neolithic representation of reindeer and elk. The elk is easily to be made out by the formation of its withers.

Catal Hüyük, Turkey
Hill of neolithic settlement discovered in 1961 with cult rooms decorated with hunting scenes. Stags and hunters are depicted in red and green.

Hunting in Antiquity

4 Artemis and Actaeon. Drawing after a painting on a Greek amphora by the
"Geras Painter", 5th century B.C. Thorvaldsen Museum, Copenhagen

From Wild to Domestic Animal

"Herds of gazelle, stag, ibex, antelope ... they allowed me to catch in nets, up in the lofty wooded mountains. I collected whole herds of them and counted their number like herds of sheep. I caught four elephants alive."

Tiglath–Pileser I, King of Assyria (1112 — 1074 B.C.)

The grassy steppes, deserts and high plateaus of the Near East and Central Asia are ancient seats of man's culture. For one and a half million years hordes and tribes of hunters and gatherers of plants roamed the valleys, savannas and forests in order to kill animals with their primitive weapons. At that time five square kilometres of hunting area was needed to support one man.

These groups of hunters in the cultures of the Ancient Orient caught beside their hunting quarry young animals which they kept for killing later in times of need.

Nineteenth–century reports show that even then the Bedouins of Arabia used similar methods to obtain "living meat reserves". Young animals caught in that way, adapted themselves after a few weeks to their new surroundings, and began looking for fodder on their own. The hunting nomads of the Near East created the first semi–domesticated herds from the wild animals they caught.

At the hunting settlement of Tosya in Upper Egypt tools (sickle blades and rubbing stones) for the working of wild grain from the fourteenth to the thirteenth millennium B.C. were found. There are also countless remains of the bones of gazelles and antelopes which had possibly been kept captive for a while. Steppe hunters were most widely spread during the tenth century B.C. when, besides hunting, they had begun cultivating grain and keeping animals in small settlements. However, we can only speak of domestic animals proper from the time onwards when wild animals reproduced in captivity, which meant breeding influenced by man. This process of development from wild to domestic animal involved the replacing of hunting as the main means of gaining a livelihood, by animal breeding and agriculture. The tamed herds became the private property of the herdsman, always a man, not a woman and this new means of production led to the first great revolution in the history of mankind, the Neolithic or Agrarian Revolution. In the Middle East this developed slowly between the tenth and fourth century B.C., culminating in the formation of a class society in the city states of Mesopotamia. The transition from an economy of acquisition by hunters and collectors to an economy of production through agriculture and animal breeding is well documented by archaeological material from the Near East. While in the finds of bones and rock pictures from caves in Southern Turkey, Beldibi and Ökeuzlu near Antalya, stags and wild cattle still dominate the Late Palaeolithic hunting settlement, in the Ukraine and in Siberia domesticated wolves as the hunter's companion begin making their appearance. All the same, the wolf–dog is probably not, as believed at one time, the oldest domesticated animal. Finds from Cayönü near the village of Ergani in Turkey about 9500 B.C., also Lehmi County in East Idaho, U.S.A. about 9000 B.C. and about 8000 B.C. prove the existence of hunting dogs in cave settlements, possibly a Pomeranian kind of dog, used as bloodhound and guard dog. Ivory carvings from Thebes, dating from between 4400 and 4000 B.C. show fast running dogs, and this type is the likely ancestor of all hunting and sheep dogs. The Phoenicians, too, had several bloodhounds, with the unmistakable long lop–ears, and fast–running dogs and lime–hounds were man's popular hunting companions long before the Celts used them. In Babylon Molassian hounds were trained for the lion hunt.

In a dig at a settlement of Palaeolithic cave hunters in Northern Irak, bone finds seem to indicate that the sheep was the first domesticated animal. Examination of the material revealed that three fifths of the domesticated sheep were less than a year old while undoubtedly the remains of older animals were quarry of the hunt. This find from Zawi Chemi Shanidar dates from the middle of the tenth millennium B.C. Excavations in Deh Wuran in the Southwest of Iran, with finds from about 7000 B.C. or from the cave of Haua Fteah in Northern Libya (about 6800 B.C.) show that the sheep was bred as a domestic animal, to supply meat for nomadic tribes. While this was true also in Anatolia and Syria Bezoar goats were bred, gazelles and antelopes in Palestine and Iran. An epitaph on a tomb in Saqqara (6th dynasty) shows that a wealthy Egyptian kept in his herd 3,998 cattle, 1,135 gazelles, 1,308 sabre–horned antelopes and 1,244 of the Mendel type antelope.

At that time, too, the first wild animal parks were made. On the Tigris archaeologists uncovered a space of over 50 square kilometres which had served as game reserve. Artificial canals made fresh water available to the animals. This kind of park formed at one and the same time important game reserves which Assyrian and Babylonian kings turned to for the planning of grand hunting entertainments. A relief from Nineveh represents a hunt for red deer of King Ashurbanipal's time (668—626 B.C.) where the escape of game is prevented by high nets.

Next to the keeping of herds of wild animals for hunting, animals were domesticated for cult purposes. In the sacred groves and temples of India and Sumer many antelopes, gazelles, elephants, tigers and all sorts of birds were kept as sacred animals, to be venerated. Through the sensational discovery of the temple settlement of Catal Hüyük in 1958 by the British archaeologist, James Mellaart, an extensive hill settlement of Anatolia in Turkey became available for examination, containing interesting religious representations of the hunt, dating from about 5800 B.C. The settlement's temple decorated with a frieze of leopards and a representation of the "Goddess clad in a Leopard Skin", was dedicated to hunters and warriors.

The hunt and war, both devoted to killing, are treated as sacred powers. The dreaded leopard and the wild bull, master of the herd, had to serve a higher, more powerful and supernatural being, a woman become goddess. In Mesopotamia, Ishtar, the Goddess of War, of the Moon and of Love, was often represented accompanied by leopards or lions.

The lion frieze, made of coloured enamelled tiles, lining the great processional road in Babylon to the Ishtar Gate and the temple of E–Sagila, counts among the finest achievements of Babylonian artists in the first half of the sixth century B.C. This processional road of the gods Nabu and Marduk, has been faithfully rebuilt in the Staatliche Museen in Berlin. The reconstructed Ishtar Gate, with original parts, shows bulls and weird dragons, mushrush. The whole imposing walls of tiles at one time displayed more than 240 lions, and about 575 bulls and Marduk dragons, all likely of cult-significance. From an inscription by King Nebuchadnezzar II (604 to 562 B.C.) we know that on the last day of the Feast of the New Year a religious procession took place at the Ishtar Gate. The fierce lion was Ishtar's sacred animal while the Weather God Adad's companion was a mighty horned bull. A strange mystical creature, the dragon, belongs to Marduk, the City God. The dragon's body was covered in scales, its neck and head were those of a snake. It had lion's claws, the hind legs were eagle's claws and the tail was a scorpion's.

The people of the Ancient Orient saw in their sacred animals not just symbols of their gods, but guardians of the sacred places, and symbolic figures protecting their herds of domestic and wild animals from hostile demons and beasts of prey. All over the Ancient Orient the lion was considered a demon which had to be con-

quered and killed in order to ban the power and the force of evil and all ill fate. This protective function embodied in the hunt, devolved mainly on the king.

5 Lion-headed demon with dead hare. Relief from Sinjirli, 9th century B.C. Staatliche Museen, Vorderasiatisches Museum, Berlin

Lion Hunts of Assyrian Kings

"I am Ashurbanipal, King of the World,
King of Assyria. For my pleasure, and
with the help of the God Ashur and
the Goddess Ishtar,
Mistress of the Battle,
I pierced a wild lion with my spear."

Ashurbanipal (668—626 B. C.)
Inscription on a hunting relief

In the older literature on hunting King Nimrod, legendary founder of the Babylonian Empire, builder of the Tower of Babel, was also considered to have started hunting. This mighty hunter before the Lord, with his huge quarries served as a model to European Renaissance princes, and even to this day he agitates the mind of many a huntsman. The Old Testament, Chapter X of Genesis speaks of the mighty Nimrod as an ardent huntsman, and great builder of cities, Nineveh and Calah among them.

However, the Tower of Babel was built under Nebuchadnezzar II, and by that time game for hunting between the Euphrates and Tigris had been severely reduced. It is erroneous therefore to think of Nimrod as the personification of the spirit of hunting in the New Babylonian Empire. His special connection with the city of Nineveh on the east bank of the Tigris is more convincing. In the ruins of the huge palace of the Assyrian king, Ashurbanipal II (883—859 B.C.) magnificent reliefs, made of alabaster, were discovered, as well as his library consisting of 20,000 cuneiform tablets. The reliefs represent scenes from the lion hunt. Excavations at Calah, the ancient Assyrian capital, Nimrod's ruined city on the Tigris, brought to light further reliefs of the lion hunt in a palace of the same king. These reliefs show hunting scenes, depicting the then current methods of hunting, symbolising at the same time the idea of the pro-

tection of game from predators and all enemies by the ruler. With pastoral tribes becoming settled, there developed along with hunting a regular protection of the herds from animals of prey. This situation determined these ancient peoples' concept of life.

In the early art of Sumer many representations show the desperate struggle of the herdsmen against attacking lions, symbolising the protection of the herd from beasts of prey. The herdsman is here shown as a hunter without the royal insignia. On a seal of the period a female animal is seen at the moment of "lying down and giving birth to a calf. Defenceless, the animal would be exposed to certain death, but the herdsman is running, lance in hand, against the attacking lion and destroying the beast." (Seibert, 1969)

With emerging kingship in the city states of Mesopotamia the word herdsman is used in the same sense as "ruler" or "king". This terminology expresses the unconditional subordination of the herd of men as well as animals to the herdsman, the ruler, the king, who was looked upon as being called by the gods to his high office. We must regard the whole tradition and representation of royal lion hunts under this very aspect, and not lion hunts only. The hunting of crocodiles, wild bulls and wild asses in the Ancient Orient follows the same line of thought. Always the king fights beasts of prey and the enemies of his country. For this reason hunting and war formed a unity in the thought of the Ancient Orient, and again and again we do discover the connection.

Another aspect to be taken into account is the fact that next to the early Sumerian, Hittite and Assyrian theme of the Shepherd–King — secular representations of the hunt — there are ceremonial scenes of feeding and hunting by royal priests. These express a solemn and symbolic act of the care and protection of game. The royal privilege of hunting, the passion for the hunt and its enjoyment were only

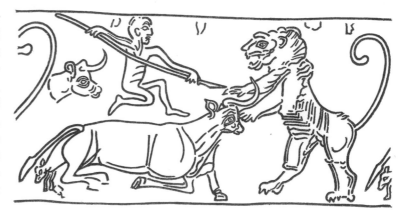

6 Herdsman defending a calving cow from an attacking lion. Impression from a seal, early Sumerian.

part of the whole picture, there were also mystical forms and ceremonies of ancient hunting cult which reflected the beginning struggle between the functions of priest and king. Early Sumerian seals depict royal priests consecrating young lions, killed as sacrifice. A hunting relief of King Ashurbanipal also shows a libation sacrifice when consecrated wine is poured over the carcasses of dead lions.

In the collections of cuneiform tablets of the Assyrian kings there are many and interesting reports about successful hunts. Here, too, the kings refer to the goodwill of the gods without which success in hunting would be impossible.

King Tiglath–Pileser I (1112—1074 B.C.) is recorded to have said: "On the order of Ninurta, my patron, I have, with a brave heart, killed 120 lions in a terrible fight, facing the animals on foot. I have also killed 800 lions from my war chariot. All kind of game of the fields and fowls in the sky I made my quarry."

The light chariot, the "miracle weapon" of the Assyrian army, made possible a new way of hunting big game, when the flight distance of the animals could be overcome by the quickly moving chariot. The use of metal tips on arrows also increased the effectiveness of hunting weapons.

Apart from the often reproduced wall reliefs of the palace in Calah there are other lesser known representations of hunting the lion, for example, the great Hittite orthostat relief in Sakca–Gözü in the North of Syria—now in the Vorderasiatisches Museum, Berlin.

Here the archer shoots at the lion from his war chariot. Everyone wears mail shirt and the horses, too, are protected by mail. This does mean that we are looking at Assyrian warriors, out lion shooting, and not at hunters. The symbol of the winged solar–disk above the chariot points to the fact the Goddess of the Sun was the protector of the hunt. Only one loincloth–girded figure in the centre might be a hunt servant. It is interesting to note that the attacking lion is met by soldiers armed with spears, and not by the king. The shot of the archer is only symbolically alluded to, for he could never hit the lion. This special feature is contained in nearly all the representations of the lion hunt in the Ancient Orient.

On the wall relief from the palace in Calah, King Ashurnazirpal II is hunting several lions. He takes his place as an archer next to his charioteer. The chariot is drawn by three stallions. Wounded lions, lions hit by arrows, are scattered all round. The king has been victorious. With the well known frieze at the British Museum the urgency of the animals depicted, is fascinating, animals represented so realistically that the different phases of the hunt are clearly recognisable. For days the lions were kept in cages, before being set free for the hunt. The keepers of the hounds with their heavy Molossian dogs drove the game together, and the king fought the beasts with bow and arrow or hunting–spear and sword. In cold blood, the demon lion, enemy of all herds, is defeated and killed. The animals hit by arrows, roll on the ground until they perish. No beast ever attacks the king, and the ruler is always represented as being victorious. After returning from a successful lion hunt he gives thanks to the Goddess Ishtar in his palace.

Ashurnazirpal II is quoted as saying: "In those days on the opposite bank of the Euphrates I have killed 50 wild bulls and 80 I caught. I killed 30 elephants with my bow and arrow, in royal combat I killed 215 powerful wild bulls. By stretching out my hand, and with a stout heart I caught 15 strong lions in mountains and forests." (Meissner, 1911)

7 Hunting scene in the mountains. Impression from a seal from Uruk, 2800—2700 B.C. Staatliche Museen, Vorderasiatisches Museum, Berlin

These splendid monumental representations of lions from the reign of Ashurnazirpal II served exclusively to glorify the victorious figure of the king who was at the head of a powerful military state. In his hunting for Big Game the king wished to assert his absolute power and rule over all beasts, people and countries. The Assyrian sculptors were masters in portraying the animals, conveying at the same time all the details of weapons and methods of hunting, so that Assyrian and Babylonian works of art have become valuable source material to the history of hunting.

8 King Ashurnazirpal offering a drink after hunting wild game. Relief from the Palace of Calah, 9th century B.C. British Museum, London

14   *Ishtar Gate from Babylon. First half of 6th century B.C. Reconstructed in the years 1899 to 1901. Staatliche Museen, Vorderasiatisches Museum, Berlin*

15   *Boar hunting. Seal impression from Babylon, 6th/4th century B.C. Staatliche Museen, Vorderasiatisches Museum, Berlin*

16   *Hunting for bull from a chariot. Orthostat relief from Tell Halaf, 9th century B.C. Staatliche Museen, Vorderasiatisches Museum, Berlin*

17   *Lion hunt. Orthostat relief from Sakca–Gözü, 8th century B.C. Staatliche Museen, Vorderasiatisches Museum, Berlin*

18 *King Rameses III, hunting wild bull. Relief on the first pylon of the Temple of the Dead in Medinet Habu, first half of 12th century B.C. (20th Dynasty).*

19 *Hunting ostrich from a chariot. Gold fan from the tomb of Tutankhamen (18th Dynasty), in the Valley of the Kings (Thebes). Egyptian Museum, Cairo*

20 *Fowling with throwing stick. Painting on stucco, from the tomb of Neb-Amon, about 1400 B.C. (18th Dynasty), West Thebes. British Museum, London*

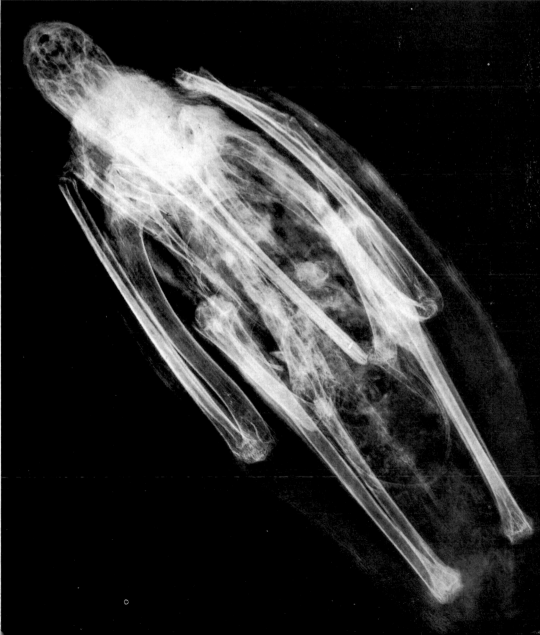

23 Sculpture of an ibis. Bronze, Egypt, late period. Staatliche Museen. Ägyptisches Museum, Berlin

24 X-ray photograph of a mummified ibis. Staatliche Museen, Ägyptisches Museum, Berlin

21 King Ashurbanipal (668—626 B.C.) hunting lions. Alabaster relief from Nineveh. Staatliche Museen, Vorderasiatisches Museum, Berlin

22 King Ashurnazirpal II (883—859 B.C.) hunting lions. Alabaster relief from Calah. Staatliche Museen, Vorderasiatisches Museum, Berlin (lost during war)

25 *Grand coursing in the presence of the emperor. Detail of a scroll. Painting on silk. China, about 1700. Deutsches Jagdmuseum, Munich*

26 *Hunting the cervine antelope. Indian miniature of the Mogul School, 18th century. Staatliche Museen, Islamisches Museum, Berlin*

27 *Feeding gazelles. Indian miniature. Victoria and Albert Museum, London*

28 *Grand coursing in the presence of the emperor. Detail of a scroll. Painting on silk. China, about 1700. Deutsches Jagdmuseum, Munich*

29 *Bird catchers. Indian miniature of the Mogul School, late 17th century. Staatliche Museen, Islamisches Museum, Berlin*

30 *Cervine antelopes, tethered. Indian miniature of the Mogul School, early 17th century. Staatliche Museen, Islamisches Museum, Berlin*

31 *Hunting for gazelles by night. Indian miniature of the Mogul School, 18th century. Staatliche Museen, Islamisches Museum, Berlin*

Hunting in Ancient Egypt

"When he (the king) spent a moment enjoying the hunt in a foreign land, his own quarry was bigger than that of the whole army. He killed seven lions by his arrows, in just one instant."

Pharaoh Tuthmosis III (1490—1436 B.C.)
Inscription on the Temple of Month at Armant.

In the history of Egypt the hunt began in the Old Kingdom as a privilege, sport, enjoyment and recreation of the ruling class. It was, in fact, the privilege of the pharaohs to hunt the hippopotamus and the wild bull. From representations in sacrificial and cult chambers of the nobles we know that from 2470 B.C. onwards fishing and hunting in the Nile delta were favourite entertainments of nobles and high officials alike. Wild fowl was pursued with nets or throwing spears. Servants now hunted the hippopotamus as it was considered too dangerous for the privileged classes who remained spectators. It is certain that in the Old Kingdom, side by side with battues of big game, traps were in use too. Rock pictures in the Sahara and on the banks of the Nile clearly depict the use of traps. A specially impressive wall painting from the early third century B.C. in a tomb at Hierakonpolis, upstream from Thebes in Upper Egypt, shows the distinct drawing of a foot trap. A herd of antelopes got into this circular trap, and five animals were caught. Side by side with foot traps, animals were hunted with the use of the throwing-stick, the tirasse and decoys, as may be seen with several representations in Egyptian papyros. The large swamps of the Nile delta with their thickets of lotus, papyros and reed, were favourite hunting grounds in Ancient Egypt. The papyros plants themselves were important for the fibre they supplied, used in the making of indispensable writing material and the construction of light papyros boats for hunting and fishing. The harpooning of fish and hippopotamuses and also the killing of wild fowl with the throwing stick, all these were typical hunting methods of the delta. In the Old and Middle Egyptian Kingdoms the killing of birds and the harpooning of fish were royal privileges. Hunting excursions were sport and recreation reserved for the ruler, who by his hunting served Sekhmet, the "Goddess of the Swamp, of Hunting, Shooting and Fishing". Quarry was considered a gift of the goddess to the ruler.

From the fifth and sixth dynasty onwards courtiers and high officials also took part in hunting expeditions to the delta, often accompanied by their wives, children and servants. The hunting of birds and the catching of fish is usually treated as one subject in pictorial representations. In the New Kingdom pictures were arranged to show the harpooning of fish on the right, and the killing of birds with the throwing stick on the left. Birds were usually killed on their nests during the breeding season. Small animals of prey were used for driving the birds, particularly cats. They were brought along in cages by the hunters, and when released, chased the birds from their nests. The birds were then killed by the throwing stick. Decoys carried by hunters and proof for the extensive use of nets also appear in pictorial representations. It is said of Pharaoh Horemheb (1342—1338 B.C.) that he had whole flights of birds caught in nets. These were tirasse as well as standing nets.

Wild geese and ducks in flight from the papyros thickets are among the most impressive pictures of fauna in Egyptian art. The quarry of hunting in the delta were mainly Nile geese, then called fox-geese, the gray laggoose, the white-fronted goose, several kinds of heron, among them the slate-coloured, purple and silver heron. There were also broadbills, white-fronted fowl, the spoon-billed duck and the red-headed duck. Wild ducks were relatively seldom killed. The hunting of ducks is reported only from the twelfth Egyptian dynasty onwards. Nor was the duck hardly ever domesticated during Antiquity, even though the keeping and fattening of game and poultry was popular with the Egyptians as far back as the Old Kingdom. A limestone relief from the

9 Pitfall, from a fresco in a tomb of a prince at Hierakonpolis. Ancient Egypt, period of Negade II, about 3200 B.C.

fifth dynasty shows the feeding of rabbits and wild geese in a poultry yard about 4,500 years ago.

Independent of the luck of the chase a continuous supply for the lordly tables with luxurious game and poultry had to be assured. Queen Hatshepsut about 1500 B.C. maintained a great game park near the temple of Dair–al–Bahri, called the Garden of Ammon, where she kept indigenous animals, big game from the North African plains and savannas and even Indian elephants.

Hunting of hippopotamuses and catching fish and shooting fowl in the Nile delta, were the most popular forms of field sports in Ancient Egypt, with little hunting of Big Game. After the early extermination of Big Game in the North African plains and savannas, it was only the rulers of the eighteenth Egyptian dynasty who again encountered Big Game. On their extensive expeditions to the Near East in the service of war or of hunting, they learnt about the hunting methods of the Assyrian Kings. In the ruins of Tell el–Amarna (about 1350 B.C.) the residence of the Pharaoh Amenophis IV, more than 350 clay tablets of Babylonian cuneiform writing were found, with reports of the hunting success of the pharaohs. According to these reports Tuthmosis III, for example, killed 120 elephants in one hunting expedition to the plains of Niya, though this feat was probably achieved by his warriors. There are also many representations of and reports about lion hunts of the Egyptian kings. They were an exclusive privilege of the pharaohs. One such representation, and an interesting one, is on a chest belonging to the finds in the tomb of Tutankhamen (1347–1338 B.C.). Of 8 lions, 7 have already been fatally wounded by the young pharaoh and a young lion in flight is about to be hit by the next arrow. Here, too, the triumphant victory of the pharaoh is assured.

An engraved scarabaeus of the time of Amenophis III says that the king, within ten years, killed 102 lions. Another report tells that in four days he killed 96 of a herd of 170 wild bulls. Rameses III had scenes from his wild bull hunts depicted in a prominent place at the temple of Medinet Habu.

With the growing power of the Persian kings hunting and catching elephants became more important with all the peoples of Antiquity. Elephants, after being caught and tamed, were used for the hunt, for war, as beasts of burden and draught animals. The famous war elephants of the Persians, in the campaigns of Alexander the Great began a new epoch in the history of war and hunting. The king owned a herd of nine thousand of these animals, which had to be supplied by the Indian auxiliary troops. Next to Assyria, Greece, Persia and Egypt, too, had elephants caught in large numbers. Under the Egyptian king, Ptolemy II Philodelphus (283–247 B.C.) grandiose elephant hunts were undertaken in Ethiopia where whole armies were sent out to catch the animals. The frightened elephants were driven into pitfalls, and from the port of Saba taken in specially constructed ships across the Red Sea to Egypt. Trade in precious ivory also increased.

The well known war elephants of Carthage, employed in the Punic Wars against Rome, were caught in Libya, Mauretania or Ethiopia. These hunting enterprises, organised on military lines, led, particularly in North Africa and the Near East, to the extermination of several species of big game. In that way the last European lion was killed in Greece, the last Berber lion in North Africa and the elephant disappeared from the Near East.

The fate of the Egyptian ibis is typical. Widely spread in Ancient Egypt, it became extinct by the end of the Middle Kingdom.

| Old Sumerian | | Old Babylonian | | Neo Assyrian | | Late Babylonian |
| Lagash | | | Middle Assyrian | | Neo Babylonian | |

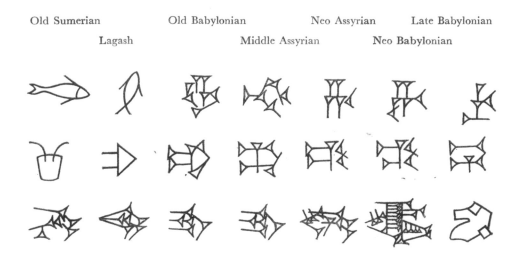

10 Example of the development of cuneiform for the words fish, bull and lion.

The Sacred Ibis—
the Egyptian Moon Bird

"Egypt would be lost
Were it not protected by the Ibis."

Claudius Aelianus (about A.D. 200)

When fowling in the papyrus swamps, it was forbidden to kill the snow–white ibis, much worshipped in the whole land as the "Sacred Ibis" *(Threskiornis aethiopica)*.

The deliberate killing of the sacred bird carried the death sentence in ancient Egypt. The bird was consecrated to the Moon God, Thoth, and was of particular significance in the city of Hermopolis where the Moon God was the local deity. There the ibis became the symbol for all the sacred animals of the country. The ibis–headed god, Thoth, was in the Old Kingdom the symbol of the heart, of wisdom, of chronology, the calendar and of writing. In many temples therefore live ibises were kept in great numbers. If a bird died, it was mummified, the mummy being shaped like a heart, with the head and neck pulled in.

During excavations at Saqqara thousands of mummified ibises were found which had been entombed with the Pharaoh Imhotep (Third dynasty). In other temples, too, cemeteries of the bird were discovered. Tomb corridors were excavated in Hermopolis whose niches held over four million pottery vessels, containing the remains of ibises. The snow–white, stork–like bird, with its black feet, its naked neck and head, was worshipped in the country mainly perhaps for its usefulness. When the ibis appeared in Lower Egypt in late summer, it was taken as a signal for the arrival of the fertile Nile mud. After the annual flooding of the river, the marsh birds with their long down–turned beaks searched the mud systematically for vermin left behind.

The literature of Antiquity contains many reports about the ibis, killing insects, locusts, scorpions and snakes. In the city temples the birds are said to have eaten the waste from fishmongers and butchers, and so played an essential part in keeping the cities clean and sanitary.

The usefulness of the ibis was stressed again and again by the priests, particularly at the feast of the "Consecrating of the Waters". It was said that where the ibis drinks, the water is sure to be clean and healthy. And the Egyptian priests then took to making their ablution in the waters. It was due largely to the cult action of the priests that in the Old Kingdom the ibis became the sacred Moon Bird, completely protected in all the land. The bird's flesh was supposed to be poisonous, only its liver could be ceremonially sacrificed. This sacred bird, once common in ancient Egypt, is now extinct. The ibis–type of bird existing on the African coast, is not related to the Egyptian ibis. These birds are imigrants from the South.

The extermination of the Egyptian bird is not due to man's passion for hunting but its cause is the "Sacred Ibis" mythos itself. The fall of the old gods and the beginning struggle for power by the priests were the bird's doom. The extermination of the ibis was accelerated when in the Middle Kingdom a new priesthood gained power, determined to abolish the old mythos of the ibis priests. The new priests spread the legend that the bird's eggs contained deadly poison, and the population was asked to destroy systematically all eggs laid. It was obviously not possible by this action alone to make the ibis cult vanish at once. And the priests thought up another story, namely that from the eggs of the Ibis comes the basilisk, that snake–like creature of fable, whose glance can kill.

11　Ibis-headed Egyptian deity Thoth, holding a risp in his hand. From: Wilkinson, I.G., 1878.

The much feared Egyptian eye disease, chronic conjunctivitis, was widespread in the country at that time. We know today that the disease is caused by a small midge, carrying parasitic organisms into the human eye. Small parasitical threadworms can thus get into the cornea of the eye, and cause blindness. The larvae of this tiny midge float in shallow water, and may attach themselves to water plants. Could it be possible that the sacred ibis was fond of eating those larvae, and that the insidious disease did spread more widely when the ibis was destroyed? Be that as it may, the fear of the dreaded glance from a basilisk, and the loss of sight that followed, did lead to the destruction of all eggs and nests of the bird in Egypt.

To decimate or wholly exterminate a popular and worshipped bird, was possible only by destroying the eggs while the bird itself still remained completely protected.

Many religions have sacred animals which must neither be hunted nor killed. It is specially in East Asia that religions—Buddhism and Hinduism—with their mystical legends, influence the relationship of man and beast. Hinduism, for example, forbids the needless killing of animals, while the teachings of Buddhism —more than 2,500 years old—demand for ethical reasons the worship of a number of sacred animals, particularly cattle and gazelles.

Indian Legends of the Gazelle King Nigrodya

"We shall protect them all, O Lord!
The gazelles in this park will be protected.
But what about all other beasts?
To them, too, no harm will be done."

12th tale in the Jâtaka

The literature of ancient India and of Buddhism contains many interesting legends, among them the tales of the Jâtaka dealing with the relationship between man and beast. In the twelfth tale the legendary Gazelle King, Nigrodya, explains Buddha's teaching concerning the meaning of hunting, and the necessity of protecting game. This ancient Indian legend is directed against the magnificent hunting entertainments of the court, and the methods used. It strongly points to the ethic responsibility of the hunter for all wild animals. The tale is one of the oldest traditions come down to us, concerning the idea and purpose of protection and preservation of game. According to the legend, Nigrodya, as a wise Bodhisatva, a later Buddha, was reincarnated in the body of a gazelle.

"Golden–coloured, he emerged from his mother's womb. His eyes were like precious stones, his horns like silver, and his mouth shone like a bright red cloth, while his hooves were lustrous as if varnished ... And he lived as the King of the Gazelles in the wood. Not far from him there was another Gazelle King, Sakya. He, too, was gold–coloured and the leader of a herd of five hundred.

At that time the King of Benares was passionately devoted to the hunting of gazelles. And to go hunting, he called up town and country people, day after day, disregarding their own work. And the people thought: 'this king disturbs our work. How would it do if we were to put feeding–places for the gazelles into the park, and carry water to these places. Then we would drive many animals into the park, lock the gates, and hand over the animals to the king?'

And they did so, then went to the king, and said: 'O Lord, if day after day you command us for your hunting, our own work will be ruined. Therefore we have driven the gazelles from the wood, and filled your park with them. From now onwards be contented with these animals.' With that they took leave of the king.

The king hurried to the park, and looked at the gazelles. When he saw the two golden ones, he granted them protection. After that, he now and then killed a gazelle, took it with him or handed it to his cook. But every time the animals saw the deadly weapons of the hunters, they fled in a great fright. Those hit by an arrow, collapsed and perished. The herd reported all that was happening to the Bodhisatva. He called for Sakya, the other Gazelle King, and spoke to him thus:

'My dear friend, many of our gazelles perish. If death there must be, we shall not allow our gazelles to be killed by bow and arrow. Rather shall they die one by one, one day one from my herd, and the next day one from yours. The animal, its fate decided by drawing lots, shall be put at the entrance of the park, to be met by the king or his cook. There it is to lie down, its head bent to the ground, awaiting death. In that way the suffering of being wounded will be spared to the rest of the herd.' And so it was done from that day onwards.

One day, however, it was the turn of a pregnant gazelle from Sakya's herd. The gazelle went to the king and said: 'O Lord, I carry a young one. Once I have given birth to it, both of us will have to suffer death some day. Therefore spare me this time.' But Sakya replied: 'It is impossible to let others meet the fate that is to be yours. You must suffer what is meant for you. Therefore, go away.' As the gazelle had found no help with Sakya she went to the other Bodhisatva to tell him of her sorrow. When he had listened to her, he said: 'Go, and I will let the lot go past you.' He then went himself to the entrance of the park, sat down, and bowed his head, ready for slaughter. The cook soon found him, and when he set eyes on him, he thought: 'The Gazelle King who is untouchable, is waiting for death. How is it possible?' And he ran to tell the king.

The King immediately got into his carriage, and hurried to the place with many courtiers. When he saw the Bodhisatva, he said: My dear Gazelle King, have I not granted you protection? Why do you lie in this place?'

And the Bodhisatva replied: 'O great King, a pregnant gazelle came to me, and begged that another one might meet her fate. But I cannot transfer the suffering of death to another animal. Therefore I will give my own life.'

Said the king: 'Dear golden Gazelle King, I have not come across a single being so full of patience, friendship and compassion. And hence I am mercifully inclined towards you. Rise therefore, and I will grant protection to you and to that gazelle.'

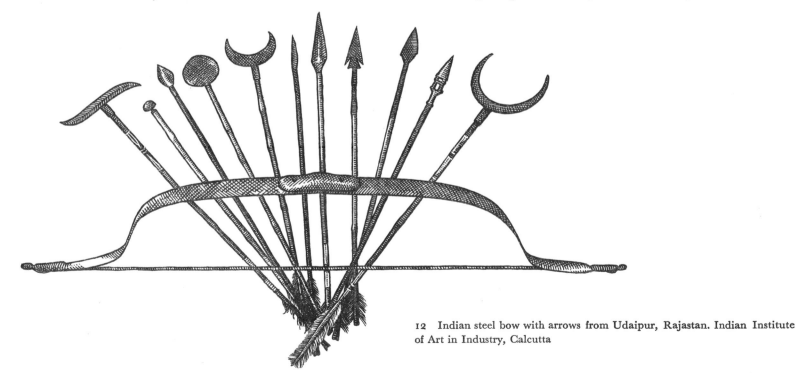

12 Indian steel bow with arrows from Udaipur, Rajastan. Indian Institute of Art in Industry, Calcutta

'Two have gained protection. But what is to happen to the rest, O King of Man?'

'We shall protect them, too, Gazelle King.'

'Then all gazelles in the park will be protected, but what about the others?'

'To them, too, no harm will be done.'

'O great King, all gazelles will then be protected, but what about the rest of four-legged creatures?'

'They will all be protected, Gazelle King.'

'O great King, all animals will be protected, and what will the birds do?'

'They, too, will be protected, Gazelle King.'

'O great King, the birds will be protected, and what about the fish in the waters?'

'I grant protection to them also, Gazelle King.'

After in that way the Bodhisatva had asked the king for the protection of all animals, he rose and most gracefully introduced the king to the teachings of Buddha. He stayed in the park for some days, and then returned to the woods, surrounded by his gazelles.''

This Indian legend originated more than 2,100 years ago. Gazelles are a sub-family in the animal kingdom, with fifty-nine different sub-species again. The beauty and agility of the slender, slightly built animals is praised in many legends and poems of the Ancient Orient. In the Middle East—Palestine, Syria, Irak and Arabia—mainly the true gazelle *(Gazella gazella)* was hunted, while in the deserts of Central and Northeast Asia the goitred gazelle *(Gazella subgutturosa)* is widely spread. In the open savannas of India and West Pakistan there existed at one time many cervine antelopes which are a species of true gazelle. Their remarkable exterior contributed to their extermination. The black male animal, weighing some 40 kilogramm, has twisted horns which may be up to 60 centimetres long. This makes the grown-up male a coveted quarry. The sandy-coloured female has no horns. The young male gazelles are grey, and only turn black when they mature.

With a tethered strong male, a herd of cervine antelopes could be lured easily, so that hunting success was assured, specially at night. This contributed much to the extermination of the species in India. Nowadays the cervine gazelle is practically extinct in the savannas.

Recently cervine antelopes were introduced to Texas from India, and bred in large herds on game farms (more than 4,000 animals), and there are now more of these animals in Texas than in India.

The milu—the later Père David's deer—suffered a similar fate in North China.

Unknown Deer in the Game Park of the Imperial Palace at Peking

''The main item in this shipload is the "ssu-pu-hsiang", a kind of big reindeer whose female has no antlers. For a long time I have tried to obtain one of this interesting species of deer, unknown so far to natural scientists.''

Armand David (1886)

The oldest Chinese literature shows that hunting was of great economic importance, and equally served as a training for war. It is, for example, said of the Shang Dynasty (1750 B.C.): ''Hunting is common in the second month, and as this was particularly for wild pigs, skill in the use of weapons was needed. Also, the exercise was dangerous, and for that reason alone, it was a preparation for war.''

And indeed, hunting in Ancient China was a training for war, as it was in so many other places. It demanded order and obeyance. Autumn hunts tended to be combined with the great autumn manoeuvres, when after the inspection of troops grandiose drives took place.

In Ancient China hunting was under the Ministry of War, and the archers were the emperor's picked unit.

Under the Han Dynasty in the second century B.C. the art of archery reached its peak. Many pictures illustrate hunting with bow and arrow, a privilege of the country's high dignitaries.

This kind of hunting in the marches and river plains of North and Central China was mainly for the milu—the later Père David's deer—which in the course of time became completely extinct. It was only in the game parks that a few specimens survived.

A Chinese manuscript from about 1120 B.C. records a successful hunt. At that time the quarry of one court hunt was 22 tigers, 2 wild cats, 5,235 stags, 12 rhinoceroses, 721 yaks, 151 brown bears, 118 grizzly bears, 352 wild boars, 18 badgers, 16 elks, 50 musk deer and 3,508 Sika deer. This enormous quarry appears to have been possible only through the hunt taking place in the game park of the King Chou Wu-wang, which was dismantled only with the fall from power of the last emperor of the Shang Dynasty. This park, measuring some 40 kilometres square, and called "The Park of Intelligence" was situated between Peking and Nanking, and made about 1150 B.C. Next to mammals, many birds, tortoises and fish were kept in it.

These game parks served one purpose only, namely to provide pleasure and recreation for the ruler. At the same time they were the biggest hunting grounds in the country. The most famous of them was the emperor's game park, south of his residence in Peking. In about 1400 it was surrounded by a wall three metres high and seventy-five kilometres long, so that for more than five hundred years no trespasser could enter this "forbidden city". Special officials bred the animals, and cared for them. Foresters supervised the park's grounds. Very little was known in public about the animals in the park.

It was by chance that the world heard about the discovery of the milu, a species of animal, unknown until then. Armand David, a French Jesuit father, teacher at the mission school in Peking, made the discovery during a walk in 1865. Through a small gap in the wall of the game park at the Imperial Palace he saw that under the old cedar trees deer were feeding of a kind, he, an experienced natural scientist, did not know. Did the Jesuit father on his morning walk really discover a species of deer, unknown to the experts so far? His casual observation kept him alert until he had exact proof of the facts.

The ancient Chinese called the animals ssu-pu-hsiang, which means "None of four" but "Four in one" (neither stag nor goat, neither donkey nor ox). The animals were strongly guarded by men of the Tartar Guard, and were not known to the general public.

Through the agency of the French embassy in Peking David received — at the end of January 1866 — as an "honourable" gift, three of the valuable broad-hooved animals from the Imperial Game Park. Highly delighted, he took leave at once and boarded a ship to accompany the animals to Europe. Two died on the long sea journey, but one deer arrived safely in Paris, to become a sensation there. Professor Milne-Edwards confirmed that this animal had long since become extinct in its wild state. In honour of the man who discovered it, the deer was called Père David's deer (*Elaphurus davidianus*).

The antlers are of a strange shape. The two front branches are the brow-tines while the two main branches grow to the back. It has been observed with some of these deer that as early as February or the beginning of March, they shed their antlers for the summer growth which they rub off in May or early June, and discard in October. The stags grow their smaller winter antlers in November, cleanse them in January, to keep them only until the end of February. These two different kind of antlers are also met, if rarely, with other deer.

The Père David's deer soon attracted general attention in other European zoos. In 1869 the British envoy in Peking, Sir Rutherford Alcock, procured a pair of deer for the London Zoo. From 1876 onwards the Berlin Zoo also began building up a small herd, known under the nickname of *Olle Chinesen* — ancient Chinamen. Until 1913 twenty-three animals were raised in Berlin. Among representations of the Père David's deer, there is a water-colour by the German painter, Adolph Menzel, supposed to represent this rare animal. It was published in an album for children under the title, *Hirsche im Zoologischen Garten* (Deer in the Zoological Garden), of 1884. It shows the characteristic features of this special deer. So far this watercolour has not been reproduced in colour in the literature on zoology and hunting, as it could not be traced after 1945. However, it does exist in the Collection of Copperplate Engravings of the Staatliche Museen in Berlin, under the catalogue number of 1,028, and next to Adolph Menzel's signature, it carries the date 1863. According to this, the work can hardly be a representation of the Père David's deer, as this was only discovered in 1865. The fact has been pointed out in German Literature on the subject, and it has been suggested that Menzel changed his picture in 1883 — before publication of the

13 Study of the head of a large Père David's deer. Drawing by Michael Kiefer.

album—in order to show the much discussed rare species. A check under ultra–violet rays, made in 1975, did, however, not reveal later changes or re–painting of the original. A perusal of Adolph Menzel's sketchbooks, also kept in the Collection of Copperplate Engravings, made clear that in 1863 the artist made the sketch as one of a red deer whose antlers and legs do not show up as well as in the later watercolour. The female animal in the foreground, however, can be easily recognised as a fallow deer, and is represented as such in the water colour also. The question whether Menzel's picture is that of a Père David's deer remains open.

Several expeditions to the marshes and reedlands of North China, on the Yellow River did look for specimens of the milu, but without success. The Père David's deer has been extinct in the wild for 3,000 years. In 1894 further bad news reached Europe. Devastating floods penetrated the Imperial Game Park in Peking, and destroyed many animals. Only few deer survived the natural disaster, and later settled again in their old area.

When in 1900 the rebellion of peasants and artisans, the I Ho Ch'uan movement or "Boxer" rebellion was suppressed, fierce fighting took place around the Imperial Game Park, and European troops killed more than one hundred Père David's deer. In 1901 only one female animal remained in the Peking Zoo. It died in 1920.

In European zoos there was little success in breeding the animal, and in 1914 the last of the species died in Hagenbeck's game park in Hamburg. It then appeared that one more species of game was extinct forever, until one day the experts were surprised by the news that the Duke of Bedford at Woburn Abbey had made it his task to save the last Père David's deer from extinction. Since 1898 he had settled in his private game park Père David's deer from several European zoos. On marshy ground and with large areas to roam and feed in, they reproduced much more quickly than in zoos. In 1922 there were 64 Père David's deer at Woburn, 182 in 1932 and about 400 in 1950. The World Register of Père David's deer, kept at Whipsnade Zoo in London for the IUCN (International Union for the Conservation of Nature), gives the number of milus all over the world.

After the Second World War the animal park at Berlin-Friedrichsfelde was also successful in breeding Père David's deer systematically, and the animal can now be found again in 69 zoos all over the world. In fact 600 animals were registered in 1971, and in the same year 141 calves were born. Thanks to the international collaboration of zoologists, the Père David's deer has been saved, in the end due to the initiative of one man, namely the Duke of Bedford. In 1954 Père David's deer from Woburn Abbey went to their ancient Chinese homeland, so that in Peking, too, they can be seen again.

32/33　*The hunting camp after the hunting party. Detail of a scroll.*
Painting on silk. China, after 1700. Deutsches Jagdmuseum, Munich

34 *Père David's deer in the Animal Park at Berlin-Friedrichsfelde*

35 *A. von Menzel: Stags in the Zoo. Water-colour from* Kinderbuchalbum.
Staatliche Museen. Kupferstichkabinett and Collection of Drawings, Berlin

36 *Père David's stag with new antler growth*

37   Hunting in the Chang-pai mountains in the province of Kirin (Northeast China).

38   Chinese archer with crossbow near the Yo-wa-lon Pass. Museum für
Völkerkunde, Leipzig

39 *Roman sarcophagus with hunting reliefs. 3rd century. Sanssouci Park,*
Römische Bäder, Potsdam

40 *Meleager and Atalante (School of Rubens). The hunt for the Calydonian Boar.*
First half of 17th century. Staatliche Museen Dessau, Mosigkau Castle
(German Democratic Republic)

41   Diana of Ephesus. Roman copy of the statue from the Temple of Artemis in Ephesus. Museo Nazionale Archeologico, Naples

42   Boar hunt. Roman mosaic. Museo Etrusco, Chiusi

43   Alexander the Great and his general Craterus, fighting a lion. Mosaic, late 4th century B.C. Pella (Macedonia)

44   Gladiator fighting a panther. Floor mosaic in a Roman villa, about 250. Museum, Bad Kreuznach (Federal German Republic)

45   *Cretan-Mycenaean bronze dagger, decorated with a scene from a lion hunt.*
16th century B.C. National Museum, Athens

46   *B. Dietterlin: Forest scene with Actaeon and Diana. 17th century. Staatliche*
Kunstsammlungen, Gemäldegalerie Alte Meister, Dresden

47 *Habibullah of Meshed: Young dandy with flintlock. Persian miniature,*
17th century. Staatliche Museen, Islamisches Museum, Berlin

48 *Bronze bowl with gold and silver inlay. Mosul, Mesopotamia, second half of*
13th century. Staatliche Museen, Islamisches Museum, Berlin .

49 King Chosrau II hunting. Iranian silver-gilt crater, 6th century.
Bibliothèque Nationale, Cabinet des Medailles, Paris

50 Oriental decorated daggers of the 15th to the 18th century. Staatliche
Kunstsammlungen, Historisches Museum, Dresden

51 Spring-lock gun with silver damascening. Turkish, 17th century. This gun
was a present from the Empress Catherine II to Augustus the Strong of Saxony, on
the occasion of his coronation at Cracow. Staatliche Kunstsammlungen,
Historisches Museum, Dresden

Illustrations on the following page:

52 Diana. Ivory figure. Hermitage, Leningrad

53 Artemis of Versailles. Roman copy of a Greek sculpture, 340 B.C. Louvre,
Paris

Artemis and Diana, the Goddesses of the Chase in Antiquity

"I sing to Artemis,
to her with the golden arrows,
the boisterous, wild virgin,
the bow–loving, the fear of the stag.
On shadowy heights and wind–swept
rocky mountains she gaily pursues the chase,
and drawing her bow
she dispatches deadly arrows."

Homer, Hymns (8th century B.C.)

Artemis, the Goddess of the Chase, was the twin sister of the Sun God Apollo. The Persians called her Anahita, and the Romans Diana.

The daughter of Zeus and the beautiful Leto, chaste Artemis, received high respect and esteem from the Greeks. As patroness of all animals, Goddess of Chastity and Fertility, Artemis is represented with bow, quiver and torch, accompanied by nymphs and roe deer.

In Finnish mythology we find tales of the beautiful wife of Tapio, the woodland god, who protected animals, both wild and domesticated. There appears to be a closer connection between the Nordic gods of the forest and the Artemis legend of Antiquity than has hitherto been assumed.

On the west coast of Asia Minor Croesus, the wealthy king of Lydia (560–546 B.C.) had a sanctuary erected in Ephesus, consecrated to Artemis, a temple which was among the seven wonders of the ancient world.

We know from the writings of Herodotus that under the direction of the architect, Chersiphro, from Knossos, and his son, Metagenes, a gigantic building was erected, the sanctuary of Artemis, surrounded by a temple supported by 127 columns.

In 356 B.C. Herostratus, perhaps in a fit of madness, perhaps anxious to perpetuate his name, set fire to the temple, which collapsed in a heap of debris and ashes. Under Alexander the Great the sanctuary of Artemis was rebuilt on the same spot, until in A.D. 263 it was completely destroyed by the Goths. Today it is a ruin, half submerged in the silted up bay of the waters of the Aegean. It was discovered in 1863 by a British engineer, Wood, and has since been excavated mainly by the Austrian Archaeological Institute. Recently plans have been mooted for the rebuilding of the temple in its original state. A few objects in the museum at Ephesus bear witness to the gigantic size of the temple.

Artemis was not only the Goddess of the Chase and patroness of all helpless beasts, she was mistress also of all wild life and was Goddess of the Night and the Moon. As Patroness of the animals she was often represented with lions, cattle, goats and stags, and the bee was sacred to her.

In the world of Homer's legends the goddess appears in the tale of Actaeon, a youth and passionate hunter who killed many animals. It was said that Actaeon had "boasted about his own hunting being superior to that of the goddess ... Soon after these rumours, Actaeon with his companions and a pack of fifty hounds went into the mountains where they happened to come upon a place often visited by the goddess. Some believe this to have been chance, others say that the angry goddess herself had lured the youth to the spot, for she was set on destroying Actaeon.

Why are the hounds so restless? Why do they whimper all the time? What is wrong with this spot? What is happening? Then Actaeon saw a small stream in the meadow grass, in which Artemis was bathing, naked ...

The youth stood startled, unable to take his eyes off the goddess: 'How beautiful you are O goddess,' he stammered. 'Let me admire you, just for a moment, one moment only.'

But the nymphs cried out: 'Flee Actaeon, flee! Don't look this way. Flee Actaeon, flee!'

Then Artemis spoke: 'Villainous wretch, you have made bold to say that you are a better hunter than I am. You deserve that an arrow should pierce your heart! But even worse shall befall you to punish you for your wickedness.'

Saying this, the goddess took water from a copper vessel, and sprinkled it on Actaeon's eyes. Hardly had the water touched him when he was turned into a stag. He fled at great speed, but his hounds, not recognising him, ran in full pursuit.

'What will I do?' thought the youth. He had kept his human consciousness and was aware of having been turned into a stag, since he saw his new image reflected in the stream. It was the wish of Artemis that the youth should experience fully all his suffering right to the terrible end.

'I am Actaeon,' he shouted to his hounds who coursed him through the forest. But instead of words, all that came from his mouth was a hollow dreadful sound. The hounds kept up the chase, and the stag ran through fields and woodlands which had been once his own hunting grounds.

At last the hounds cornered him, and again he wanted to cry out: 'I am Actaeon, let me go, I am your master.'

But the pack attacked him and pulled him down.

The hounds bayed to call Actaeon to the place, so that he could see the conquered stag, and take pleasure in his victory. Nobody could tell the faithful hounds that it was their beloved master himself who lay on the ground before them in the shape of a stag, and who looked at them, his staring eyes breaking."

So far the re–telling* of the legend of Antiquity about the passionate hunter. It can be traced back to the Roman poet Ovid (43 B.C.—A.D. 17) who tells the story in the third book of his *Metamorphoses*. The Hrabanus Maurus Codex from the eleventh century A.D., kept at Monte Casino, also contains the Artemis legend.

Huntsmen and nature conservationists of our own day keep stressing that moral principles of hunting and the protection of wildlife are a modern concept. However, many oriental tales and legends of Antiquity do reflect early thought on conservation. These legends, transmitted by word of mouth, speak of the true meaning of hunting.

We know from Homer that the people of his day valued huntsmanship. They knew how to protect themselves from predators, and hunting for game provided them with much of their food. They did take delight in drawing a bow, throwing a spear and coursing game, over and over again.

In Greece and Rome the hunting of game was neither restricted by ownership nor time. Only in the close surroundings of Athens, it was forbidden to hunt by night in order that "no commercial butchers might exterminate the animals".

Classical Antiquity knew neither hunting laws nor close times for game.

After the hunt, according to Homer, people told stories of "the daughter of Zeus and Leto, the chaste goddess Artemis. Songs of praise were sung and sacrifices and gifts offered which would please the proud Goddess of the Chase."

As a hunting companion of Artemis, Callisto is often mentioned, the huntress who was changed into a she–bear by the jealous Hera.

Later on the Romans took over the cult of Artemis. Her most famous statue, the so–called "Diana of Versailles" is a marble copy of a Greek original from the second half of the fourth century. Found in the ruins of Hadrian's villa in Tivoli, it now stands in the Louvre. The statue was on loan to the World Exhibition of Hunting in Budapest in 1971. Servius Tullius (578—534 B.C.), the legendary sixth king of the Romans, in the course of his political reforms, had a temple built on the Aventine Hill in Rome, on the model of the temple of Artemis in Ephesus. Consecrated to Diana, it served the whole of Latium, and glorified the protectress of women, the chase, fertility, growth and the Goddess of the Moon.

In the second century B.C. Greek influence kept increasing in Rome. The Greek gods, the Olympian pantheon, became a standard component of Roman thought. There were also popular sanctuaries of Diana on Lake Nemi at Aricia and at Capua, both on the Via Appia. The hunting cult of Artemis was not completely transferred to Diana, centred on her great temple on the Aventine Hill but also spreading to distant provinces of the Roman Empire.

This was particularly so in the hunting regions of the Ardennes. Here many altars were sacred to Diana Arduenna, continuing the cult of the Celtic goddess Arduenna, the Goddess of Wild Boars. The French kings were later on to introduce their own cult of Diana, and in the mid–sixteenth century King Henry II (1547 to 1559) built a château for his mistress, Diane de Poitiers, in the village of Anet (Eure et Loire) and there established a new sanctuary to the goddess. Many representations of Diana date from this period, for example, Benvenuto Cellini's celebrated "Nymph of Fontainebleau" which is now in the Louvre.

The passion for hunting during the Renaissance and Baroque periods often found pictorial expression in hunting themes from Antiquity. The Venetian painters, Titian, Tiepolo and Tintoretto, in particular, found stimulation for their work in the legends of Antiquity. Raphael, Rubens, de Ryckers and many others were similarly inspired.

---

* From Mitru, A., *Die Sage des Olymp*. Bucharest, 1962.

Gladiatorial Contests and Animal Combats in Ancient Rome

The Emperors Hadrian and Gallienus often held these infernal combats, while the Emperor Antonius Caracalla shuddered, watching them with tears in his eyes, and condemned the blood-thirsty spectacles.

H. F. von Fleming (1724)

The anniversary of the founding of the temple of Diana, the 13th of August, was one of the few holidays granted to slaves. On such days the slaves in Ancient Rome were allowed to watch the magnificent contests, the races of chariots and horses in the Circus Maximus or the Colosseum, and the gladiatorial contests in the Flavian amphitheatre. The Colosseum alone held 50,000 spectators. Under the motto *panem et circenses*, the Roman emperors produced grand combats of animals —*venationes* —to entertain the crowds, and to court popularity. It is well known that next to chariot races, gladiatorial contests —taking place in the Roman arenas since 264 B.C. —formed the main attraction for all classes of society.

There were three types of contest: The bitter single combat of life or death between differently armed gladiators; combats of gladiators and beasts, or beasts fighting each other; *naumachias* —luxurious spectacles of sea battles, with artificially flooded arenas or specially made artificial lakes.

We are here particularly interested in animal combats. The famous schools for gladiators at Capua and Ravenna trained gladiators in single combat —*myrmillos* —fighting with the sword and also —*retiarriones* —fighting with nets and tridents. Special gladiators were trained for the fighting with wild beasts —*bestiarii*.

It had become boring "to watch all day men fighting each other, and so beasts were brought into the arena for a change. Either a man might fight beasts or the beasts might fight each other. More interesting even to the spectators was to see specially trained men meet the wild animals, or somebody condemned to death, naked, armed only with a cudgel, fight a starved beast and so enter into a hopeless combat." (O. Keller, 1887).

The first Roman Emperor, Augustus (63 B.C.—A.D. 14) organised grandiose spectacles to strengthen his political and social position in the slave-keeping society. He employed more than 10,000 gladiators. Reports in the ninth Book of the *History of Rome* by the historian, Livy (59 B.C.—A.D. 17) say that in combats in the Roman arenas more than 3,500 animals were killed.

The people bestowed honour on whosoever produced these spectacular events, especially if so far unknown animals were driven into the arena. In that way, lions, bears, tigers, cheetahs and also African Big Game: elephants, rhinoceroses and hippopotamuses caused loud applause.

It is told of the Emperor Marcus Aurelius that he had 1,000 African ostriches driven into the arena for one spectacle only. Wild animals from northern countries —bulls, bisons, elks and wolves also featured in the spectacles.

We know from Pliny that for the combats elks were brought to Rome from the forests of the Barbarian countries. In the Hercynian Forest of the Roman province of Germania —the region between the Rhine and the Carpathians —elks then existed in largish numbers in the wild.

Julius Caesar (100—44 B.C.) in the fifth book of his *De Bello Gallico*, when relating his campaigns in Gaul, gives interesting details about encounters with elks, and the way they are caught. There is perhaps hardly a huntsman who will not take the stories with caution.

These tales certainly are among the first huntsman's yarns, and so we shall quote a little from them:

"In the Hercynian Forest there are animals, called elks whose shape and colour is not unlike that of goats; only they are bigger. They have legs without ankles or joints." And Caesar continues: "They do not lie down to rest, and are unable to rise again if by some chance they have fallen. Trees are their places of rest, as they lean against them, and enjoy some repose. When through following the scent the huntsmen have found out the haunts of these animals, they dig up all trees by the roots or saw into the trunks of trees which still look firm. Then, when the elks come to rest against them, they pull down the unsteady trees, and fall down themselves."

According to Caesar, the huntsmen have only to come and chain the elks, lift them, and, complete with their antlers, spanning almost 2 metres, drive them to the amphitheatres. Pliny took over this tale into his *Naturalis historia*, and transferred it to the species of *alces* which lived in Scandinavia. Pliny differentiates between animals of land, water and air while usually in Antiquity animals were divided into domesticated (including edible game) and wild animals. The meaning of the Latin word *bestia* has changed several times. If, to begin with, the word applied to all animals, it later on only meant wild animals and beasts of prey.

In Antiquity concepts of zoology were still broadly based on the ideas of the Greek philosopher, Aristotle, and his work on animals which proves him a careful observer of nature. Knowledge about game animals was limited until late in Antiquity, compared, for example, to the knowledge available on fish or horses. From reports on combats and from representations in Roman frescoes and mosaics from Pompey and particularly those of the Villa Erculia in Piazza Armerina in Sicily, we can increase our knowledge of the methods of catching wild animals, their transport and the way they were kept in Ancient Rome.

According to Roman law animals in the wild were unprotected, and everyone, except slaves, could catch or kill them.

Roman law considered property only that which was under a person's personal power and authority. Hence an animal belonged to whoever caught or killed it.

In the Roman Empire legionaries were ordered to requisition during their campaigns prisoners and wild animals for the Roman spectacles. From the travel writings of the Greek geographer and historian, Strabo, (about 63 B.C.—A.D. 20) we learn of extensive Roman expeditions to Central Africa—up the river Nile to the Sahara—through the Arabian desert, and journeys of discovery on the Atlantic to the Canary Isles and far into the northern Atlantic Ocean.

The *lanista*, organiser, fencing master and manager of the gladiators, was also responsible for the supply of wild animals, so that next to the slave trade, there developed a flourishing business in Big Game. The splendid Berber lions, in particular, which came from the Northwest of Africa—Gaetulia, the present Algiers and Morocco, were caught in great numbers. They soon became extinct. The North African Atlas elephant was also exterminated.

It is said that in the animal reserve of Emperor Augustus one hippopotamus *(Hippopotamus amphibius)* lived for over forty years. Since the year 58 B.C. the hippopotamus was regularly used in spectacular combats. Well experienced catchers and wardens were needed to get these animals to Rome alive. Animals were caught mainly in pits. Young goats or sheep were used for tethering in the pits to lure lions with their bleating. Several kinds of cloths and nets were also used—*laxarum vestium*—for the catching of animals. They were transported mainly by sea in quick rowing boats, and a good knowledge of the keeping of animals was needed to convey them as speedily as possible and with the least possible loss to Rome. According to Pliny, Lupinus the Roman, began the systematic feeding of wild animals.

In the cellars of the amphitheatres the beasts were kept in pits, also special animal parks were established to keep them in readiness for the next combat. A few days before the bloodthirsty spectacle the animals were starved in order to give a special edge to their appetite.

14 The Calydonian boar hunt. Drawing after a marble sarcophagus from the 3rd century. Museo Nuovo in the Palazzo dei Conservatori, Rome

The following table provides an idea of the animals used in combat: —

Organiser of contests and combats (Reign)	Occasion of the spectacle	Species of animals used
Marcus Flavius Nobilior 180 B.C.	Aetolian War Gala Spectacle, lasting for ten days	Lion and panther hunt
P. C. Scipio Nasica and P. Lentulus, noble aediles 168 B.C.	Spectacles in the circus	63 panthers 40 bears and elephants
Censor Eneus Domitius Ahenobarbus	Circus	100 bears fought against 100 men
L. Cornelius SULLA (138—78 B. C.)	On the occasion of Sulla being elected praetor in 93 B.C.	many rare animals from Africa, among them 100 lions.
Consul POMPEIUS (106—48 B.C.)	Contests and combats in the circus	more than 600 lions. Special attraction: fight of a rhinoceros against an elephant
Pompeius (Second Consulate)	Circus	Africans from Gaetulia fight against elephants
Julius Caesar (Third Consulate)	Circus	20 elephants against 500 men on foot
Emperor AUGUSTUS 27 B.C.—A.D. 14	26 contests and combats, "to amuse the people"	nearly 10,000 gladiators fought against 3,500 animals, among them 200 lions
Emperor TRAJAN (A.D. 98—117)	After the victory over the Dacians (106) Trajan ordered 123 days of spectacles to celebrate the Dacians' defeat	more than 10,000 prisoners of war fought as gladiators, and over 11,000 animals were killed
Emperor PHILLIPPUS ARABAS (A.D. 244—249)	From a war against the Persians he brought back to Rome:	32 elephants, 10 elks 10 tigers, 60 lions 30 leopards 40 wild horses

The animals were specially cared for and injuries treated with the utmost concern. This made veterinary medicine —already developed with the Greeks, particularly concerning horses —reach a high standard with the Romans. It was also used more and more in dealing with wild animals.

Staff for feeding and caring for the animals in the enclosures of the amphitheatres consisted both of specially trained slaves and experienced huntsmen. In Rome as before that in Greece, professional hunters, venatores, were a recognised organisation.

In the late Empire the catching and killing of lions was strictly forbidden. Only by a decree of the Emperor Flavius Honorius (393—423) did the killing of lions become an imperial privilege in 414, while trade in lions remained prohibited. A total prohibition of combats with wild beasts did not come until the sixth century through the Emperor Anastasius (491—518) who made it an offence under threat of punishment.

On the Ancient Roman pattern animal combats took place between the fifteenth and eighteenth century at many German and Spanish courts. They are continued in the bull fights in the area of the eastern Mediterranean, mainly on the island of Crete. In contrast to animal combats in the Roman Empire, a completely new type of hunting was developed in Persia, the spectacular hunt.

Hunting Scenes on Persian
Silver Craters and Damascus Blades

"The golden crater makes the round with us,
decorated with many a picture made by Persian hands.
The crater's base reflects Chosroes,
And speedy antelopes run along its sides, fleeing from the horse-men's arrows."

Abū Nuwās (about 747–815)

The Great Kings of the Persians, "ruler over all men from the rising to the setting of the sun" with their spectacular hunts greatly influenced court hunting and the art of hunting in general.

Cambyses and Cyrus, the two most prominent kings of the Achaemenides dynasty saw hunting as a mere extension of war. They organised great battues on military lines. With these hunts 7,000 to 8,000 men were employed, and game was driven from as far away as 100 to 150 kilometres. Stags, wild asses and pigs as well as antelopes and roe deer were kept in large herds in great animal parks.

These parks in the royal domain were called *paradeisos* by the Greeks. In these "paradise" parks in Persia proper forestry and hunting economy were practised in order to keep the herds alive and healthy for the day of the court hunt. There were even tree nurseries where foreign plants were being acclimatised to assure fodder for the animals. Thousands of courtiers accompanied the king on a big hunt, and after the king had shot the first arrow the great carnage began. With spear, sabre, bow and arrow, the herded game was killed, mainly from the saddle. The use of horses in hunting saw a peak in Persia. Many ancient Persian carpets and reliefs show scenes from court hunts. Under the rule of the Sassanidae dynasty (3rd to 7th century A.D.) and the Arabian khalifs too, the hunt occupied an important place as a theme in art, especially in the art of engraving metal. The flat silver bowls in particular with their fine representations of hunting scenes are perfect accomplishments of this courtly craft.

These precious examples of the art of metal engraving show the hunting under the Sassanidae of lions, panthers, bears, wild boars, stags, gazelles, antelopes, as well as buffaloes, wild bulls, asses and tups.

Representations of lion hunts at the time of Shahpur II show a completely different artistic concept from that of Assyrian or Egyptian artists, portraying the same subject.

The flat silver, partly gilt, drinking vessels are now in several of the world's big collections. The art of exquisite metal working and the representation of hunting scenes has survived to this day. At the Budapest Exhibition of Hunting in 1971 the country of Iran showed excellent silver craters continuing the ancient tradition.

Damascus became an important centre for metal art in the Near East. Two hundred years after the fall of the West Roman Empire the Arabian tribes of the Near East united under the religion of the prophet Mohammed (about 570—632). The khalifs of Baghdad (representatives of the Lord on earth) with their armies conquered—from the seventh to the eleventh century—the Ancient Oriental lands from North Africa to India.

In 635 the Arabs stormed Damascus, and flourishing Arabic-Islamic science, culture and skilled craftsmanship created in the city of Damascus a centre of the armourer's art. The blades of daggers and swords of Damascene steel, the so-called Damascus blades, with their great elasticity and keenness of hard edge became the wish-dream of many a huntsman.

The technique of these magnificent weapons rests on the welding together of several rods of metal of varied strength. These steel rods are then twisted and through further welding and treating with acid the blades get their "flamed" or damask-like appearance, irregular in design and colour.

By the addition of metal threads or massive gold inlay, hammered under the incisions of the blade, any pictorial representation stands out well against the blue steel background. These splendid Arabian weapons were of superb artistic quality. Shaft handles and hilts were further embellished by jewels and precious stones. In fact, these weapons became a symbol of fairytale oriental splendour and synonym for all the glamour of the Arabian Nights. Damascus blades and the jewel-studded Arabian hunting weapons conquered the world's trade, and became much coveted gifts. Many can still be admired in art and historical collections. The art of horsemanship and hunting, as practised by Persians and Arabs, became the model for early medieval hunting in Europe.

Hunting and Game Conservation
in the Middle Ages

15 Coursing. Drawing from the manuscript *Vie et Histoire de Saint Denys*, about 1250. Bibliothèque Nationale, Paris

The Hunting Capitularies of Charlemagne

"He practised constantly riding and hunting as was the custom with his people."

Eginhard, Vita Caroli Magni, about 830

With the strengthening of the central power of the ruler, and the expansion of Feudalism, the Frankish Empire of the Merovingian and Carolingian dynasties developed in Western Europe.

In the eighth and ninth centuries the Carolingian empire reached from the Ebro to the Theiss, from the North Sea and the Baltic to the Apennine Peninsula. Carolingian imperial castles, estates and monasteries decided the social and economic life of the country. The peasants' hard work and endurance had created fertile arable land from a huge wilderness of moorland, marshes, forests and wastelands. The foundation of Carolingian imperial power was the enormous possession of real estate. Many decrees, capitularies, together with the royal prerogatives, ruled the strict handling of natural resources in the framework of Feudalism. This was reflected also in the hunting laws which underwent a decided change. According to the law of several West Germanic tribes, fishing and hunting was free within the bounds of tribal law. Whoever was entitled to carry arms, could also kill game. Basically the king had, until the fifth and sixth century, no favoured position concerning hunting, though young noblemen already practised hunting as a sport. Hunting prohibitions and close seasons for game cannot be traced in Germanic national law.

With the beginning and expansion of princely ownership of forests a new period for hunting laws began in the early Middle Ages. The concept of *forestis* appears for the first time in a parchment, from the year 648, for the royal forests of the Ardennes. The order was made by the Frankish King Dagobert, and belongs to the oldest hunting laws of Europe.

Under increased Carolingian power the forests became protected and reserved for royal hunts only: they belonged to the king's territorial rights. Through the claims of rulers to all unclaimed ground, wasteland and waters, the eighth and ninth centuries saw the rise of large continuous royal forests. Game in these forests was protected, and only the king could hunt in his own forests.

The Carolingian rulers were passionately devoted to hunting and organised splendid hunting entertainments. Royal Frankish hunts became the model for the later conduct of hunting, based on absolute royal privilege.

The creation of vast hunting grounds which by royal order could not be entered or hunted in, made court hunts possible and the methods they employed. Charlemagne's capitularies fixed a fine of 60 schillings for entering the royal forests. At that time the price of a cow was 1 schilling, a mare cost 3, a stallion 6 and a hunting falcon 3 to 12 schillings. Comparison makes the fine a very hard one.

The capitularies regulated—as edicts given by the ruler—all public life in the Frankish realm after 779. The best known edicts were the *capitulare de villis* and the *capitulare de missis*. These discuss in detail the management of the crown lands and estates, giving concrete directions for the men put in charge by the ruler. From this much may be learned about hunting. The inventories of crown estates mention among other things that peacocks, pheasants, ducks, pigeons, partridges and turtle-doves, also magpies, jackdaws and starlings are to be kept live. It was ordered also that falcons for hunting should be kept and cared for as well as sparrow-hawks, eagles and gun dogs, and special mention of this is made in chapter 36 of the *Landgüterordnung*—the estate regulations. Huntsmen were first-class experts, for example *bersarii* (for large game), *veltrarii* (for greyhounds), and *beverarici* (for those dealing with beavers and otters). There were also falconers and men hunting the wolf.

Charlemagne himself was a passionate hunter from his young days. At the good age of seventy-two he was still hunting. Many written sources tell of the emperor's hunting expeditions and the places he stayed in. The following are just a few examples: in the summer of 802 he hunted roe deer and wild boar in the Ardennes; in 803 it was aurochs in the Hercynian Forest, and from the end of September to the beginning of November in 804 the hunting was again for roe deer in the Ardennes. In July 805 until the autumn there were hunts ranging from Aachen via Thionville to Metz in the Vosges. During a hunt for bison in the Ardennes the king was injured in the leg by an angry bull, and his trousers and boots were torn to pieces. We owe the epic description of a court hunt of Charlemagne to his son-in-law, Angilbert, contained in a manuscript from the year 799 in the St Gall monastery, the *Carolus Magnus et Leo Papa.*

In the beautifully situated game park of Brühl near the residence at Aachen, a favourite hunting ground of Charlemagne, he ran the game with hounds and shot with his quick bow. Praising and glorifying the ruler in the poetic style of Antiquity is typical of the reports on court hunts of the early Middle Ages. The retinue gathered at break of day in front of the royal palace. Shouts of the huntsmen on foot mixed with the noise of servants hurrying to and fro, and the neying of the horses snatching at the bit, the king's horse was richly harnessed, decorated with gold and other metal ornaments. Trumpets sounded as the king at the head of his brilliant retinue of nobles and town dignitaries rode off. According to legend the king often punished severely the vanity of his noble followers by taking the hunt through thick undergrowth, making the sorry objects return with their clothes torn.

Young men carried the hunting equipment; spears with iron heads and huge nets for trapping. These young men were also in charge of the leashed hounds. Arrived at the hunting grounds the hounds were let loose to search in hedges and thickets. Game was then encircled by the mounted huntsmen, and with the hounds they followed the fleeing animals. They were out for wild boar, and at long last a boar would be sighted even though not all the hounds had taken up the scent but the remainder of the pack were ready to chase it. Shouting with joy the huntsmen drove the game, "encouraging" the boar with the sound of their horns. The enraged boar then tried to escape, but the pack continued the chase and at length they cornered the tired animal on a hillside. The boar courageously tried to get away from his persecutors, right and left hounds were overthrown, heavily hit by the angry boar.

When the huntsmen reached the boar the king himself took charge, plunging his keen sword into the beast's heart, and killing it. Hardly had the boar expired, when the ruler gave orders to continue the hunt. "... Large numbers of wild boars were the day's quarry. Everywhere they fell and were killed. The king divided the bag among his followers. In the end the hunting party would turn to a shadowy place for the hunting breakfast, taken preferably near a well. Here richly decorated tents had been erected where the meal was being prepared. Falernian wine refreshed the tired hunters, until long after sunset and very drowsy they lay down to rest."

This type of hunt in game parks was carried out at the courts of German princes until the eighteenth century.

The hunting calls for huntsmen and hounds were sounded on the oliphant, a horn made of an elephant's tusk, richly decorated.

It is said that the horn's call could be heard over a very great distance, even though only few notes could be sounded on it. Some horns had mouth pieces and decorations of gold and precious stones. The carrying of an ivory horn was a sign of special rank, and reserved for the nobility.

A few of these valuable horns are still kept in the great museums or the treasure houses of cathedrals. They may be seen also in hunting collections. Among the treasures of the cathedral at Aachen is a hunting horn, said to have been given to Charlemagne by Haroun–al–Rashid (Ill. 61). Its genuineness has, however, been questioned, as the carvings appear to have been made in the tenth century. There are many and impressive representations of early medieval horns.

The capitularies of Charlemagne say nothing about close seasons and conservation of certain species of game.

It is quite different with the protection of forests. From a dispute between the St Gall monastery and some peasants on the monastery estates, it becomes clear that the use of the forest for cutting wood, grazing animals or fattening pigs by the peasants, was carefully watched by the foresters who warned the peasants not to cut down oaks recklessly, as this would be to their and the monastery's disadvantage.

Hunting Prohibition to the Clergy

"Also we forbid all servants of God, to hunt or roam about the forests with hounds. Neither may they keep hawks or falcons."

Second Resolution of the Concilium Germanicum of 21. 4. 742

Though all hunting was officially prohibited to the clergy, many princes of the church were as passionate hunters as their feudal peers. The Council of Agde in Southern Gaul decided as early as 506 that priests, bishops and deacons should be barred from keeping hounds or falcons. Many other councils renewed this hunting prohibition, as the hunting passion of the spiritual dignitaries kept increasing. In 747 St Boniface complained to Pope Zacharias about many unworthy priests and bishops who indulged in their hunting passion. Often by falsifying documents, the monasteries tried to obtain hunting rights under the pretext of "needing the skins for binding bibles and using game hunted for relishing the weak". So it appears that in a decree by Charlemagne from 26 March 800 the abbot and monks of St Bertin were allowed to have servants hunt red deer in their own forest, in order to obtain skins and leather for gloves and belts as well as for the binding of books.

Bishop Jonas of Orléans (821—844) strongly attacked clerical dignitaries and the nobles for "spending money on birds for falconry and hounds, but little only on the poor". He also pointed to the harsh and cruel treatment meted out by the nobles to the poorer people, and this only to pursue their own pleasures. The noble gentlemen, he said, missed attending mass because of their hunting passion, and so did harm to the good of their own souls.

In the eleventh century Adam von Bremen reported in his Hamburg church history that many bishops and abbots paid little attention to the obligations of their calling. Worldly affairs seemed to take all their time, so that they neglected preaching and the care of their community. In their ways and their behaviour they hardly differed from secular princes. They would rather mount a fine horse than the steps to the chancel.

Bishop Interville of Auxerres had a falconer crucified because he had sold a falcon owned by the bishop. It is reported from Hungary that at the Council of Ofen (Budapest) in 1278 Ladislaw, the Saint, excluded the members of his order from hunting and falconry.

As late as the sixteenth century the council of the town of Münster in Westphalia, demanded that the clergy should not hunt, "as the *jus canonicum*," they said, "had many references to the clergy being prohibited to hunt. Rather should they spend their time exclusively in the business of the church, praying, reading and managing the church's estates and such matters. From all this, they are kept by hunting. Hounds and falconry birds must not be kept, and fed from clerical income or estate".

At this period of discussion about the right of the clergy to hunt, the legend of St Hubert originated.

The St Hubert and Eustace Cult

"And when he came into the forest to hunt, he saw many stags, and among them there was a specially beautiful one, who shone among the rest.
This stag turned round and spoke thus: 'Why do you chase me, Hubert?'"

The Jesuit Father Robert's Historie St Huberti, 1621

St Hubert's Day, the 3 November, was celebrated at one time with magnificent masses and splendid hunting entertainments.

According to legend, this was the day when Hubert, the passionate hunter, lost his way during a hunt in the forests of the Ardennes. Suddenly in his wanderings he saw in front of him a very fine stag who bore a radiant crucifix between its antlers. At the same time Hubert heard a warning voice, telling him to abandon unrestricted hunting and profess his Christian faith. Hubert was so impressed, says the legend, that he left the court, gave up all worldly vanities, and entered a monastery at Maastricht. It is from this time that we have the first documented proofs of his existence.

Hubert is said to have been born about 658, the son of Bertrand, Duke of Aquitania. He entered service at the court of Pépin of Héristal, who was a passionate hunter. It was at the court of his father that Hubert learnt about the cruelty of hunting, and decided to turn away from worldly pleasures, to become a monk at Maastricht. Here Bishop Lambert of Tongeren invited him to take part in a pilgrimage to Rome, and about 700 he is said to have been made Bishop of Liège by Pope Sergius I after Lambert of Tongeren had been assassinated. Hubert died on 30 May 727 in Vura in Brabant, and was laid to rest in Liège. He was soon accepted as a saint among the people and worshipped as the "Apostle of the Ardennes".

He was canonised only a hundred years later, and his remains were then taken to the Benedictine monastery of Andagium (Andain) in the Ardennes. The St Hubert Basilica was erected on the foundations of the old monastery church. From 827 onwards the name of the Abbey of St Hubert is mentioned, and it became a popular place of pilgrimage.

It is here that the famous gun dogs of the monastery were consecrated and branded with the mark of the golden St Hubert Key. Until the French Revolution the abbot of the St Hubert monastery had to supply the French king with six trained guide–dogs annually, from the monastery pack.

There are reports about the life of St Hubert, written down by a brother monk seventeen years after Hubert's death. From this *Vita Sanct Huberti* it is, however, not absolutely clear that, before being elevated to the bishopry, Hubert was actually a passionate hunter. Only in the tenth century did St Hubert become the patron saint of hunters.

It is interesting to note that in the town of St Hubert in the Ardennes the guild of butchers ("Genootschap van de Beinslagers") chose St Hubert as their patron in the twelfth century. Every year on the 3 November they organised a procession to the cathedral. At that time it was never mentioned that Hubert was honoured as the patron saint of hunting. The legend of the miraculous stag gained popularity in the fifteenth century, at a time when several Orders of St Hubert were founded, and the saint increasingly became the ideal of the sophisticated hunter.

In 1621 the Jesuit Father Robert's *Historie St Huberti* contained the description of the miracle of the golden cross. St Hubert's day, 3 November, which at one and the same time marked the end of the shooting season for larger game, was first celebrated in 1744.

In 1444 on St Hubert's Day Duke Georg V of Jülich founded the Order of the Knights of St Hubert as an act of thanksgiving for a battle won on that day. To begin with the Order was not connected with hunting, and only 300 years later did hunting entertainments become accepted on St Hubert's Day in place of other celebrations.

Sometimes these hunting parties and pleasures took several days, and the celebrations were of high moral value as they took a stand against unrestricted hunting and for the protection of game. They served to improve the image of hunting, and at the same time demonstrated the hunter's love of animals. Yet, these magnificent entertainments and court celebrations did not always follow the humane concept of preservation.

StHubert's Day has remained the festival of the huntsman. The 3 November no longer means the end of the shooting season for larger game, however, it is still a reminder of proper ways of hunting and the protection of game and all wildlife. In many countries of Western Europe St Hubert's Day begins traditionally with Holy Mass in a cathedral while elsewhere, especially in Eastern Europe, there are hunts on horseback or shooting parties, usually ending with a festive dinner.

In the town of St Hubert in the Ardennes a great festival takes place, enjoyed by countryfolk, artisans and shopkeepers of what is considered there the patron saint of the butchers and all country people. In 1960 huntsmen, especially from the Federal Republic of Germany, came flocking in for the festive procession, and St Hubert is now claimed by an ever increasing crowd of followers.

The literary content of the miraculous stag may be found early in the legends surrounding the Roman general Placidus. In charge of the army under the Emperor Trajan, he is known to have been a passionate hunter. After meeting the miraculous stag, he became a Christian, and was later canonised as St Eustace. His cult goes back possibly to Indian and Buddhist literature of the third century B.C. A golden stag is mentioned at the period whose eyes are as bright as precious stones and whose antlers are of pure silver.

No documentary sources of the St Eustace legend have been traced yet, and as far as the history of hunting is concerned the legend gained in importance only at the height of the Middle Ages. The relics in the Church of St Eustace in Paris appear to have little real significance. The 20 October is the Day of St Eustace.

The first pictorial representations of the miraculous stag date from between 1138 and 1147. They are contained in the hymn books of the monastery of Zwiefalten in Germany, and this fine manuscript is now in the keeping of the Württembergische Landesbibliothek at Stuttgart.

The stag motif and St Hubert were represented by many artists in the centuries to follow, and became increasingly associated with hunting. The legend of St Eustace is depicted impressively in the stained glass windows of Chartres Cathedral which date from the beginning of the thirteenth century. The reference here is to Placidus and not, as customary, to Eustace or Hubert.

The vision of the saint and martyr, Eustace, was described at the end of the thirteenth century by the Genoese Archbishop Jacobus de Varagine in the *Legenda aurea*.

16 St Hubert. Engraving from the Lower Rhine, about 1470.

The Art of Falconry

"I trained myself a falcon
for longer than a year.
You know how tame and well–bred
the beautiful bird was then.
When I dressed its fine plumage
with the richness of gold,
the bird took off into the clouds
and flew to distant lands."

Der von Kürenbnrg (about 1150—1170)

Through the Crusades the feudal nobility of Europe became acquainted with Arabian and Byzantine methods of hunting.

Falconry originated in Asia, and was popular at the courts of emperors as a noble and chivalrous sport. It was an expensive pleasure with much ceremonial splendour and precisely regulated usages and rules attached to it. There are many and different methods of falconry but only some interesting historical and social aspects of the sport will be discussed here.

The earliest sources concerning falconry go back to a Chinese king, ruler of the kingdom of Ch'ou, who organised falconry at the Lake of Tung–t'ing in the Province of Hunan between 689 and 675 B.C. Reports from Ancient feudal Korea also speak of falconry birds being strictly protected. All falcons in the land were under the direct protection of the ruler.

In Japan falconry was introduced only in 335 B.C. by the sixteenth Emperor Mintoku when as many as forty–three kinds of hawking birds were known. In the eighth and ninth centuries the War Ministry of the Japanese Imperial Court had a special department of falconry. Five ancient Japanese families undertook falconry training according to traditional rules and instructions. At the height of the Middle Ages great training schools for falconry evolved from these training grounds, and became known as falconry courts. Special methods of catching and training the birds, as well as caring for them, were taught together with other aspects of falconry. This time also saw the beginnings of an extensive literature on the subject. More than six hundred books on falconry are known to have originated in Japan alone, among them an eighty–one–volume work by the Emperor Mintoku himself.

Falconry in Asia reached its climax at the time of Genghis Khan (1155—1227). Over seven thousand families of falconers were under the direct jurisdiction of a prince of the ruling house of the Monguls. It was Genghis Khan's order "to hunt regularly, as hunting is the training ground for war". He formed regiments of hunters, with falconers as his own body guard. Under Genghis Khan, too, falconry came under the Ministry of War, and a gold falcon was the messenger symbol of his couriers.

Since 1304 Persian princes ruled supremely over falconry in Asia, and Persian falconry became the model for European practice.

Marco Polo reports from the second half of the thirteenth century that falconry was very popular all over Asia, from the Black Sea to China. "They keep a great number of falcons and gerfalcons, carrying the bird on their right hand. They tie a small leash to the bird's neck which reaches about half way down the body. When they release the bird to catch prey, they press head and body down a little."

Marco Polo also reports that the Emperor of China went hunting in Manchuria, and that his hunting camp consisted of over ten thousand tents, and more than two thousand falconers took part in one hunt.

It is said of the Turkish Sultan Amurath II (end of the fourteenth century) that he employed over six thousand falconers. Sultan Bayazid (1389—1402) had as many as seven thousand falconers and six thousand keepers of hounds in his service.

Hunting with falcons was introduced to Europe in the third century, and one of the first written accounts comes from Paulinius of Pella who lived in Bordeaux in the fourth century, and mentioned a *speciosum accipitrem*. In the laws of King Gundobad (about 505) falconry is included in chapter 86 of *Leges Burgundiorum*.

As early as about the year 530, chapter 36 of *Lex Ribuaria* speaks about punishments for the prohibited snaring of birds of the chase. It was, however, not until the height of the Middle Ages that falconry developed rapidly in Europe, obvious among other things through the writing of the first falconry textbook by the Emperor Frederick II (1194—1250). Frederick's son, Manfred, issued his father's manuscript in 1260, under the title, *De Arte Venandi cum Avibus*.

Frederick II acquired his passion for falconry during the Crusades when he came to know the falconry courts of the Near East. His comprehensive work contains detailed observations of nature and descriptions of the behaviour of different species of falcons. It is illustrated by drawings, made most likely from sketches by the emperor himself. The emperor's study is the first scientific one in Europe, dealing with ornithology and hunting of the period.

The eventful history of this manuscript is interesting: the original of the splendid imperial codex with its hundreds of miniatures, was lost in 1248 during the siege of Parma. A part copy, probably ordered by King Manfred of Sicily, between 1258 and 1266, was for long in the possession of the Count Palatine of the Rhine, and after that at the University Library of Heidelberg. During the Thirty Years' War the manuscript came as booty to Duke Maximilian of Bavaria (1573—1651). In 1623 he made a present of it to the Vatican in Rome where the manuscript is kept to this day. The first printed edition was published by M. Velserus (Prätorius) in 1596, and a complete modern facsimile edition became available in 1968. A further copy, dating from about 1300, is a rendering into French, with the miniatures supplemented and brought up to date.

Hunting played an important part in the courtly epics and poetry of the twelfth and thirteenth centuries. The producers of much of this work in Germany were the minnesingers who modelled themselves on the troubadours, the wandering minstrels of Provence. Their poems and songs treat of courtly love but also of the beauties of nature and the countryside. Wolfram von Eschenbach, Heinrich von Morungen and Walther von der Vogelweide are outstanding representatives of this period.

A precious manuscript, now in the University Library at Heidelberg, contains a great number of songs and poems of the minnesingers. It is said to have been collected by a Swiss Knight, Rüdiger Manesse, and has become known as the *Manessische Liederhandschrift*. The codex contains 138 miniatures, likenesses of some of the most important poets in the Middle–High German language. The miniatures are full of details from the life of these knightly poets, including scenes from hunting, as, for example, a representation of falconry with King Conrad the Younger and Wernher von Teuffen.

There are many detailed descriptions of falconry in Europe in the hunting manuals published from the fifteenth to the eighteenth century. The oldest printed book on hunting, *Meysterliche stuck von Bayssen und Jagen*, published in Augsburg in 1531, survives only in one original copy. A facsimile edition of this appeared in 1971, and other important books on falconry have also been reissued in facsimile in recent years. In 1576 George Tuberville published a book on falconry in London. Mention should be made here of Albertus Magnus's book *Von den Falken und Habichten*, of the work *New Falcknereybuch* by Johann Wolff, published in 1584 and of French books on falconry by Jean de Franchieres, Mallopin, Cassianus, Guillaume Tardiff, Artebouche of Alagona and Charles de Arcussia.

Falconry is a subject in the literature of ancient Russia as early as the fifteenth century, when the courage and skill of falconers and all huntsmen is praised in the manuscript *Sadonstchina* by Ryasnev Sofonia.

17 Duke Heinrich of Meissen hawking. Manesse Manuscript, about 1300. Universitätsbibliothek, Heidelberg

Tardibus in his *New Jagd– und Weydwerck* of 1582, demands that a falconer should be: "straight, congenial, gentle, kindly and of good graceful deportment and manners. He must be courageous and friendly, possessed of a love for falconry. He must not get angry when a falcon is idle, and shout at the bird, scold or even pinch, push or beat it. On the contrary the falconer must keep calm and patient, redressing the bird's faulty behaviour by treating it carefully and skilfully training it. The falconer must be diligent, not afraid of work by day or night. He must always think of his falcons, and neither wind, weather, heat or cold must diminish his eagerness to work with them." The very same principles might well be applied today.

In the late Middle Ages falconry was popular at all courts, and the ladies took part in the hunt. Queen Elizabeth I (1558—1609) took delight in falconry and her Grand Master was a lady too, Mary of Canterbury.

Next to precious horses, weapons and jewellery, a trained falcon was a highly valued gift, one of the most attractive exchanges between diplomats and rulers. Many courts were supplied with falcons from hunting grounds in Eastern Europe which had become accessible through feudalist progress to the East. The training school for falconry founded in 1390 by the Grand Master of the Order of Teutonic Knights in the fortress of Marienburg, became one of the chief suppliers. The following list shows some of its customers:—

In 1401 —the King of Bohemia, the King of Poland, The Duke and Duchess of Austria, the Elector of the Rhine, the Margrave of Meissen, the Count of Württemberg, the Burgrave of Nuremberg.
In 1402 —Duke Luitpold, the Bishop of Freysing, Duke Wilhelm of Austria, the Duke of Saxony, the Archbishop of Mayence.
In 1405 —the Dukes of Cleves, Holland, Geldern and Saxony, also the Archbishops of Cologne, Mayence and Trèves.
Very frequently falcons were dispatched as official presents: in 1408 80 falcons to the Pope, the King of Portugal and others. The Emperor in Vienna received 14 of these. In 1509 the Emperor again received 12 birds, the Pope 8, and the Kings of France, England and Portugal 6 each. The Duke of Saxony got 4 birds. Between 1533 and 1569 one thousand eight hundred and eighteen falcons were given by the Grand Master of the Order of Teutonic Knights to foreign princes and rulers. Others, too, were involved in these diplomatic exchanges. In 1615 the Elector of Brandenburg sent 18 birds to the Emperor in Vienna, 12 to the King of France, 10 to the King of England, 18 to English princes, 12 to Moritz of Saxony, 2 to Jacobus Moravius in England and 9 to the Elector Johann Sigismund.

Hungary sent hunting falcons as special presentations to the Belgian court.

In Europe the bird most frequently trained for hunting was the peregrine *(Falco peregrinus)*. The rue falcon *(Falco pusticulus)* is specially valued, occurring in different habitats, and consisting of several species. The best known are the Icelandic, the Greenland falcon and the gyr–or gerfalcon. Danish falconers pursued the bird in Greenland, and sent shiploads to Europe. This trade in white falcons earned the island large sums of money until well into the eighteenth century. The St John's Knights of Malta also carried on a flourishing trade in falcons. The stock of falcons decreased rapidly in the late Middle Ages, so much that the demand for young birds could scarcely be satisfied.

18 J. E. Ridinger: Autumn. Staatliche Kunstsammlungen Greiz, Kupferstichkabinett, (German Democratic Republic)

Falconry reached its glamorous peak during the sixteenth century at the French court. Under Francis I (1515 – 1547) three hundred falcons were kept. The *Grand Fauconnier* of the king, René de Cossé, commanded ex officio fifteen nobles, fifty masters of falconry and many other servants. He had the sole right of selling falcons all over France, and he took a customs duty of every bird bought or imported.

Fierce competition existed between hunters and falconers at the court. It quietened down only when in the spring, with the beginning of the moulting of falcons, the hunters gained the upper hand. On 3 May the green–clad huntsmen rushed into the castle forecourt, sounding their horns, and using green twigs, symbolically drove out the falconers. Now the time of stag hunts began, to last until 14 September when the stags "were no longer any good". This was the moment for the grey–clad falconers to return to the forecourt. Now the huntsmen had to confine their hounds to kennels. March was the height of the season for falconry. Heron hawking was one of the finest hunting experiences of the time.

In 1755 Margrave Wilhelm Friedrich of Bayreuth reported as his quarry of twenty–five years 37,238 items of game altogether, including 4,174 herons, 1,763 kites, 14,087 partridges, 5,059 hares and 6,563 crows of all kinds.

With the rise of firearms and quite specially the invention of finely grained shot, the stock of herons was much reduced, so that falconry as a most luxurious and expensive sport lost in importance quickly, and for a long time to come.

Nowadays the art of falconry is again carried on in many countries, with all its traditions intact. The impressive language of falconers is used once again. According to manuals of falconry the equipment of the falconer—glove, bag, jessel, soft leather straps, bell, bewit and varvels are made, mostly by the falconer himself, and from historical models.

Falconry more than any other way of hunting makes for a close relationship between man and animal. The skill and experience of the falconers of old are praised in all modern books on the subject, and the many facsimiles of ancient books on falconry find a well deserved market.

54 *Fresco with stag hunt. Museum, Paestum (Italy)*

55 Ladies hunting with ferrets. Miniature from the Psalter of Queen Mary of
England, about 1340. British Museum, London

56 Theoderic (Dietrich von Bern) hunting for stag. Relief on the West Portal of
San Zeno Basilica, Verona. Second half of 12th century

57 Blade of Charlemagne's hunting knife. Cathedral Treasury, Aachen

58 Small box, decorated with the "hunt of the wild people". Rhenish, about 1470.
Kunsthistorisches Museum, Vienna

59 The Bavarian Order of the Knights of St Hubert. Schatzkammer der Residenz

60 Pisanello: The Vision of St Eustace. About 1439. National Gallery, London

61 Charlemagne's hunting horn. Inscription; "deyn eyn". Ivory, about 1000.
Cathedral Treasury, Aachen

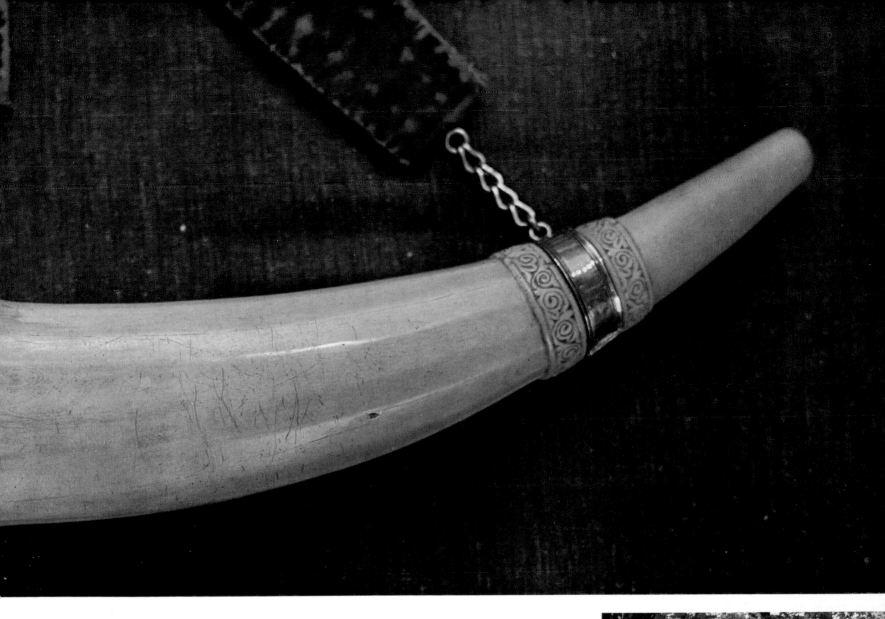

62   *Mass of St Hubert. The trumpeters of* Le Saint Hubert *sound their hunting horns at the St Hubert Mass of Obry, while in the shade of the castle wall a Catholic priest performs this rare religious ceremony at an ancient stone altar.*

*63   E. Grawert: St Hubert Hunt in the Grunewald with the Emperor Frederick
William IV, 1857. Staatliche Schlösser und Gärten, Jagdschloss Grunewald,
Berlin (West)*

64   Crozier of the Prior of the Order of St Hubert. Schatzkammer der Residenz, Munich

65   L. Cranach the Elder;
St Eustace. Pen
drawing, about 1530.
Museum of Fine Arts,
Boston

A reit Gessila an der gav
ain her von Bayren

66 *Master of the Pollingen Altar:*
Altar of the Monastery Church
at Pollingen.
Huntsmen with cross-bow and horn
accompany Duke Tassilo of Bavaria
on his way to the hunt.
Early 15th century.
Alte Pinakothek, Munich

67 Rayah Dhyan Singh, out hawking. Indian painting, about 1830. Victoria and Albert Museum, London

68 Camping after a hunting party. Detail from a scroll with the camp of the falconers. Painting on silk. China, after 1700. Deutsches Jagdmuseum, Munich

72 *Gerfalcon. Drawing by M. Wolf.*
From: H. Schlegel, Traité de
Falconnerie. *Rijksmuseum van*
Natuurlijke Historie, Leyden

73 *Kazakhstan huntsman with golden eagle*

74 *Russian falconer. Drawing by Samokish.*
From: N. Kutepov, Die grossfürstliche
und Zarenjagd. *St Petersburg, 1896*

69 *Hawking with a heron. Detail of a Japanese scroll. About 1800. Deutsches*
Jagdmuseum, Munich

70 *The Emperor Akbar and his son Djehangir, with a hawk. Indian miniature,*
about 1700. Staatliche Museen, Islamisches Museum, Berlin

71 *J. H. Tischbein the Younger: Falconer. Etching, 1785. Staatliche Museen,*
Kupferstichkabinett and Collection of Drawings, Berlin

75 F. Traini: Gentleman with hawk. Section from the
"Triumph of Death", about 1355. Camposanto, Pisa

76 Hawk. Indian miniature. Staatliche Museen, Islamisches
Museum, Berlin

77 Sakers. Miniature from the Falkenbuch of Frederick II,
first half of 13th century. Biblioteca Apostolica, Vatican

78 C. A. Hirsch: Falconer of the Margrave. 1752. Kreis-
und Stadtmuseum, Ansbach (Federal German Republic)

94

79   Prayer Book of the Emperor Maximilian I. Pen drawings by L. Cranach, 1515. Bayerische Staatsbibliothek, Munich

80   Title page from a textbook of hunting of 1580. German translation of Jacques de Foilloux, La Vénerie. Sächsische Landesbibliothek, Manuscript Collection, Dresden

81   J. Collaert, copperplate from J. Stradanus, Antwerp, 1578. Staatliche Museen, Kupferstichkabinett and Collection of Drawings, Berlin

82 *Hunting chamois. From:*
Weisskunig, *illustration*
by Hans Burgkmair the
Elder, 1512—1517.

83 *School of the Breviary of*
the Duke of Bedford.
Miniature from Gaston Phoebus,
Le Livre de la Chasse.
Bibliothèque Nationale, Paris

84 *Hunting roe buck.*
Section of a carpet from
Chatsworth, Derbyshire. Arras,
mid-15th century. Victoria and
Albert Museum, London

85 *Boar hunt. Section from a carpet, the hunt for bear and wild
boar. Arras, mid-15th century. Victoria and Albert Museum, London*

86 *Stag hunt. From the* Jagd- und Fischereibuch *of the Emperor
Maximilian I, Innsbruck Master (Jörg Kölderer?), about 1504.
Österreichische Nationalbibliothek, Vienna*

Glancing through the Pages of Old Hunting Manuals

"Game should be killed nobly and with decorum so that there may be good sport and yet enough game spared."

Gaston Phoebus (1391)

In the twelfth and thirteenth centuries hunting laws were set out precisely in all kinds of documents, capitularies and rulings of nearly every European country. The first comprehensive publication regarding methods and customs of hunting was *Le Livre du Roy Modus* of 1338, a small manuscript, kept at the National Library at Liège.

A French didactic poem about the hunting of red deer, *La Chasse du Cerf*, written anonymously about 1275 is, apart from the already mentioned works on falconry, one of the oldest manuscripts concerning hunting in Europe. This manuscript is in the Bibliothèque Nationale at Paris. These two manuscripts are not illustrated. Their text was used over and over again in later hunting manuals.

In the *Instructions of Prince Vladimir Monomach of Kiev for his Children*, from the twelfth century, hunting is likened to the life and success of the battle, and moral issues of hunting are given special consideration.

The most important document concerning hunting in fourteenth-century France is the *Miroir de Phebus* manuscript by the French Count Gaston III, also in the Bibliothèque Nationale.

Gaston III, Comte de Foix et Béarn lived in his castle of Orthez, close to the Pyrenees, from 1331 to 1391. With six hundred hunting horses and a pack of one thousand six hundred hounds, used in coursing, he was one of the most prominent huntsmen of Europe. In 1357/58 he visited the Teutonic Knights at the Marienburg where he hunted wolf, bison and elk. Here, too, he saw frescoes and reliefs with impressive representations of hunting scenes, before returning to France from East Prussia. Because of his striking appearance and his head of fair curly hair, he was called Phoebus—the Radiant. Gaston was one of the first to describe the hunting methods of his age when in 1370 he published the textbook of hunting, *Le Livre de la Chasse*. Dedicated to Philip the Bold of Burgundy, it became one of the most popular treatises of the Middle Ages. The manuscript was later on copied many a time, and was also translated (1507). Some forty copies are known to exist, with the most interesting one now in the Bibliothèque Nationale. It contains eighty-seven illustrations from the workshop of the limner of the Breviary of the Duke of Bedford, from between 1405 and 1410. These instructive miniatures on parchment show many different hunting scenes, in which the hunting of red deer occupies a special place. "Stags are pursued with hounds, greyhounds, nets, ropes and other equipment. Game is caught in pits, shot with bow and arrow, trapped or coursed on horseback," wrote Gaston. He died in May 1391 after a bear hunt at a hunting breakfast in the Forest of Sauveterre in the province of Navarre.

Edward II, Duke of York, who was imprisoned in the Castle of Pevensey since 1406, on account of a plot against the king, translated Gaston's treatise into English. Under the title, *The Master of Game*, the manuscript was finished in 1410. The translator who had been Master of Game to King Edward I, was well acquainted with hunting in England, and in his work he did not limit himself to the hunting of deer, but preceded its description by a chapter on the coursing of hare, a very popular sport in England then.

In the centuries to follow there appeared many and different hunting manuals and chronicles, listing quarry, often accompanied by illustrations. The wish of the ruling classes of seeing their successful hunting methods and records of quarry published in magnificent folios, richly illustrated, kept increasing. Outstanding among the many manuscripts is the *Jagdbuch* of the Emperor Maximilian I (1493—1519).

The "Last Knight", as he was called, Maximilian was a great huntsman, a patron of Humanism and all the arts. He founded one of the most important book collections in Europe, now incorporated in the Nationalbibliothek in Vienna. Among his many interests reflected in the library, hunting was an important one. He had his own hunting adventures recorded in a *Geheime Jagdbuch*—a secret book of hunting. His own work, *Weisskunig*, published in 1515, also contains some curious hunting reports, glorified as the emperor's grand achievements. Maximilian particularly boasted of his feats as a master of the crossbow, maintaining to have shot one hundred out of one hundred and four wild ducks on the wing. He treats in detail the hunting for chamois in the Alps. He ordered strict close seasons for chamois and ibex, also for heron, duck and partridge, installing special officials to watch over his laws being kept. In the interest of hunting the emperor preserved game carefully and intensely, making strict rules for its protection.

Illustration and lay-out of his works were commissioned from the most prominent artists of his time. Lucas Cranach, the Elder, for example, drew the wild animals for the margins of the emperor's famous prayer-book, and also Albrecht Dürer created impressive pages. The woodcuts in the *Weisskunig* were made by Hans Burgkmair, and the coloured miniatures in the Emperor's book on shooting and fishing are by Jörg Kölderer.

With the invention of printing and the improvement in the techniques of woodcut and engraving, a quicker and wider distribution of books on hunting was achieved, with the previously mentioned Augsburg publication of 1531 — *Meysterliche stuck von Bayssen und Jagen* — an outstanding example. Even though printing existed, for some time to come, hunting manuals kept appearing as manuscripts. They were printed eventually, but only much later.

One of the most important books of the sixteenth century is Jacques de Fouilloux's *La Vénerie* of 1561. There are twenty-nine French editions of this work, and it has also been translated. Taking Gaston Phoebus's treatise as basis, French hunting methods are discussed in detail, using also *La Chasse Royale* by the young King Charles IX (1550 — 1574). This book about red deer did not appear in print until 1625. It contains among other things a study of hunting calls of the period, and the way they were sounded on various horns. To this the author remarks:

"There are nowadays few people who can sound the horn well, the way our ancestors did." It is worth remembering that the hunting calls then were not written out as music, but the rhythm of the call was indicated by longer or shorter squares on a picture representing the hunting scene, appropriate to the call. This kind of morse code is used in a manuscript published in the South of France in 1394, *Hardouin*, the earliest hunting music. The seigneur of Fontains-Guerin was the author of *Trésor de Vénerie*, a song in praise of hunting, written in verse. Fourteen different hunting calls were given for the hunting of large game in the forests of Anjou and Maine, interpreted in pictorial writing.

George Tuberville's book on falconry (1576) included an English translation of *La Vénerie*. A German edition was published in Strasbourg in 1590 (facsimile of this in 1972).

In the following decades literature about hunting increased in all countries, and extensive bibliographies exist in many languages. There are, however, relatively few sources for the survey of early hunting in the eastern countries of Europe. The oldest Polish hunting manual appears to be one on falconry, published in Cracow in 1584. In 1768 the first Russian one appeared in St Petersburg. It was a translation into Russian of a work by G. F. Möller, published in Frankfort on the Oder in 1753. There followed in 1779 a Russian translation of the three volumes of *Der vollkommene Jäger oder die Kenntnis über alle Erfordernisse der Flinten und anderer Jagd* by H. F. von Göchhausen. There are many descriptions of hunting in Russian fiction and belles-lettres.

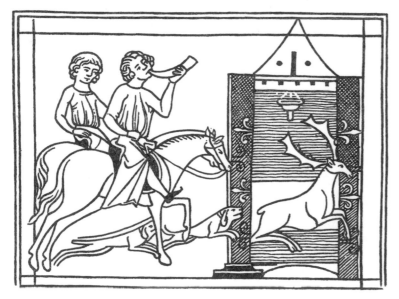

19 Coursing. Drawing after a miniature of the manuscript *Vie et Histoire de Saint Denys*, about 1250. Bibliothèque Nationale, Paris

Hunting and Gamekeeping under Absolutism

20   Wild boar hunt. Drawing from an *Augsburger Spiegel*. Mid-18th century.
Bayerisches Nationalmuseum, Munich

The Renaissance of Hunting

"Every day can be a hunting day,
But not every day brings quarry."

Hans Sachs (about 1555)

At the beginning of the sixteenth century the ideas of Humanism and the Renaissance, originating in Italy, spread widely in Europe. This progressive thought influenced decisively all cultural life between the fourteenth and the sixteenth century. Through returning to the culture of Antiquity, science, art and literature produced outstanding work. There was a great longing to explore the sources of all that is fine and beautiful in man and his surroundings. Several courts and universities became centres of the new Humanism, and in these places next to the mastery of language, literature and the furtherance of the arts, the study of economics, natural history and science was demanded. Renaissance and Reformation shaped the life of the period, bringing about powerful social, political, economic and cultural changes.

Naturally hunting was influenced, and it experienced its own Renaissance. Hunting was now reorganised on rational economic principles, and carried out according to the laws of natural history. Literature on the subject often describes the period from the sixteenth to the eighteenth century as the Golden Age of field sports, following ages of much unrestrained passion and suffering. Looking at the age with a critical eye, we shall find that much passion remained and even more suffering.

Hunting regulations of the sixteenth century show clearly how hunting was organised then and what principles underlay the orders of Renaissance rulers for the execution of hunting so that it would comply with new economic thought. During the sixteenth century special rules laid down principles, for example, how the prerogative of the sovereign to the exclusive right of the chase *(jus banni ferenti)* was to be interpreted. According to the regulations the ruler had to see to everything concerning the welfare of the state, including everything concerning game and hunting. The ruler then issued special hunting laws, and his will decided times of hunting, control of vermin and punishments for poachers etc.

Hunting law *(jus venandi)* gave the ruler the sole right to hunt anywhere where no private person had exercised hunting rights since immemorial times or had been invested with these by his prince.

Forest, game and hunting thus gained in importance during the sixteenth century, and became a definite component of the commercial transactions of Renaissance princes. The centralisation of hunting reserves led to the creation of large conservation areas, set up on commercial lines. Forests grew in importance as an indispensable source of raw material, and were suppliers to a quickly developing industry. Large amounts of timber for building, potash, bark for tanning and charcoal were needed to supply a growing manufacture of glass and textiles. Wood was used also in the mining of ore. The salt–panners alone used big quantities of fire–wood. Trading in wood became big business beyond the frontiers of individual regions. Through taking into forestry cultivation large areas which had been wasteland, the growing of timber and hunting were intensified.

From the fourteenth century onwards the economic situation in the countryside had steadily deteriorated. The agricultural crisis showed itself particularly in the sale of grain, while animal products did not suffer quite as much. With the growing population in towns in the fifteenth and sixteenth centuries the demand for food increased (meat, fat, berries, mushrooms, honey) also such commodities as leather, furs, fire–wood and timber, and prices rose. Game and all kinds of food began yielding good profits, but the three–field system and contemporary methods of animal rearing did not make for much improvement. The main factor was still the intensive use of woodland for grazing, with relatively small yields of milk and meat. Fattening pigs in oak forests was the only way of some sort of intensive animal rearing. Regular breeding and keeping of animals indoors was still impossible because of the shortage of winter fodder. Rearing pigs in forests became specially important again after the devastation of the Thirty Years' War when princes were anxious to make as much profit as possible from their woodlands. According to Brandenburg forest laws of 1622 a local peasant had to pay one *thaler* and twelve *silbergroschen* for each pig driven into the forest. Townspeople had to pay one *thaler* and eighteen *silbergroschen*, and for a foreigner the fee was two *thalers*, with monies to go to the ruler's forestry administration. A document concerning the elector's forests, from 1672, stated that all domestic pigs within the area were to be driven into the elector's forests only. In that way in the Electorate of Brandenburg alone 20,000 pigs were fattened in the woodlands each year. Until 1750 this type of rearing continued in Prussia, and in 1780 there were still some 190 cattle in 100 hectars of forest. In 1784 on the Schorfheide, north of Berlin, there were 9,408 head of cattle, 2,402 horses and 45,726 sheep. With this intense rearing of animals in the forests ecological conditions for game became severely limited. Wild game retreated further and further into untouched wildernesses wherever this was possible. Virulent diseases among domestic animals increased difficulties from time to time. The huntsmen's stocks of game escaped those risks, and supplied more quickly and more cheaply than domestic animals all animal products much in demand. In 1512, for example, the board of finance of the Grand Master of Teutonic Knights bought from the huntsman in charge all skins and furs of game quarry for 16 *schillings* per skin. He sold altogether 15 skins of male bison for 18 *marks*, 30 of wild horses, elks, cows and calves of bisons for 15 *marks*.

The Order made a profit of 44 *schillings* from each bison skin. Also the meat of game was salted and taken for sale to the towns. In 1565, for example, the town of Königsberg was supplied with 46 barrels of venison, 4 of elk meat, 6 of aurochs, 3 of wild boar

and $^3/_4$ tuns of the mouths of elk and stag. Large amounts of game meat played an important part in the nutrition of the people, particularly in mining areas there existed a big demand.

From the documentation available* it may be seen that from the elector's provision store and smoking chamber, close to the Jägerhof in Dresden old town, the following supply of freshly salted or smoked game was offered for sale between 1.1.—31.12.1669:

861 red deer	20 Indian geese	170 foxes
616 wild boar	4 swans	55 badgers
646 hares	15 bears	17 beavers
751 partridges	74 wolves	27 otters
65 woodcocks	15 lynxes	13 squirrels

It is interesting to note that the elector's kitchen at the court of Dresden was supplied mainly with meat from animals which themselves hunt for prey. This consisted at one time of seven eighth of bears, weighing 11 centners and 88 pounds, salted, together with the bears' heads and 24 claws, 52 wolves, 10 lynxes, 12 foxes—whole for roasting and 52 foxes for stewing (1 centner = 51,420 kg).

* From the files about game supplied between 1636 and 1737, in the collection of manuscripts of the Sächsische Landesbibliothek, Dresden, MS. R. 17—42.

21 J. E. Ridinger: Boar Park. "How wild boar is caught in a boar park." The animals are lured into the park by spreading fodder. When eating, they touch a wire which automatically closes the gates, and traps the boar. Etching, mid-18th century. Staatliche Museen, Kupferstichkabinett and Collection of Drawings, Berlin

Similar numbers are quoted for the year 1637 when the supply included: large quantities of wolf, bear, tiger, lynx, fox and the meat of wild cats.

The preference of court kitchens for the meat of animals of prey may well be based on the widely spread superstition that the strength and cunning of animals passes to the man who eats their flesh. Large amounts of game were eaten at court festivities, for example, at the wedding of the Polish Duke Johann Sigismund in 1594*:

"13 bison, 20 elks, 10 red deer, 22 does, 36 wild boar, 29 sounders, 2 bears, 48 roe deer, 272 hares, 5 wild swans, 123 woodcocks, 279 heath cocks, 433 hazel grouse, 47 partridges and 413 wild ducks."

From all this it is easy to understand that the ideal of the feudal lords was the possession of large forests and big stocks of game. With this end in mind close seasons were fixed periodically for certain species. On 2. 7. 1572 a police regulation in Mecklenburg fixed close seasons for hare, wild duck, goose, bustard, partridge and other fowl.

According to this regulation it was prohibited to catch, shoot or stalk game, take eggs or young birds from nests, from Shrove Tide until St James's Day (March to 25th July). It was prohibited also to hunt any game in deep snow or shoot a hare in its form.

In a ruling of 4. 2. 1575 and a later supplement to it of 22. 3. 1598 Duke Friedrich Wilhelm of Weimar ordered, under threat of punishment, his subjects, whether belonging to the nobility or not, to refrain from hunting with hawk, club, lime rod or any other means. He also ordered them not to destroy young birds or eggs, and not catch, shoot and the like during close seasons. This meant between Shrove Tide and St Bartholomew Day, 24th August. It is interesting to note that the fine was fixed at 100 *Scheffel* (old German corn measure) of oats as well as fifty *gulden*. Of this half was to be kept by the authorities, and the other half to go to whosoever had denounced the criminal. An order of the Elector of Brandenburg of 6. 3. 1582 forbade the shooting of swans.

Trade in swan's feathers was a royal privilege in many European countries. Hunters and fishermen had to take live swans to the courts each year, where they were plucked and then set free again. (England 1590, Prussia until the end of the eighteenth century.) Forest regulations from Württemberg specially protected falcons. In 1606 the Prussian Diet in Königsberg noted that everywhere in the country there was much abuse through hunting and coursing and that shooting and fishing was carried out during the wrong seasons. To protect game and fish, the Diet unanimously agreed that fishing in spawning time as well as the shooting of fowl, coursing and hunting should be forbidden at close seasons, namely between Shrove Tide and St Bartholomew Day. Under the prohibition gentlemen of rank and nobility paid a fine of ten Hungarian *gulden*. Should a commoner be concerned who in any case was forbidden to shoot, course or hunt in any other way, he should lose his gun, and be punished by imprisonment.

This ruling shows the typical class distinction made in the measure of punishment meted out under feudal hunting laws. These very contradictions contributed much to the dissatisfaction among impoverished country people which eventually led to the revolutionary risings in many parts of Europe during the early sixteenth century.

To live up to the new aims of Renaissance rulers concerning the management of forests and woodlands, highly qualified and specialised staff was required in order to assure the systematic and economic handling of forests. The professions of huntsman and forester developed in the sixteenth century. This development was similar to that of the craftsmen's guilds in the towns. The huntsman needed specialised knowledge only to be gained by extensive training over the years. His apprenticeship lasted for more than three years. During the first year he was a boy huntsman or hound boy. During the second year he was called a huntsman's lad, and was allowed to carry the hunting horn over his shoulder. After completing a third year, an examination made the lad a fully-fledged huntsman, and as a symbol of this, he was given a hunting knife. Compared to this training, the hunting squire had a relatively easy time in qualifying as a competent huntsman. It was the privilege of the nobility only to begin as a hunting page or secretary, and then rise to becoming a master-huntsman. This strict order of rank can be clearly seen in representations of the so-called huntsman's parade.*

A fully-fledged huntsman had to recognise the slot of a stag to be hunted, by twenty to seventy-two indications. He had then to be able to find the animal by scent, droppings and other ways.

The keeping of gun dogs, too, required special training. In 1592 in the game park of Duke Heinrich of Brunswick more than six hundred hounds for the hunting of wild boar were kept. The

---

* From files in the Central State Archives, Hist. Abt. II, Merseburg, *Königl. Hausarchiv*, HA Rep. 18 Tit. 16 No. 2, *Wildbretgeschenke zu Hochzeiten, Taufen usw. 1590—1693*.

* From documents in the collection of manuscripts in the Sächsische Landesbibliothek, Dresden. MS. J 18 "Abriss vnd Verzeichnis aller Inventionen vnd Auffzüge, welche an Fassnachten Anno 1609, als Christian den Andern Johann Casimir vnd Johann Ernst, Hertzogen zu Sachsen so wol Christian Marggraff zu Brandenburg besuchet, vff die im Churf. Schlosshoff zu Dresden auffgerichtete Rennbahnen gebracht worden. Verfertigt durch Daniel Bretschneider, Bürger und Mahlern zu Dresden."

Duke of Zweibrücken in the Palatinate kept more than one thousand. A hunting lad was responsible for twenty dogs at a time. In 1724 a German, called Flemming, wrote about the training of huntsmen: "The hound boys should not let their faces fall if now and again a box on the ear comes their way. No boy has ever died of it. He should get the hound's feed ready in good time, clean the kennel, and put down clean straw. However, should a lad become lazy, begin drinking and gaming before his time, sleeping in and all that sort of thing, it is only right that his master should drive him from his bed with the hunting whip."

At that time, apart from the rules concerning gun dogs, many other hunting customs developed. These were, among others, rules regarding hunting prerogative, huntsman's language and the green twig worn by huntsmen in their cap. Today the language of hunting in German consists of more than six thousand different expressions, and this very language began to emerge in the sixteenth century.

In written hunting regulations and chronicles we find many expressions still in use today. With the introduction of new methods of hunting, trapping and the use of weapons, new concepts arose constantly. In the fifteenth and sixteenth centuries the speedy development of the technique of weapons lead to basic changes in the ways of hunting and trapping. The publication of the first printed textbooks of hunting allowed for practical experiences in various hunting methods with the new weapons to be spread more widely and more quickly.

Small-arms are known since the mid-fourteenth century.

Wrought-iron hand guns with lighted match were the first to introduce a completely new range of weapons. Blunderbuss, arquebus and musket are the prototypes of hand-fired weapons which as early as the late fifteenth century allowed shooting at a distance of three hundred paces.

Match-lock muskets were not suitable for hunting because the evil-smelling burning match could be seen from a distance and game could catch the scent. Thus at the time hunting-spear and cross-bow still remained the chief hunting weapons.

The hunting-spear, used for bear and boar hunting, consisted of a long, leaf-shaped blade and a strong wooden staff. To insure a firm grip the staff was covered with leather strips, embossed or ornamented with brass nail heads. At right angles to the staff, below the blade, was fastened a projection of horn, which was to prevent too deep entry of the spear into the game.

Along with the spear a special sword was used in boar hunting. It had a straight blade, widening out, and, like the spear, it had a crosspiece. This weapon of the mounted huntsman originated in the late fifteenth century, and was popular as a hunting weapon until the end of the sixteenth. The hunting sword of the fifteenth and sixteenth centuries was superceded by the hunting knife, carried by huntsmen to this day as an ornament or actual weapon.

Many richly ornamented hunting-spears and hunting-swords from princely armouries and treasuries were handed down to us.

If spear and sword were the main weapons in dispatching the prey, bow and arrow and the crossbow were the typical weapons

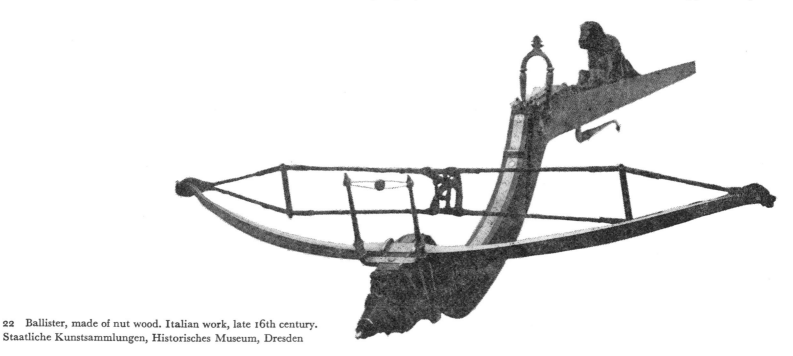

22 Ballister, made of nut wood. Italian work, late 16th century.
Staatliche Kunstsammlungen, Historisches Museum, Dresden

for hunting from a distance, and they remained that even when fire arms had begun to spread widely. Though the crossbow was known in China since the second century B.C., the Romans only began to use similar weapons in the fourth century A.D. After that the crossbow appears once more as a weapon of war and of hunting in written and pictorial sources of the tenth century. It was used increasingly in Europe after the Crusades, though at that time there existed a papal prohibition to use it as a weapon of war, and the rules of chivalry considered it an "un–Christian" weapon.

In the fourteenth and fifteenth centuries, however, archers, using the crossbow, formed the nucleus of the foot–soldiers in the armies of mercenaries. Particularly the Swiss crossbow men were much sought after abroad as mercenaries and as huntsmen. At one time France and England used crossbow men and archers as élite units, this was so until well into the seventeenth century. The Japanese army used them until 1869. English archers shot 10 to 12 arrows in a minute when heavy arrows were accurate to 150 metres. With crossbow men the range was 300 to 500 metres and an accurate hit could be assured at 200 metres. The bolt penetrated without difficulty a helmet and plated armour of the knights at a short distance. For hunting specially the crossbow was an excellent weapon with outstanding qualities: wide range, relatively quick follow of shots, exactness of aiming and all without noise. The crossbow's disadvantage was its relatively heavy weight.

The hunting crossbow consisted of a stock, the bow and string, the catch and the trigger mechanism. The bow itself was made of solid wood or several layers of horn and fishbone, but steel bows are known since the fifteenth century. It was fixed to the stock by strong hemp ropes. Splendid engraved work of metal or ivory, usually represented hunting scenes.

The trigger mechanism, consisting either of a long lever or a short hand–worked trigger, was later on furnished with gearing in which the catch released the shot. The strings consisted of 60 to 80 thin threads of hemp or twisted gut. Since the fourteenth century a simple tenter hook was also used, but later German and English bows had winches, strong enough to cope with the heavy bending of the almost rigid bows. But in its turn this made shooting relatively slow.

The missile was a pointed arrow or a blunt one just to numb the animal. To hunt large game, mainly red deer and wild boar, two–pronged arrows were also used in order to cause greater injury.

A special form of the crossbow for hunting was the so–called balista. This light crossbow, developed in Italy, was constructed on the principle of the projectile military engine of Antiquity, which projected several missiles of lead or clay at the same time. Between the double strings there was a small bag from which the missiles were projected. This weapon was used mainly for fowling. Apart from the Italian one, there was also a light one of German make.

Hunting weapons and equipment were kept in the armoury of hunting boxes, palaces and castles of the Renaissance.

87   *The Castle of Fontainebleau was the centre of the royal hunting grounds near Paris.*

88 *The Castle of Weikersheim, Knights' Hall. Coffer-work ceiling with representations from hunting by B. Katzenberger from Würzburg; the walls decorated with trophies on prepared hides. 1586*

89/90 *Coursing on the River Elbe near the Jägerhof at Dresden 1614. Moritzburg Castle near Dresden*

...n von der Schulenburg.
...ar Schwalenschbi.
... Von Thür.

Henrich von Sunteradt.
Hanns Georg von Osterhausen.
Sebastian von Berbsdorff.

Hanns Chaspar Corbitz.
George von Wolfframbsdorff.
Hanns Beer.

Wendel ...
Sebastian ...
Sigismundt ...

Ander Fuchsi Kasten.

Ander Haasen Kasten.

91/92 D. Bretschneider: Huntsmen's procession in the castle yard at Dresden 1609 ("Abriss und Verzeichnis aller Inventionen vnd Auffzüge, welche an Fassnachten Anno 1609, Als Christian den Andern Johann Casimir vnd Johann Ernst, Hertzogen zu Sachsen so wol Christian Marggraff Brandenburg besuchet, off die im Churf. Schlosshof zu Dressden auffgerichtete Rennbahnen gebracht worden. Verfertigt durch Daniel Bretschneider, Bürger und Mahlern zu Dresden"). Sächsische Landesbibliothek, Manuscript Collection, Dresden

93/94 Report of Duke Johann Casimir's Master of the Hunt, given at the fortress of Coburg. Sheet 7 and sheet 27 of Wolfgang Birkner, Jüngeres Jagdbuch, after 1639. Landesbibliothek, Gotha (German Democratic Republic)

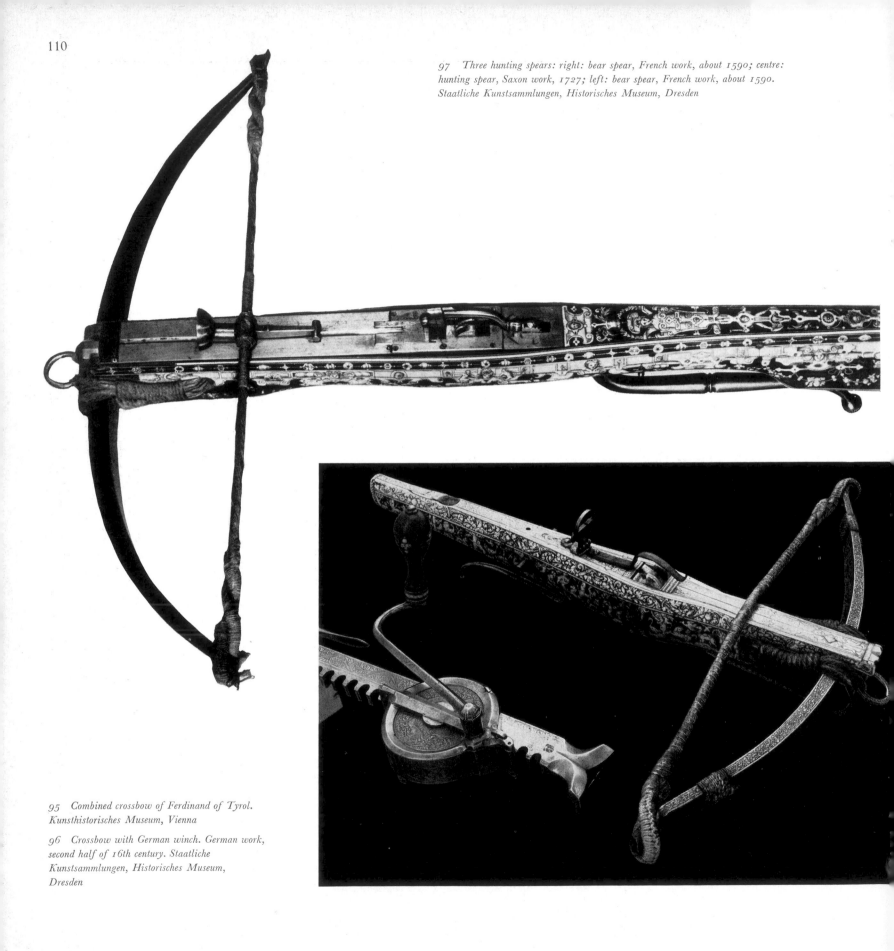

97   Three hunting spears: right: bear spear, French work, about 1590; centre: hunting spear, Saxon work, 1727; left: bear spear, French work, about 1590. Staatliche Kunstsammlungen, Historisches Museum, Dresden

95   Combined crossbow of Ferdinand of Tyrol. Kunsthistorisches Museum, Vienna

96   Crossbow with German winch. German work, second half of 16th century. Staatliche Kunstsammlungen, Historisches Museum, Dresden

98 *Philipp Galle: Catching duck. Etching after Hans Bol, 1582. Sheet from a series of 54 hunting scenes, under the title* Venationes, Piscationes et Aucupii Typi. *Biblioteca Nazionale, Florence*

Sic per et infidias finuofa in retia mollis   Allectatur Anas, cane per dumeta natante.

99 *Bernhard van Orley: Stag hunt (Month of September). About 1530. Brussels tapestry from the series "The Hunts of Maximilian". Louvre, Paris*

Hunting as reflected in Renaissance Art

"As often as a prince will take you hunting, you carry a half-finished picture with you, to complete it during the hunt. Or you draw a stag which Friedrich has brought to bay, or a boar Johannes is coursing. And all this is known to give the prince no less pleasure than the hunt itself."

Christoph Scheurl, Eulogy for Lucas Cranach, 1508

As hunting was of chief importance in the life and entertainment of Renaissance rulers, it naturally supplied new impulses to all the arts. While in the fifteenth century representations of hunting were limited mainly to impressive French and Burgundian miniatures, decorating prayer books and manuscripts of all kinds, completely new forms of pictorial representations appeared during the Renaissance. This was due to the growing need of princes for status symbols and luxury. The height of the Renaissance saw hunting pictures with realistic representations of country and animals. This change was linked to general artistic and social developments in different European countries. Splendid hunting scenes were painted of many kinds and in many techniques.

In France the large *pièce de chasse* dominated; in the countries of the Middle Rhine hunting was represented in stained glass work; in Brussels magnificent hunting tapestries were popular, while in Southern Germany many books were illustrated by impressive copperplate engravings and etchings with hunting as their theme. The goldsmiths of Nuremberg and Dresden used hunting as a subject in their craft, while in Flanders there were large hunting pictures with many figures. Holland became famous for its emotive hunting still lifes.

Early in the sixteenth century French builders and architects created castles on the Loire for courtiers and the nobility, and French secular architecture, in its transition from the Gothic to the Renaissance, reached a climax. With the taking over of décor from the Italian Renaissance there developed a specifically French architectural style which was called after King Francis I.

Renaissance secular building did not continue the tradition of the old feudal keep, but erected hunting castles and country seats as places of recreation and pleasure; always situated close to good hunting grounds. The castles of Chambord and Fontainebleau became prototypes of the Renaissance hunting castle, built in the sixteenth and seventeenth centuries in the so-called Henri-deux-style. This splendid Renaissance architecture was followed by the way castles were built and parks laid out in the Baroque manner under Louis XIV. The hunting castle was transformed into a representative palace. The famous castle of Versailles was originally planned as a royal hunting box and pleasure seat in the style of the Renaissance and it was actually completed in 1678 as a monumental Baroque palace, to become the model for a new period in the architecture of castles and the lay-out of gardens all over Europe.

Next to France's famous castles, in the sixteenth and seventeenth century important buildings—particularly in England and Germany—were erected which owed their existence to hunting. It is impossible to give a proper impression or even do justice in a few pictures to the abundance of building and the different styles which appeared all over Europe. These castles' architecture and their interior decoration are one of the most important achievements of Renaissance art in Europe.

Artistic manifestations to the subject of hunting may be found in the castles in two main features: hunting friezes and tapestries. A hunting frieze was painted in the main rooms of the castle directly on to the fresh rough-cast. Under a special theme hunting scenes full of movement were portrayed or studies of the movement of certain species of game. Red deer was the most frequent motif when the stag was often represented life-size. Occasionally these pictures were even decorated with genuine hunting trophies. The representations demanded skilled animal painters.

As the frieze was static and could not be changed, large hunting pictures or tapestries frequently took its place. Tapestries in particular quickly gained in popularity during the Renaissance. These wall hangings could be constantly changed as whole series of them were made. They became favourites in the hunting castles and palaces during the sixteenth and seventeenth centuries, not least in their action of keeping out draughts.

In 1565 the inventory of the Dresden court lists altogether two hundred and thirty different pictorial wall hangings, then called *Tapezirei*, meaning tapestry. Many Flemish tapestries with fine presentations of animals are among the treasures left by King

Sigismund II Augustus Jagiello in the royal castle on the Wawel rock at Cracow. These hangings date from between 1553 and 1565, and were created in the workshops of weavers from Flanders and the Netherlands. Full–size designs by well known artists served as models for the tapestries.

One of the most important of the artists involved was the Dutch painter Bernhard van Orley (1492—1542) who made designs for the series of tapestries representing the hunting adventures of Emperor Charles V. This series is now known as *The Hunting of Maximilian*, with part of it kept at the Louvre and part at Fontainebleau. The tapestries were made in the workshops of Franz Geubels.

This type of wall hanging eventually became known as gobelin after the French firm which made them, and which had in 1667 discovered the secret of dying scarlet. Through the royal manufactory, Paris became the centre for making gobelins.

Because of the religious wars of the sixteenth century many weavers from the Low Countries and from France were driven from their homes, and founded workshops in the many European capitals which gave them asylum. The Flemish painter, Jan van

23   L. Cranach the Elder: Stag hunt. Woodcut, 1506. Schlossmuseum, Weimar

der Straet (1523—1605) worked in Florence where he called himself Johannes Stradanus or Giovanni della Strada. Here he created splendid designs, commissioned by the Duke of Florence for his castle Poggio a Caiano. The tapestries displaying hunting motifs are now in the Palazzo Vecchio in Florence.

Hunting, as mentioned previously, was in fact reflected in all artistic activities of the sixteenth and seventeenth centuries. The German artists, Lucas Cranach, Hans Burgkmair, Albrecht Dürer, Hans Holbein, Jost Amman are among the great masters of the Renaissance, and all of them created works which have left their mark on the artistic history of hunting. Hans Holbein, the Younger (1497—1543) became court painter to King Henry VIII, and created excellent pictures of his master out hawking. The realistic drawings of Hans Burgkmair (1473—1531) in Augsburg served as designs for the woodcuts in Emperor Maximilian's book, *Weisskunig*.

The famous painter, Lucas Cranach, the Elder (1472—1553) worked in Wittenberg since 1505 as painter to the court of Saxony. He and his son, Lucas Cranach, the Younger (1515—1586) made important hunting paintings and woodcuts in their workshop. More than eight hundred works by Cranach have survived to this day, among them forty paintings and drawings of hunting and game animals. His panoramic presentation of big court hunts in Saxony are specially impressive. In the woodcut, *Hirschjagd* (Stag Hunt), of 1506, which belongs to the earliest large woodcuts in Germany, the different phases of a big court hunt are vividly depicted, and representations of countryside, people and animals are well blended. These paintings usually represent scenes from a particular court hunt with special emphasis put on the master of the hunt and his guests. In a painting of 1544, for example, a court hunt for stag, wild boar and fox, the scene is the start in front of the castle of Torgau. The hunt was arranged by the Elector Johann Friedrich of Saxony for the Emperor Charles V, and the painting is now in the Prado at Madrid.

Written sources confirm that the painter had to take part in the hunt in person, to be able to make sketches on the spot. On 3. 12. 1583 Cranach, the Younger, received an invitation to a boar hunt. On 13. 10. 1583 the Elector August killed a large boar in the forest at Colditz, which he wished Cranach to draw (according to a letter of 27. 11. 1583, giving an order for six representations of the boar for the elector). More than twelve orders for the "Colditz Boar" have been traced in the records.

The many woodcuts of the Augsburg artist Jörg Breu (1510—1547), of Jost Amman (1539—1591) in Nuremberg, Tobias Stimmer (1539—1584) in Schaffhausen or the Brothers Beham who were banished from Nuremberg in 1525 because of their revolutionary convictions, all represent memorable scenes from hunting.

24   Peasants working in the fields. Woodcut from S. Brant's edition of Virgil. Strasbourg, 1502

25   Petrarch Master: Peasants ask for the right to hunt. Woodcut, 1519/20

Glasses, goblets and table services equally took up the inexhaustible subject. There were serving dishes of embossed metal representing hunting scenes, and even furniture showed the popularity of the subject.

If magnificent representations of hunting scenes found their place in the castles and palaces of the great, ordinary folk were content with woodcuts and etchings, and quite specially coloured pictures on glass. The glass pictures do not represent only scenes from court hunts or different kinds of game, but most often show motifs of small hunting. This is due to the influence of a growing middle–class in the towns who hardly ever possessed the right to hunt for large game. Coloured ornamental sheets of glass may be found in bay–windows of the high–gabled houses of townsfolk in the central part of the Rhine valley and in Southwest Germany.

Representations of ordinary huntsmen or peasants are relatively rare in Renaissance art. Lucas Cranach's portrait of the head of a peasant huntsman — *Kopf eines bäuerischen Jägers* (Portrait of a Peasant Hunter) — (a water colour study of 1515) or the woodcuts by Sebastian Brant in an edition of Virgil (Strasbourg 1502), also the ones of the master of the Petrarch edition (1519/20) are exceptions.

Call for the Abolition of Hunting Privileges

"Water, game, forest and heath, shooting game, snaring birds and fishing, have been the privilege of princes, great gentlemen and priests. We now want all this to be free and open so that every peasant in the land may cut wood, hunt or fish, without hurt or hindrance, at all times, and in all places."

From the demands of Bundschuh — an association of rebellious peasants — worked out by Joss Fritz, a serf, of Untergrombach in the diocese of Speyer, in 1502.

The pomp and circumstance of feudal hunting entertainments has come down to posterity through magnificent works of art. There are fewer sources documenting the life of the people to whom this very hunting was a burden and a nuisance. Faded records, petitions and legal documents testify to the saddest period of hunting. Quite often they are shocking witnesses to the need and the suffering of the peasant. He had to do forced labour for his feudal lord, had lost all privileges, added to the terrible losses through game devastating his fields and grasslands. Peasants and serfs groaned under the weight of want and bitterness, and despair prepared the ground for rebellion. Large stocks of game, fierce punishment for poaching, as well as the dreaded *corvée* contributed much to the peasant rising of the sixteenth century in Germany. Everywhere embittered charges were made as can be seen from the chronicles of the period.

At the beginning of the Peasants' War, the theologian Dr. Martin Luther (1483—1546) published warning words, directed at the ruling princes, and the way in which they carried out hunting. A sermon says: "Our princes do not sin only by not attending to their duties nor caring for their poor sufficiently, they sin heavily by their unrestricted hunting when they steal from the poor by destroying the peasants' fields and the fruit of their labour.

They devastate the fields, and in no way are the peasants allowed to drive the game from their fields and gardens. They must suffer the game to destroy what they themselves have achieved with the sweat of their brow. In that way the princes do not only fail to protect their subjects, they do them actual harm which they could easily prevent. And so a Turk or some other huntsman will come and forcefully take hunting nets and spears from the German rulers."

After the outbreak of the Peasants' War, Luther no longer had pity with the hard lot of the peasants. His radical change of mind becomes evident in his pamphlet *Wider die räuberischen und mörderischen Rotten der Bauern* (Against the plundering and murderous peasant hordes).

However, it was not the Turks, after all who took the hunting spear from the German princelings. In the spring of 1525 crowds of peasants in Upper Swabia, Württemberg, Franconia and Thuringia stormed the fortified houses and hunting castles of the princes. They issued a declaration which stated among other things:

"It has been the custom so far for no poor man to have the right to hunt game in the forest, fish in the waters or shoot birds in the air. This seems not proper to us, and void of brotherly love, selfish and not according to God's word. Also in many places those in authority bear us ill–will and do us damage. We have to suffer that whatever the good God has allowed us to grow, is wantonly destroyed by foolish beasts. And with all this we are expected to keep silent, which is against God and our fellow creatures."

In a declaration of peasants from the Black Forest of the spring of 1525 similar demands were made for the curbing of hunting services. The just demands of the peasants were made particularly against compulsory services expected of them. These included the provision of transport for equipment, game and followers, supplying beaters for court hunts, bigger hunts and boar and wolf hunts. Labour was required also for the building of hunting equipment and hunting castles. In the building of the hunting castle of Augustusburg in the Erzgebirge—from 1568—1573—for example, peasants loaded rubble, did building work in the cellars, carried old timber while wives, daughters and maidens carried 1,100 tons of loam in baskets to the building site.

The peasants had to repair hunting runs on heath and moorland, plough and work them, prune the trees in deer forests, repair old fences and do more such labour.

The peasants from Stühlingen in the Southwest of Germany forcefully demanded to be free of all this in a declaration to their superior of 6. 4. 1525. Article 24 of this says of compulsory hunting services: "...this means repairing game fences, providing beaters, taking along ropes for catching game, and when game is caught, conveying it to the castle. Also at times we have to transport game from the castle to Thann (Alsace), Engen (Baden) or any other places which may please our lord and master ...

Also we have to raise gun dogs for as long as our masters wish us to do so, which not only deprives us of some of our own food, but causes damage to chicks and other poultry.

We beg you therefore to recognise that it is not our duty to raise these dogs, but that we want to be free of it."

But the peasants did not only want to be free themselves, the game was to be free too. Article 41 has this to say:

"We are forbidden under threat of severe punishment to catch, hunt or drive off game. And should anybody fail to comply with this order, his eyes are gouged out or he is tortured in some other way, whatever pleases the lord and master and his henchmen.

We do beg to recognise that in future, according to the laws of God and Men we should without punishment be allowed to hunt game, large and small, shoot and trap, to use it for our own needs ...

At least we should have the right ... to carry guns and crossbows which we have been denied so far, also not to have to attach sticks to our dogs as we have been made to do."

Woe betide the peasant who tried to drive the game from his fields and gardens, or, worse, set his dogs on it. He was brutally punished as a poacher. Duke Ulrich of Württemberg made an order in 1517:

"Anybody, whoever it may be, met with a gun, crossbow or similar weapon in the duke's forests and hunting grounds, in woods or fields or any place where game may be about, away from public roads, or is seen to move in a suspicious way, even though he is not in the process of shooting, will have his eyes gouged out." In the same year the duke had a poacher sewn alive into the skin of a stag, and coursed by his hounds.

A similar cruel deed is reported by the Superintendent M. Nic. Rebhan in 1621 of Archbishop Michael of Salzburg. He writes:

"In 1537 a miserable tale has been publicised in word and picture about an archbishop or rather a horrible monster, a savage and cruel tyrant, called Michael of Salzburg.

He was keen, almost mad on hunting, and a man, accused of poaching a stag, he had not only put into a vile prison, but he ordered a judge to pronounce the death verdict on him. However, the judge being a more conscientious and pious man than his master, refused and apologised. Then the godless bishop elevated himself to be the judge, pronouncing an even worse and more barbaric sentence on the poor man.

He was to be sewn up into a stag's skin, coursed by hounds, and then be exposed to wicked mockery, saying that on condition he could escape from the hounds, he would be free. And so the poor man went to his execution. The hunt was held in the market place for everyone to see, and the man sewn into the stag's skin, commanded his soul to God, as he was brought along. The horn was sounded, English hounds were then let loose, and, taking the poor man for game, they mauled him cruelly and tore him to pieces, all of which the brutal tyrant watched with pleasure."

One of the leaders of the Anabaptists in Germany, Thomas Müntzer, (1490—1525) fought with revolutionary passion against the despotism of the feudal nobility, proclaiming the community of goods and the equality of all Christians. In his writings and sermons, as usual at the period, hidden in religious concepts and including numerous quotations from the Bible, Müntzer spread his social ideas of a general popular reformation all over the country. In his *Fürstenpredigt* (1523) he sharply attacked clerical and worldly princes, prophesying a great peasant rebellion.

The "apostle of the poor and oppressed" openly denounced the wrong done by the overlords, "causing the common man to be their enemy". "They seize hold of all creatures, and make them their own: fish in the water, birds in the air, and all that grows on the land. They want to possess it all. And to the poor they preach God's law. God, they say, commanded you not to steal. But they themselves do not believe in this very law. They exploit the poor countryman, and do him harm, as they do to those who make things with their hands, in fact all those they consider lesser beings. If anyone does the slightest wrong, he'll hang for it."

"How can all that lead to any good in the long run? If I say this, I am bound to be called rebellious!" This rebellious spirit, Thomas Müntzer, spent the winter of 1524/25 in the Southwest of Germany, and there had great influence on the shaping of the *Artikelbriefe* of the peasants in the Hegau and the Black Forest.

In April and May 1525 great crowds of peasants stormed the castles of the feudal lords, and gave the signal for the storming of fortified houses and palaces on the Rhine, in Alsace, Württemberg, Swabia, Lower Franconia and the Palatinate. The notorious *Bauernkrieg*—the Peasant War—had begun. Everywhere in Germany the movement grew spontaneously, until, hardly supported by the townspeople, the peasants suffered a resounding defeat by the united armies of the princes. Thomas Müntzer himself was captured and executed. Terror ruled and bloody persecution, as the nobility took revenge on the revolting peasants. Thousands perished in a horrific bloodshed of arbitrary killing. Great suffering and need again ruled in the countryside. Taxes and compulsory labour increased, and the dream of freedom from hunting services died a sad death.

In 1587 a preacher in Thuringia wrote: "If anybody would ever add up how many hundreds and thousands of people in the German countryside are every year kept off their own work for weeks, even months, to serve the mad passion for hunting of their lords and masters, there would no longer be a question as to why the soil yields less than ever."

In 1632 Colerus remarked in his *Opus oecunomicum*:

"The huntsmen do great harm to the people through their game getting into the cornfields, also in the way they do with their horses and hounds. Not to mention that the wretched poorly clad people have to go with the hunt in a hard winter. Those having to hold nets, get so badly frozen that often they have to have their legs amputated or are even found dead or frozen behind trees."

Poachers among their lord's game were as severely punished as before, often even shot on the spot. In fact, anything could happen when there were no witnesses. A decree in the Mark Brandenburg of 1669 states that poachers in the elector's hunting grounds should be shot on the spot, and that smaller offences should be punished severely. Many cases of brutal and ruthless treatment of poachers are known. An abbot of Kempten, for example, had a poacher, caught in winter, tied to a pole in the water, so that under extreme suffering he froze to death.

In principle the carrying of a weapon in the princely hunting grounds, forests and woods, was taken as poaching, even if no killing of game could be proved.

26 Peasants chasing game from their fields. Woodcut, 1517

Gunpowder and Lead decide the Development of Hunting Weapons

"The farthest distance for shooting with a gun is taken to be one hundred paces. And he who needlessly shoots from a greater distance, is not a true huntsman."

Dietrich aus dem Winkell, Handbuch für Jäger, Jagdberechtigte und Jagdliebhaber. Leipzig, 1806

During the Renaissance, in the sixteenth century, newly acquired knowledge in natural science and technology, greatly influenced the technique of weapons. Next to the wheel lock, the spring lock came into use. Through rifling the barrel and incorporating a trigger, hunting guns achieved greater accuracy. Also, repeating arms were developed, and these are only a few examples of the many technical developments of this particular period.

With the specialisation of the making of weapons by a number of highly skilled craftsmen, like gunsmiths, ironworkers, makers of shafts, founders, gilders, even goldsmiths, cutters of ivory and engravers, large centres grew up for the production of hunting weapons. The craftsmen formed guilds, and in Suhl in Thuringia a guild of gunmakers and gunsmiths was founded in 1555. In 1563 they were joined by the makers of gun locks, barrels and winches. Specialisation and division of labour made it possible to achieve technical and artistic perfection in many European countries. Hunting weapons and equipment from the sixteenth to the eighteenth century were of excellent quality, bearing witness to superior craftsmanship, high precision and technical excellence.

Looking at this development more closely, we find that at the beginning of the sixteenth century the wheel lock was invented in Italy—other sources say Germany. The oldest drawing of a wheel lock mechanism, anyhow, was made by Leonardo da Vinci. The spark created on the same principle as the modern flint lighter, lit the priming powder on the powder pan. Through

a hole bored into the barrel, the flame made the charge of the front loader explode. As the powder was protected in the pan, the huntsman could carry the loaded gun. This had not been possible with the matchlock gun.

With hunting guns the wheel lock is on the outer side of the lock plate. Through the turning of a small hardened steel wheel with a key, the huntsman cocked a two-armed leaf spring. When he pulled the trigger which carried the burning match, the wheel with its large teeth was set in motion. The spark it caused, fired the main charge.

Gun shafts are of different kinds. Wheel lock hunting guns usually are fitted with the so-called German barrel, with a short straight butt. After 1600 a lighter wheel lock gun of smaller calibre was developed. The *Teschings* or *Tschinken*, with their short pointed-down barrel and butt, of Italian, French or Spanish make, could be pressed against the shoulder, which was impossible to do with the German type. This was pressed only against the cheek. The *Tschinke* was mainly a lady's gun, its name stemming from the place where it was made, Teschen (Ceský Tešín, Bohemia), now Czechoslovakia.

Since the end of the fifteenth century smooth-bore barrels were used in hunting. Rifle barrels were introduced in the mid-sixteenth century. There are several types of hunting guns with a wheel lock: the heavy wheel lock gun with smooth-bore barrel, for shooting with a single shot. Then there is the light wheel lock gun (*Tesching*) with smooth-bore barrel and the wheel lock gun with smooth-bore barrel for shooting with small shot. And finally, there was the gun for wild-fowling, specially for shooting geese, duck and bustard. This had a specially long barrel (3 metres), mounted on a carriage.

Until well into the eighteenth century the hunting gun played a more dominant role in the development of weapon technique than military weapons. The love of splendour and the hunting passion of princes constantly demanded more efficient and lighter weapons. Guns for the use of bullets and small shot were developed as early as the sixteenth and seventeenth centuries. Double-barrelled and revolving guns appeared, the two barrels fired usually by one lock. There were also three and four-barrelled guns, and weapons with a drum magazine which could fire four shots through one barrel. Special air guns were made for deer and wild boar. They usually had a ball-like reservoir with compressed air which supplied the impulse for about twenty shots. The precious wheel lock hunting guns were covered with magnificent ornaments for representational purposes. Cherry or nutwood inlay was inserted in the dark brown barrels, or bone, mother-of-pearl, gold and silver wire ornaments were incorporated. The decorations often consisted of very fine representations of animals. The gun makers of Augsburg and Nuremberg in particular produced masterpieces for the court of Charles V (1519— 1558).

The German painter, engraver and goldsmith, Heinrich Aldegrever (1500— 1562), a pupil of Albrecht Dürer, and members of the Sadler family of artists of Munich, made many designs and models for all types of gun barrels. Also the Flemish painter, Jan van der Straet, and the *Künstlerbüchlein* of the Nuremberg graphic artist, Jost Amman, supplied much material for the gun makers. Nearly all engravers and woodcutters of the sixteenth century made splendid designs for decorative weapons. They were put together in sample books, and used as well by craftsmen. Through this close cooperation by first–class artists and skilled gunsmiths magnificent and luxurious weapons were created, ornamentated with interesting scenic and hunting representations.

From the sample books of the French draftsman, goldsmith, engraver and chaser, Etienne Delaune (1518— 1583), excellent designs of animals—stags, roe deer, hounds, hares and squirrels— were used as gun decorations. In the seventeenth century the artistic work of Theodor de Bry, Philippe Cordier Daubigny and above all the famous French gun makers and engravers, Jean Baptiste Bérain (1639—1711) and Bertrand Piraube decided the form and wealth of luxury weapons.

At the beginning of the seventeenth century the wheel lock was superseded by a new system of ignition, the flint lock. The principle of the flint lock invented in France in 1612, is similar to that of the wheel lock save that in the flint lock the flint is held by a hammer device which holds the flint and which when the trigger was pulled struck sparks. These fired a small load of powder which in time fired the main charge in the gun. The German name, *Flinte*, for a certain type of hunting gun, derives from this flint lock weapon.

There are four types of these guns, the Spanish or Dutch spring lock, the English and the French lock. Until a few years ago the Spanish–type lock was widely used by African tribes. Spanish-made barrels were considered the best in the world, with the centres of Spanish gun making in Madrid, Seville and Eibar.

French hunting guns with flint lock were usually very luxuriously decorated, particularly the representational weapons of King Louis XIII. This French flint–lock gun, very solidly made, was used as a military weapon until the 1830s. Shooting experiments in 1806 showed that of two guns, used as early as 1789 for the firing of 10,000 shots each, only one burst after 14,443 shots and the other kept going up to 15,000. Also, it is said of the Prussian King, Frederick William I, that on some days he went shooting partridges for twelve hours on end, firing some 600 shots a day. His gun–loaders constantly handed him newly cocked rifles, so that always several guns in a set were available to him.

The magnificent decoration of hunting weapons was supplemented by highly decorative hunting equipment. Gabriel Gipfel, for example, goldsmith to the court of Dresden, made at the beginning of the seventeenth century splendid hunting sets for the electors of Saxony. In general, a hunting equipment, beside the guns, contained a hunting hanger, a set of knife and fork, powder flask, dog collar and bugles, all decorated to match. Precious sets of this kind were often diplomatic gifts from one ruler to another, and from country to country. Sets made in Saxony can be found in the collections of Polish and English kings. They are also in the Tsar's collection in the armoury of the Kremlin at Moscow. The hunting sets of the sixteenth and seventeenth centuries show rich ornamental decor and the use of colourful precious stones. Sets, belonging to the Elector Johann Georg I of Saxony, are unrivalled masterpieces.

A hunting set often contained a number of different knives, forks, larding–pins and the like, also a whetstone for sharpening the blades. All these utensils fitted into the compartment of the sheath which itself was decorated with silver, gilt or enamel clasps. Hunting bag and powder flask were equally richly decorated.

After the hunt the hunt servants skinned and carved the game, while special rules covered the procedure. Several kinds of table sets were used for the hunting breakfast which followed. Dishes were decorated with hunting scenes as well as glasses and tankards. In all this work the representations of game animals was very realistic during the seventeenth century, as is shown in our illustrations. The climax of craftsmanship was achieved in the equipment for the hunting of absolute rulers in the Baroque period.

27 Hunting lad with falcon and arquebus. 16th century

Hunting in the Age of Baroque

"O noble passion of the hunt, Come, come, Lords, knights, horsemen and servants. Come, all you good fellows, who want to accompany me on the hunt. Come, noble ladies and maidens, Let us take part in the hunting with diligence and pleasure and let us fear nothing."

Verse from the hunting chronicle of Duke Casimir of Coburg, 1564—1633

Between 1600 and 1750 in the heart of Europe Baroque developed as an important style. It influenced the artistic, intellectual and cultural activities of the courts and the aristocracy. Masterpieces of the Baroque were created for the courts of princes, the nobility and the church, reflecting the social order of late Feudalism and the absolute power of the monarch. A longing for movement, rhythm, light and colour marks the splendour and magnificence of a court and aristocracy–orientated society. This society was self–assured and addicted to representation and monumental display.

The idea of the absolute monarch to be ruling by the grace of God, was to be confirmed not only by the subjects but equally by animals and innate things, such as gardens and parks. The grounds and parks of castles and great houses in the Baroque period were laid out in the typical way of the formal gardens of the French court. Together with formal layout, the strange and exotic was stressed through the building of pavilions, orangeries and menageries, all in an effort to be spectacular.

These tendencies and the general artistic trends in seventeenth–century Europe also decided the pictorial representation of hunting. Italian Baroque must here be considered, also Dutch Realism and French Classicism.

The most impressive witnesses to hunting in the seventeenth century are undoubtedly the large Flemish hunting pieces. In the second half of the sixteenth century Antwerp became the centre of Flemish art, with Peter Paul Rubens (1577—1640) the most outstanding representative of the Flemish school. His work greatly influenced all painting concerned with hunting. As in all his other work, Rubens's hunting pictures also reflect two themes. One is the mythology of Antiquity, the other hunting scenes rich in figures. These are, like most of his paintings, very impressive, full of contrasts, voluptuous and colourful. There is movement and passion, with the separate figures full of dynamic. Obviously the composition was thought out according to Baroque taste, yet the representation of hunting itself is realistic in detail. The animals in these pictures were often painted by different disciples of the master, and on the whole they achieved representation true to nature. All the same these somewhat pathetically theatrical pictures of hunting were pure and solely status symbols for the castles of princes and nobles who commissioned them.

Rubens's favourite disciple was van Dyck (1599—1641) who surpassed his master, particularly in the painting of portraits. His greatest success came at the English court of Charles I where he painted many portraits of courtiers. Several paintings in subtle shades of colour show the typical hunting dress of the period, for example, "Charles I in Hunting Dress", now in the Louvre. These paintings, too, were, of course, made for display.

Among other Flemish painters of large hunting pieces and animal still lifes are Paul de Vos (1590—1678) and Jan Fyt (1611—1661). The most gifted painter in Rubens's workshop was, however, Frans Snyders (1579—1657) who painted some remarkable still lifes.

The turbulent and luxurious life in castles and palaces included hunting banquets lasting for days. To increase the enjoyment of these feasts, the walls of dining halls were covered with highly coloured large representations of fruit, poultry, lobsters and other culinary delights.

Thus Snyders's paintings mainly represent festive tables, heavily laden with all kinds of game together with fruit. A masterly example of this type is the so–called "Hunting Still Life", a characteristically Flemish painting, and in contrast to the later Dutch still lifes of a much more modest type, showing simple hunting equipment and small quarry, arranged in fine composition. All these still lifes, however, reflect reality as it is and great truth of detail. Snyders's still lifes, in particular, are convincing realistic representations with sharp contrasts. His large pictures were made mainly for the halls of great castles while the Dutch still lifes and animal paintings decorated the walls of the homes of huntsmen and townspeople, representing, as they did, the lives of ordinary people. In the seventeenth century Holland became the home of highly developed animal breeding, and because of this the Dutch still life and animal painting gained special popularity. Such painters as Paulus Potter, Melchior de Hondecoeter or Jan Weenix the Younger, were masters in representing the domestic animal realistically. Their animal pieces were surpassed only by hunting still lifes and "kitchen" scenes, showing fruit, vegetables, poultry and game. In the Dutch hunting still lifes the small man's game, the roe deer, the hare, the pheasant and other birds were portrayed with exact precision, often together with hunting weapons and utensils. Among this type of painting are the pictures by Adrian Cornelius Beeldemaeker (1625—1701) and Christoph Pierson (1631—1714) with huntsmen or the equipment for the small hunt carefully and clearly represented.

In France—in complete contrast—the absolute monarchy under Louis XIV demanded the splendid decoration of luxurious castles and parks. The best known example, next to Versailles, with its castle frontage of 580 metres, is the most perfectly preserved castle of Vaux–le–Vicomte, near Melum (Seine–et–Marne), completed between 1657—1661. Here André Lenôtre (1613—1700) created for the first time a geometrical park, with shrubs and trees clipped into ornamental shapes, decorative formal flower beds, fountains, grottoes and menageries. There were also numerous statues, vases and reliefs in the large French parks of the seventeenth and eighteenth centuries. Their layout remained the model for parks and gardens all over Europe. In these parks, too, nature had to submit completely to the will of the absolute monarch.

The hunting palaces of Baroque and Classicist design contained next to the large–scale Flemish hunting pictures and representative portraits, also paintings by French artists. The portraits of the favourite dogs of Louis XIV took pride of place and served as models for others. They were made by François Desportes (1661—1743) who, as a twelve–years–old, was a disciple of the Flemish animal painter, Nicasius, and went to Warsaw in 1695/1696 to work at the court of the Polish King, John II Sobiesky. In Paris he became a member of the Academy of Fine Arts, creating excellent paintings of animals and hunting scenes, among others, for the hunting castle of Anet, belonging to the Duke of Vendôme. From 1702 onwards he worked at the hunting box of Marly where he painted the portraits of the most valued bitches from Louis XIV's pack. He often took part in hunting in order to make sketches of animals in motion. Later works of his related to hunting are in the castle of Meudon, some serving as designs for wall hangings in the hunting box of Choisy.

The most famous of the French artists creating hunting pictures at the time was, however, Jean Baptiste Oudry (1686—1755). Under his direction the huge paintings of *parforce* hunts (352: 667 cm.) — coursing game by mounted huntsmen—in the castle

of Fontainebleau were made, where they may be seen to this day. Oudry deserves special mention for his work as chief inspector of the Royal Gobelin Manufactury in Paris which in his day made all carpets, furniture and jewellery for the royal household. The system of creating whole sets for furnishing was carried out also in the making of wall hangings, so that several pieces were made for the decoration of one room. The enormous tapestries of the series, "The Hunts of Louis XV", produced between 1733 and 1746, from designs by Oudry, represent hunts in the forest of Compiègne near Fontainebleau. They are now kept in the Louvre, with duplicates at the Palazzo Pitti in Florence. As a director of the Beauvais branch of the Gobelin Manufactury Oudry worked also for the Danish and Swedish courts as well as Duke Christian Ludwig of Mecklenburg–Schwerin. There are still forty–three of Oudry's paintings in the State Art Collections of Schwerin.

Next to the large hunting scenes of the seventeenth and eighteenth centuries, many copperplates were widely distributed. Representing hunting scenes or rare specimens of game, they, too, decorated the walls of hunting palaces. Of particular importance is the work of Johann Elias Ridinger (1698—1767) who, living as a painter and engraver in Augsburg, created many hunting scenes—paintings, drawings, etchings and printed graphic work. More than 1,600 engravings by this artist are known to exist, among them the following series: —
Grosser Herren Lust in allerhand Jagen (8 sheets), 1722;
Vorstellungen der vortrefflichen Fürsten–Lust oder der edlen Jagtbarkeiten (36 sheets), 1729;
Gruendliche Beschreibungen und Vorstellungen der wilden Thiere (8 sheets), 1733/1738;
Vorstellungen ... wie alles Wild ... gefangen wird (30 sheets), 1750;
Besondere Ereignisse und Vorfallenheyten bey der Jagt (46 sheets), 1752;
Die von Hunden behaetzte Jagtbaren Thiere (21 sheets), 1761;
Die Jäger und Falkoniers mit ihren Vorrichtungen (26 sheets), 1764;
Vorstellungen der Hirschen ... als anderer besonderlicher Thiere, welche von grossen Herren selbst gejagt, lebendig gefangen oder gehalten worden (101 sheets), 1768;
Abbildungen interessanter Jagdtiere und zoologischer Abnormitäten (aus der Zeit zwischen 1615 und 1765), 1740/1767.

These series whose titles, in the taste of the period, are long and complicated, were popular visual aids for the huntsman in training. In 1825 all of them were published in one book under the title, *Naturhistorisches Original–Thierwerk*, and Ridinger's work still counts among the most widely distributed and best known representations of hunting in Europe.

The Great Lords' Passion for Hunting

"Noble lords and fair ladies should be well served but rarely trusted."
Inscription on a cog–rail winch in the Historisches Museum, Dresden (1556)

Great lords and princes pursued their passion for hunting with ever increasing pomp and circumstance. In fact, they degraded hunting by making it first and foremost a show and a status symbol, which, according to strictly enforced rules, gave pleasure to the assembled courtiers. Hunting, as everything else, had, in all its methods to surrender unconditionally to the principles of Absolutism. It had to satisfy the exaggerated ambition of the princes for enormous quarry, representative trophies and excesses of all kinds. Hunting was, in the spirit of the time, in the service of the extraordinary, an aim never lost sight of. The morte, sounded on the horn, at the death of a stag, was the signal for lengthy and splendid entertainments to follow. A report from Dresden about typical Baroque hunts of the court says: "There was hunting on horseback for stags and other large game in the country's forests, wild boar hunts were held in the boar park, pheasants and partridges were shot in the Grosse Garten, combats with wild animals in the castle yard and fox–tossing in the royal stables." At the European courts of the seventeenth and eighteenth centuries several types of hunting were popular: the *Deutsche Jagen*, consisting of different ways of coursing the animals; the French or *parforce* hunt, stalking in open hunting grounds or specially made constructions. There were also hunts on water, hunts for gaining special experience and special entertainments including animal combats. "Grace and Favour" hunts were held by princes for specially invited guests.

According to decrees concerning forestry, hunting and the keeping of game, the privileges of the overlord were firmly laid down. These decrees were to serve the conservation of game and the protection of hunting. The rules also divided game into large and small game for hunting. In some regions, Saxony, for example, there were even three divisions:

Large game:
Bear *(Ursus arctos)*, stag *(Cervus elaphus)*, buck *(Dama dama)*, lynx *(Lynx lynx)*, swan *(Cygnus olor)*, bustard *(Otis tarda)*, crane *(Grus grus)*, mountain cock *(Tetrao urogallus)*, pheasant *(Phasiaunus colchicus)*, bittern *(Botaurus stellaris)*, night heron *(Nycticorax nycticorax)*;

Medium–size game:
Roe deer *(Capreolus capreolus)*, wild boar *(Sus scrofa)*, wolf *(Cyanus lupus)*, heath cock *(Tetrao tetrix)*, hazel cock *(Tetrastes bonasia)*, common curlew *(Numenius arquatus)*;

Small game:
Hare *(Lepus europaeus)*, fox *(Vulpes vulpes)*, badger *(Meles meles)*, beaver *(castor fiber)*, otter *(Lutra lutra)*, marten *(Martes martes)* wild cat *(Felis silvestris)*, polecat *(Putorius fetidas)*, squirrel *(Scirurus vulgaris)*, weasel *(Mustela erminae)*, hamster *(Cricetus cricetus)*, snipe *(Scolopacidae gallinago)*, partridge *(Perdix perdix)*, wild goose *(Anser)*, wild duck *(Anas)*, heron *(Ardea cinerea)*, crested grebe *(Podicipedea)*, gull *(Laridae)*, moorhen *(Gallinula chloropus)*, coot *(Fulica atra)*, and several other water birds, wood pigeon *(Columba)*, plover *(Vanellus vanellus)*, quail *(Coturnix coturnix)* and whimbrel. Also fieldfares, comprising fell fare, ring ouzel, missel thrush *(Turdus viscivorus)*, European thrush *(Turdus merula)*, song thrush *(Turdus philomelos)*, redwing, land rail *(Crex crex)* and larks *(Alaudidae)* together with other small birds.

This list makes it quite clear that it was legitimate to shoot or trap all kinds of birds, and this was done in big numbers.

To hunt large game remained the sole right of the prince, though he had given up this privilege where medium and small game was concerned.

In 1629 in the Electorate of Saxony, for example, court hunts were held on 133 days annually when 6,161 items of game were killed.* However, of 167 court hunts, only 6 were attended by the elector himself. Yet, all the quarry was recorded by the chronicler as the monarch's personal hunting success.

With the strengthening of power of the nobility and landed gentry in the mid–eighteenth century, some of them gained the privilege of hunting large game on their own properties. This

* From files in the collection of manuscripts in the Sächsische Landesbibliothek, Dresden, R 7 b, "Vorzeichnis was Ihre Churf. Durchl. zu Sachsen in viertzig Jahren von den 11. July Anno 1611 bis auff den 20. Dez. Anno 1650 an Hohen und Niedrigen Wildpret in Jagen, Pirschen, Streiffen und Hetzen geschossen, gefangen und gehatzt."

was, for example, confirmed in Mecklenburg in 1755. According to the new law, the ruling duke had for all time to give hunting privileges to the nobility. A tenant, too, could lease the hunt for small game and some large game from his superior. All state forests, however, were the sole domain of the ruler, and were administered by his Master of the Hunt. Game was sold in the towns, and an order by King Frederick II of Prussia, of 1747, demanded that game to the value of 10,000 *thalers*, and again in 1751 5,000 *thalers* worth of game, should be killed.

In the territories of the towns which in the eighteenth and nineteenth centuries included bigger and smaller woodlands and fields, hunting was regulated by council decision, with the employment of special town foresters and huntsmen. Hunting for small game was leased on an annual basis or given to special persons. The snaring of singing birds and shooting of vermin was open to many townsfolk. From the seventeenth to the nineteenth century the hunting of singing birds became the hunt of the common man. With net, limed rod, snare, sling, ring net and decoy,

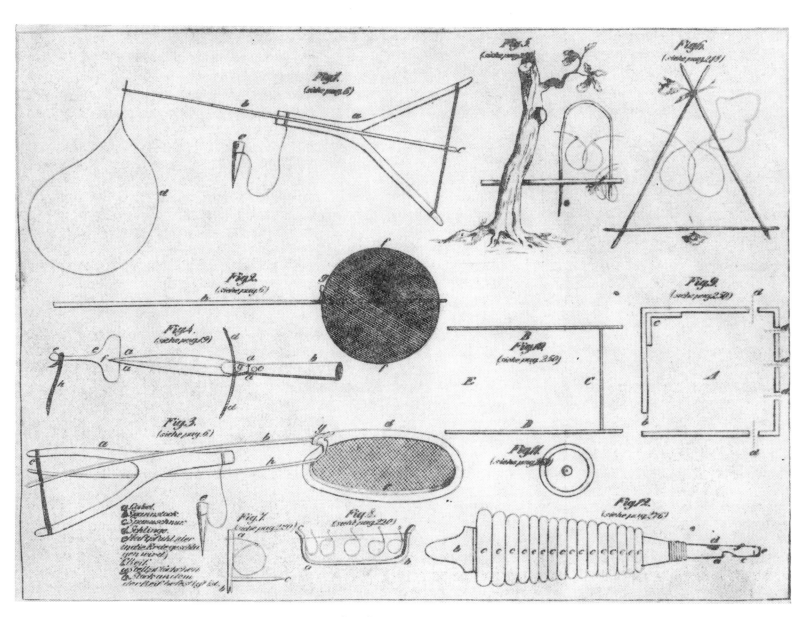

28 Birdcatching equipment. Illustration from C.L. Brehm, *Der vollständige Vogelfang ...*, Weimar, 1855.

birds were caught for centuries. The German ornithologist, Johann Friedrich Naumann, as late as 1849, described in great detail the hunting of birds in Central Germany. The bird catchers set up their expensive decoys, which had often been blinded, quite specially in the autumn, to catch thousands of small birds. The birds were plucked, put on skewers, and offered for sale in the market. A Thuringian speciality was *Kleine Vögelchen mit Klössen*—small birds with dumplings. Larks, in particular also fieldfare and quail were in great demand. In the eighteenth century birds were often considered destructive vermin, and hunted by order of the authorities. This applied, for example, to sparrows and crows. By a decree of the government of the state of Lippe–Detmold, from 23. 7. 1665, peasants were ordered to shoot or snare a certain number of sparrows annually, and display the birds' heads at government offices. In the town of Halle/Saale, too, war was declared on sparrows in 1701, with the intention of totally destroying them. King Frederick William I of Prussia made orders on 11. 12. 1721 and 8. 1. 1731, according to which farmers should deliver to the authorities 12 heads of sparrows, a cotter 8 and a crofter 6. In that way 359,928 sparrows were accounted for in Prussia in 1736. This massacre of sparrows went on in Prussia every year until 1767. How many singing birds, mistaken for sparrows, were also killed, nobody will ever know.

In Europe the Romance countries around the Mediterranean, on the main migration routes of birds, have specialised in the killing of birds. In Italy there developed a number of methods for snaring and trapping, for example, the *brescianella*, a decoy put into a group of trees and the *roscolo*, nets surrounding large stretches of woodland, allowed for the catching of thousands of birds a day. In mountainous areas the *passata* or the *copertoni* caught low flying birds in nets. A small limed rod, the *paniuzze*, some 30 centimetres long, was used in Italy alongside the *panie*, several limed rods tied together. Often for the snaring of singing birds limed rods were used in connection with decoys, lanterns or owls. The *laccio*, a net made of horsehair, with slings, was used for the snaring of quail and thrush. In it the birds were strangled. On 4. 10. 1901 a bird catcher on Lake Garda caught 5,000 in a single day, half of them thrushes. In the harbour of Marseilles in 1895 some eight million quail were handled, received from Messina and Brindisi. Between 1 and 10 May alone Messina exported over half a million live quail. They were dispatched in small boxes of one hundred each to Great Britain and France. In 1897 from the port of Alexandria over two million live quail were sent to Europe. There were also many other small birds: finches, tits, larks, golden–crested wrens, garden warblers etc., sold for centuries in Italian markets. Reports of some six hundred thousand to one million small birds sold annually in a town, are not rare.

St Francis of Assisi who lived from 1182 to 1226, is—among other things—known for his great reverence for all nature and his particular love of birds, as can be seen from his sermon on birds held at Bevagna ("My brothers, the birds."). He lived according to the doctrine he preached, and his Name Day is celebrated all over Italy on 4 October. It is ironical that at these very celebrations ten thousands of song birds are eaten.

The murder of birds goes on in Italy to this day. According to a notice in the press of 1962 about one hundred million song birds are killed there each year, with "17,000 guns at the ready to kill the birds on their flight north from Africa, or nesting in Italy when they become easy prey. The authorities have also granted licenses to 3,232 bird catchers to use nets, and 5,325 have permanently situated constructions for the snaring of birds. For all this the state has received 3,584 million lire in licence fees."

Many huntsmen and animal lovers are against the mass–killing of birds, and have published strong protests again and again. In Turin, for example, an international committee, the "Comitato Internationale Anticaccia" was formed to combat the killing of birds. Also, as early as 1910, the "Pro Avibus" Society was founded in Italy, with its main aim the full protection of birds.

Snaring or shooting birds in large numbers cannot be regarded as hunting for "fair game", even though sometimes traditional hunting methods are used. Let us now turn to the hunting methods at the courts of the seventeenth and eighteenth centuries.

Deutsch Jagen—German Hunting for Large Game

"When a good stag has been sighted, the horn is sounded, the animal is coursed and brought to bay, where some great lord will finish it off."

H. W. Döbel, Neu eröffnete Jäger–Practica, 1746

In the seventeenth and eighteenth centuries one special method of hunting became more and more popular at the courts of German princes.

To make hunting more pleasant for the prince and his noble guests, also to avoid accidents, the company had often been exposed to when following hounds on horseback, game was coursed in big numbers to certain places where the hunting party assembled and could kill the game with ease. This type of hunting reached its climax when stags were well-fed and in good condition, during the months of August and September.

After the number of game, their routes and habits had been ascertained by huntsmen, the Master of the Hunt had to report to his superior about how much game could be expected at each hunt. Long preparation was needed to have sufficient game ready for the main hunt, and much equipment had to be carted about in order to drive the game from the nearby forests. According to detailed plans whole areas were surrounded by nets, and with the cry of "Jo ho, hoch do ho", the animals were driven to enclosed places. A large number of foresters, huntsmen and peasants who had to give compulsory service, was needed for arranging a big hunt. The compulsory service was required mostly at harvest time, and a report of 1730 states that for a great court hunt of King Frederick William I of Prussia more than 600 foresters and over 4,000 beaters had to be kept in readiness. Nets and similar equipment to surround an area of more than 110 kilometres of woodland and fields had to be transported on 90 carts, each

drawn by 4 to 6 horses, and these had to be changed constantly. When the game had been driven into a comparatively small space, thick sheets were used to enclose this area, day and night, which was then guarded by huntsmen until the hunt began.

The hunting itself was surrounded by ceremony: The game area still enclosed, contained a special shelter from which the noble lords would shoot the game. Next to this was a shelter for the hounds which were to course an injured animal. There were also facilities to use, should one of the lordly company feel the need for being completely alone for a minute.

The distance between shelter and net or sheet—as may be seen from the illustrations—was fixed at no more than seventy paces. The company arrived in their carriages at the hunting canopy to the sound of hunting music. After a good breakfast they took their stand in the shelter ready to shoot. On the order of the Master of the Hunt sheetings were rolled back, and the first stags were driven into the small enclosure by hounds. Once in there, the animals rushed in a panic around the hideout, trying to escape, and were then shot by the noble lords. In 1746 a German writer, Döbel, explained that if a stag was not killed outright, but only wounded, and did not fall or die at once, a few hounds were taken from their shelter to course the wounded animal.

The best stags were finished with the hunting knife, the lesser ones with a stab in the neck. All game caught and killed was laid out on the righthand side of the shelter, heads and antlers towards it. The best animals were put into the most conspicuous place, and all game was covered with green twigs. When stags and other game were finished, the huntsmen sounded the morte on their horns to announce the end of the hunt. As a finishing ceremony the Master of the Hunt went to the prince and his guests, carrying green twigs which he presented to the prince, and then fastened one to the prince's hunting cap. All the courtiers and their ladies also attached twigs to their headgear.

Reports of quarry from these great hunts are harrowing: "On 12th January 1656 on Dresden heath 44 stags and 250 wild boar were killed; in 1730 in Moritzburg the quarry was 221 antlered stags, 116 does, 82 fallow–bucks, 46 fallow does and 614 wild boar. In 1748 during a great hunt in Württemberg 500 out of 800 animals were killed, and the rest set free after the slaughter.*

The German poet, Friedrich von Matthisson described and Friedrich Müller, an artist, made drawings of the cruel scenes,

* In the literature on hunting 8,000 head of game are usually mentioned. This, however, seems to be due to a writing error, as sources state that during a court hunt on 8. 10. 1748 in Leonberg, arranged as an entertainment on water in honour of the Duchess of Württemberg, only 800 head of red deer and wild boar are accounted for.

bearing no resemblance to noble sport, which took place during a hunt in Bebenhausen, to celebrate the birthday of King Frederick of Württemberg (1812). The game was not given the slightest chance for flight, as great numbers were driven down the mountainside to certain death. In the end wild boar was coursed by 350 strong hounds, clad in armour like knights.

A bag of 823 animals was the result, 116 stags among them, and the bloodthirsty pleasure cost altogether more than one million *marks*.

This kind of hunting continued until the end of the nineteenth century. For the imperial hunt on the Schorfheide, north of Berlin, a special railway was built through the forest, in order to ease the transport of huntsmen and game. A memorial stone bears the inscription that here "on 20. IX. 1898 His Majesty, the Emperor William II killed his thousandth stag with twenty branches."

During the last royal hunt in the Grunewald near Berlin, on 16. 12. 1901, between 11 o'clock in the morning and 4 o'clock in the afternoon 739 fallow deer were shot. Of these the Emperor William II killed altogether 39 strong bucks, and 27 were shot by the Russian heir to the throne. In 1902 the royal hunting grounds in the Grunewald were abandoned, and the last hunt on horseback just outside the gates of Berlin was held then.

29 The "run" of a Big Hunt, with the shelter in the centre. In the foreground the killing of red deer with a throwing spear. From: Fleming, *Der Vollkommene Teutsche Jäger*, 1719.

The French Parforce Hunt

"Volez! Volez! Mes chiens! après! après mes valets! mes amis! bonne chasse!

Hunting call at the beginning of a parforce hunt

"Prendre à force de chiens", hunting by the strength of hounds, is characteristic of *parforce* hunting, and is often described in the older French literature as coursing game forcefully with hounds, until it is at bay, without being shot or injured by any weapon. There is hardly a method of hunting described so often and in such detail in hunting literature as the *parforce* hunt itself.

After the model of the peoples of the steppes of Europe and Asia, Sassanid kings, Persian shahs and Turkish sultans followed the baying pack of hounds on fast horses, merciless coursing the fleeing stag. Arabian emirs, Celtic or Burgundian nobles and those of the time of the Carolingians did likewise.

Hunting on horseback was said to be paradise on earth, and fulfilling the desire for this sort of paradise demanded huge numbers of huntsmen, horses and hounds. Coursing one particular animal for hours, became the climax of the hunting passion of princes.

Under the French kings in particular *parforce* hunting reached such perfection that ceremonies were arranged according to their ways, and these became known as *la chasse à course de France*. King Louis IX (1226—1270) hunted mainly with white hounds from the Orient, while Louis XII (1498—1515) preferred grey-coloured packs. The greatest luxury was reached with the mounted court hunts of Henry IV (1589—1610) and Louis XIV (1647—1715).

When originally coursing had demanded much skill from everyone engaged in the hunt, courage and endurance on horseback became more and more pleasure without risk with these elaborate *parforce* hunts. Through the construction of special star-shaped paths through the forests, suitable for horses and transport, hunting had no longer to be done across rough ground. The illustrous company might even follow the hunt in carriages. In the centre of the paths cut across the forest, there was usually a hunting box (in Germany: Jagdhaus Stern near Potsdam or the Hellenhaus near Moritzburg/Dresden, for example). Heinrich Döbel said in his *Jäger–Practica* that, should "a prince ride with the hunt, he does not need to go over rough ground like his huntsmen, but can stay with the hunt in comfort, listen to the pleasant music of the pack and the huntsmen and their horns. For the true labour of the hunt, directing it, keeping the hounds in order, belongs to the huntsman in charge, the special *piqueur* of the *parforce* hunt and to the hired servants."

To a medium–size *parforce* hunt, the following staff was needed — as reported by the hunting department of the Electorate of Saxony at Dresden Hubertusburg, of 1737: one commander, one vice commander, one young nobleman, two pages, one *piqueur* (in charge), four *piqueurs* (mounted huntsmen), four hired servants (huntsmen on foot, with hounds to follow the scent), one mounted inspector (for the prince's horses), one stable boy, one saddler, one blacksmith, one veterinarian for the horses, two coachmen, one keeper of harness, twelve grooms, one cymbalist, six trumpeters and other musicians as well as eighty–eight horses, 273 hounds (among them two hundred old ones, accustomed to coursing the stag and fifty–one young hounds) led by the hound boys and twenty–two lime hounds for the hired servants.

In 1748 Duke Ernst August of Saxe–Weimar kept altogether 1,100 hounds and 373 horses for hunting only.

Every hunting pack had its own music, as much attention was paid to the putting together of several types of hounds in the same pack. The mixture made the music more varied and interesting. As a rule three different kinds of stag–hounds ran in a French pack:

small basset hounds; medium–size hounds, like the Bleu de Gascogne—which included a *grand* and *petit* kind, and

large long–legged hounds of the White Billy type, and several kinds of lime hounds with a deep bay.

The high and cheerful sound of the small and medium–size hounds was specially appreciated. These hounds, some 40 centimetres high, formed the main part of a French hunting pack in the eighteenth and nineteenth centuries, while earlier on larger and heavier lime hounds and bloodhounds had been preferred, for example, the *Chiens blancs du Roy* or the reddish–brown *Chiens de Saint Hubert*. These bloodhounds with a fine nose for picking up scent were used a great deal later on as lime hounds for tracking game. Lime hounds, in general, are used in hunting still in our times.

100 L. Cranach the Elder: Wild boar. Drawing, about 1530.
Staatliche Kunstsammlungen, Kupferstich-Kabinett, Dresden

101 Peter Candid: Copperplate from a design for the hunting carpet
in the Bayerisches Nationalmuseum. Deutsches Jagdmuseum,
Munich

*102/103 J. M. Mancher: Ivory bowl with representation of Diana and Actaeon in the centre,
and hunting scenes on the walls. Late 17th century. Hermitage, Leningrad*

*104 Goblet, cut glass, ornamented with bear hunting
scene. Silesian or Bohemian, late 17th century.
Staatliche Museen, Kunstgewerbemuseum, Berlin*

*105 Glass tankard, ornamented with hunting scenes
in enamel and the inscription: "Jäger sauf
dich voll, so laufen dir die Hunde woll"
(Huntsman drink your fill, and your hounds will
run well). German work, 1585. Staatliche
Museen, Kunstgewerbemuseum, Berlin*

106 Chair, made of the antlers of roe deer and red deer, decorated with hunting scenes. Hunting Museum, Ohrada (Czechoslovakia)

*107 L. Cranach the Elder: Portrait of a peasant huntsman. Water-colour,
about 1515. Öffentliche Kunstsammlungen, Kupferstichkabinett, Basle*

108 Stag hunt, window in the cloisters of the Monastery at Muri, Switzerland, 1562

133

109 *Gabriel Gipfel: Hunting set, decorated with turquoise, 1607. Staatliche Kunstsammlungen, Historisches Museum, Dresden*

110 *Wheel-lock gun, the so-called Curland "Tschinke", early 17th century. Staatliche Kunstsammlungen, Historisches Museum, Dresden*

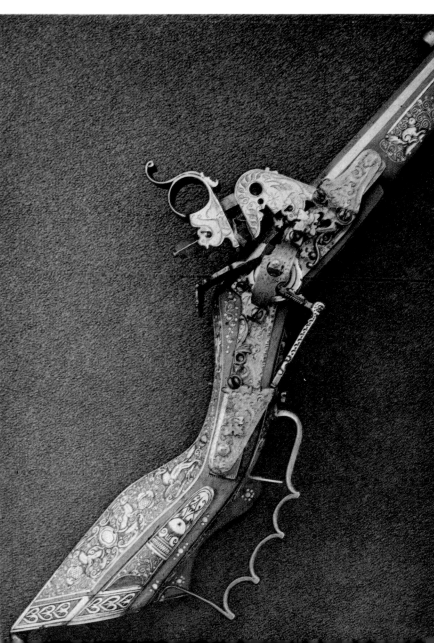

134

111 M. Merian: Game enclosure. Etching from: Ansichten von Schwalbach. *Staatliche Museen, Kupferstichkabinett and Collection of Drawings, Berlin*

112 Peasants doing compulsory labour; putting up large sheets and nets, taken from the equipment wagon. Detail, sheet 4 from Wolfgang Birkner, Jüngeres Jagdbuch, *after 1639. Landesbibliothek, Gotha (German Democratic Republic)*

113 Frans de Hamilton: Still life with hunting equipment. Late 17th century. Staatliche Schlösser und Gärten, Jagdschloss Grunewald, Berlin (West)

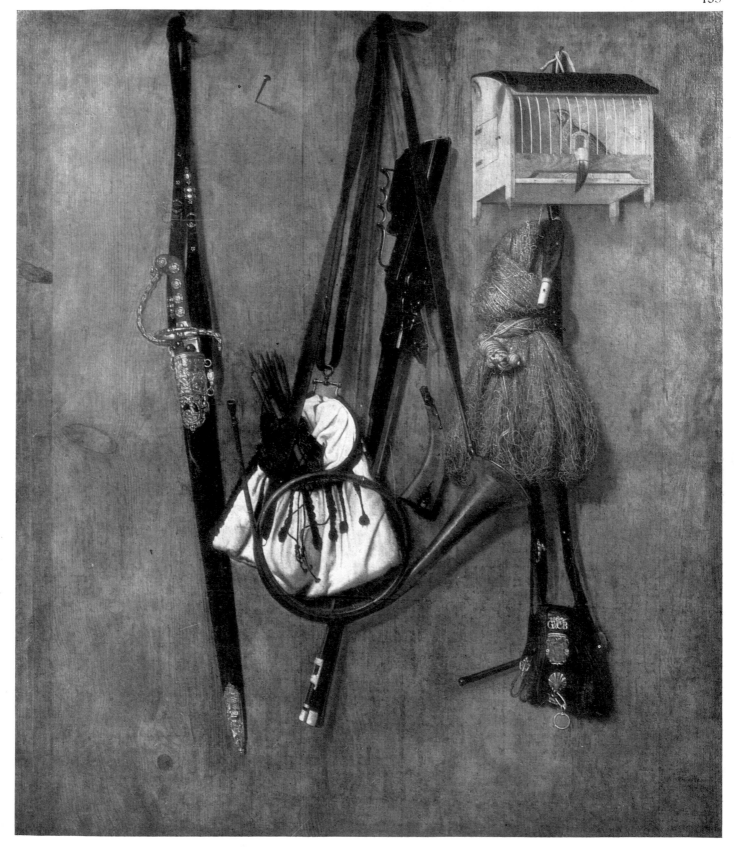

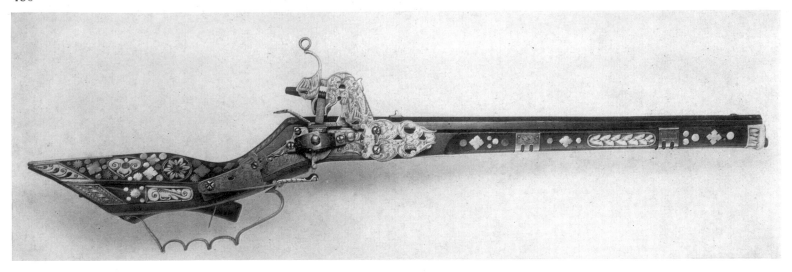

114 "Tschinke" with outside wheel-lock. Early 17th century. Waffenmuseum,
Suhl (German Democratic Republic)

115 Five-shot revolver with flint-lock. About 1720. Staatliche Kunstsammlungen,
Historisches Museum, Dresden

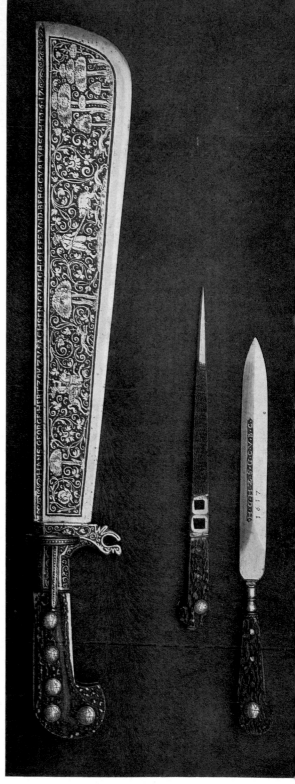

116 *Garden set, consisting of tethering pegs, scraper iron, grafting bore, saw,*
several knives and pricking steel. Dresden work, mid-16th century.
Staatliche Kunstsammlungen, Historisches Museum, Dresden

117 *Carving set, as used by huntsmen. German work, 1617. Staatliche*
Kunstsammlungen, Historisches Museum, Dresden

118 Powder flask, made of ivory, decorated with a representation of Endymion setting out on a hunt. Augsburg, about 1690. Schatzkammer der Residenz, Munich

119 Powder flask with bullet pouch and bandelier; decorated with the coat-of-arms of Saxony and initials (Christian II Duke of Saxony, Elector). German work, early 17th century. Staatliche Kunstsammlungen, Historisches Museum, Dresden

120 Banqueting hall in the hunting box of Ohrada, Czechoslovakia. Tables and chairs made from antlers and hides of red deer, 18th century.

*121   Abraham Hondius: Wild boar hunt. Second half of 17th century.
Galleria Palatina, Florence*

122 *J. A. Corvinus: Prospect of the beautiful hunting palace of the King of Poland, Elector of Saxony, Moritzburg Castle. Copperplate, after 1726. Stadtmuseum, Dresden*

123 *P. P. Rubens: Wild boar hunt. Staatliche Kunstsammlungen, Gemäldegalerie Alte Meister, Dresden*

124 *Jean-Baptiste Oudry: Dead game. 1721. Staatliches Museum, Schwerin*

125   Vittorio Cignaroli: Parforce *hunt for red deer.
About 1770. Hunting Box Stupinigi near Turin.*

*126   Wild boar hunt with nets. Painting behind glass,
late 18th century, Augsburg.*

127 *J. Bruegel the Elder: Archduke Albert and Isabella in the park of Coudenberg Castle. Rubens' House, Antwerp*

128 *François Desportes: Fowling. The bitches, Bonne, Nonne and Ponne, from the pack of King Louis XIV. Louvre, Paris*

129 *M. Carree: Red deer, driven together. Early 18th century. Staatliche Schlösser und Gärten, Jagdschloss Grunewald, Berlin (.West)*

Parforce hunting was carried out to strict rules and traditions. The Master of the Hunt was informed by the huntsman in charge about the number of strong stags in the hunting ground. This information was obtained by the hired servants who searched the terrain for game with the lime hounds. Droppings of the animals were collected in the powder horn, and shown to the Master. After this report the Master of the Hunt confirmed that a good stag was there for the hunting.

Auxiliary huntsmen, keepers of hounds and hound boys with their stag hounds, were then placed in small groups along the suggested routes of game, and could be changed about at any time. Also fresh horses were kept in readiness by the grooms, and only then did the hunting begin in earnest. Once the horn sounded, the pack, led by the chief huntsmen, was in full cry followed by the hunting party, to course the roused stag. When the hounds had taken up the scent, "good hunting" was sounded by the chief huntsmen, while the sound of *hourvari* meant "bad hunting", implying that the scent was lost. Using a short–handled *parforce* whip with a 3 to 4 metres long leather strap, the hounds were whipped in to try and recover the scent.

Generally a *parforce* hunt lasted for some two hours, but a skilled stag might run for six to nine hours before the pack held the exhausted animal at bay. The stag, frightened to death, then took up the fight against the attacking hounds, a scene represented in many paintings. Once the stag was truly at bay, the so–called "prince call" was sounded on the horn, for the lord of the hunt to dispatch the animal. It is, however, reported of the period that should a stag be very wild and angry, a hunt servant would be sent to hamstring the animal from behind, for the prince to be led to the spot in safety to finish off the stag.

After the morte had been sounded, the hunt was over. The lordly master was not given the antlers as a trophy, but the right foreleg. Only then did the hounds get their well deserved reward, the *curée*.

On the coat of the dead stag the entrails, brains, blood and other parts of the animal were spread, and at a given signal the hounds fell to and greedily devoured the lot.

Only few courts could afford the costly equipment of *parforce* hunting. It was carried out side by side with falconry and the German–type of hunting. In Germany neither the gentry nor townspeople could ever aspire to it. About 1720 there only existed ten hunts in Germany. They were:
the Royal English of the Electorate of Hanover, in Celle;
the Mecklenburg hunt in Schwerin;
the Royal Prussian in Potsdam;
the Royal Polish of the Electorate of Saxony in Dresden/Huber-tusburg;
the hunt of the Prince of Anhalt–Dessau in Dessau/Mosigkau;
the hunt of the Prince of Anhalt–Bernburg in Ballenstedt (Harz);
the Duke of Weimar's in Weimar;
the Duke of Württemberg's in Ludwigsburg and Schlothweise;
the hunt of the Prince of Waldeck in Arolsen;
and the hunt of the Landgrave of Hesse–Darmstadt in Darmstadt.

30 *Parforce* hounds.
From: Fleming,
Der Vollkommene Teutsche Jäger, 1719.
German hound;
Polish hound;
French *parforce* hound;
English *parforce* hound.

Among the most impressive representations of a *parforce* hunt are the large oil paintings at the castle of Fontainebleau, painted in 1736 by Jean Baptiste Oudry, and covering a wall space of some 10 metres. They show stag hunts in the vicinity of Compiègne. These pictures of the hunts of Louis XV served as models for the fine tapestries made at the Gobelin manufactory at Paris, as mentioned in a previous chapter.

Hunting castles were the avenue for grand hunting entertainments, particularly the feasts of Diana and of St Hubert. The Baroque hunting palaces with their vast gardens and parks no longer bore any resemblance to the intimate little hunting boxes of the sixteenth and early seventeenth centuries. Their luxurious surroundings often included artificial lakes, coursing grounds, menageries, houses for huntsmen and gamekeepers. Many princely hunting establishments were built in the days of the Absolute Ruler, and some have now been made into public museums.

The grand festivities held in the castles and grounds might include colourful theatrical performances and splendid banquets. Menageries were admired as were spectacles of hunting on water. These took place often at enormous expense on the occasion of weddings and jubilees. More than 4 million *gulden* were spent when on 18. 9. 1719 a Diana Fête was arranged at the Dresden court, to celebrate the marriage of the son of Augustus the Strong to the emperor's daughter.

Bitter protest against the cruel methods of hunting under Absolutism was increasing, however, arising from a growing middle–class. Among the pamphlets of the early literature of the Enlightenment in Germany was one by Johann Georg Hamann (1730—1788), a German philosopher and writer, known as the "Magus of the North", *Schreiben eines parforcegejagten Hirsches an den Fürsten, der ihn parforce gejagt hatte,* letter from a hunted stag to the prince who coursed him—(some sources give as the author the poet Matthias Claudius, 1740—1815).

The pamphlet says: "Your Most Serene Highness, most merciful Prince and Master! I had the honour of being coursed by you today, but I do ask most humbly that it may please Your Highness to spare me in future. If your Most Serene Highness should only once experience being hunted, my request would not seem unreasonable. Here I lie not able to raise my head while blood runs from my mouth and nostrils. How can Your Serene Highness have the heart to hunt to death a poor innocent animal that lives on grass and herbage?

Rather have me shot dead, which would end my life quickly and well. Once again it may be that Your Serene Highness finds pleasure in hunting, but if Your Highness only knew how my heart beats, Your Highness would not repeat the performance. I have the honour to be, with all I possess, and unto death etc."

Even today this hunting method is still practised sometimes; in France the *parforce* hunt on stags is quite common.

31   Lead dog at work. From: Fleming, *Der Vollkommene Teutsche Jäger*, 1719.

Hunting from specially built Hiding Places

ordered on 11 November 1620 that a special hunting installation should be put up for him at the Riesenecke near the town of Jena. This was extended in 1717, and stands to this day, an interesting monument to the history of hunting. Close to the spots where game gathered at rut racks with fodder were stationed as were places where the animals could lick salt. Here the courtiers watched the feeding of game.

The original paths leading to these places were in 1725 replaced by subterranean passages. Three of these, some 200 metres long and built of stone, connected five prepared hunting installations; a means to approaching the animals unnoticed. At intervals of several metres special holes in the ceiling admitted light and air thus allowing for subterranean walking completely at ease.

To keep any possible scent away from the animals, a high wall was erected also, so that the court and its guests could travel in coaches right up to the place.

Today this historical installation near Weimar is unique in Europe. Only one similar place exists in the Böblinger Forest in Württemberg, but the paths leading to it are made of wood.

Along with all the various ways of hunting, the courts still arranged traditional spectacular hunts and combat displays in the castle forecourts.

"Hunting is not for mighty lords only. It also gives much pleasure to the huntsmen, and it is of great use."

H. W. Döbel, Neu eröffnete Jäger–Practica, 1746

With the improvement in weapons technique in the sixteenth century and the use of heavier shotguns, "shooting" became more and more popular. Shooting game, driven into a very constricted space, had been easy, but stalking over a wide area, trying to get close to the game without being noticed, and then shoot, required much greater skill and expertise. In contrast to the German–type of killing game in a small space, stalking gives the animal a real chance for escape and success is therefore considered a genuine proof of the huntsman's skill.

But stalking game in open ground was not always successful. The very smallest mistake could destroy the luck of the chase, and so seventeenth and eighteenth century huntsmen tried to create places for their masters where game killing was secure. Huntsmen and gamekeepers naturally sought good hunting grounds so that they could set up special hides and stands.

This was done mainly in areas where the game collected at rut. Extra feeding places were erected to accustom the animals to gather on the spot, and high fences were put up to make it impossible for game to escape from the forest.

In the mid–sixteenth century the Elector of Brandenburg had a fence built, 80 kilometres long, from the river Havel near Zehdenick, across the Schorfheide to the Oder, in order to prevent his game from getting into Mecklenburg territory.

If red deer and wild boar came to the feeding places regularly, stands and installations of various kind were built there for the huntsmen to lie in wait. Also special paths were made through the forest, leading to the hide. The Duke of Saxony–Altenburg

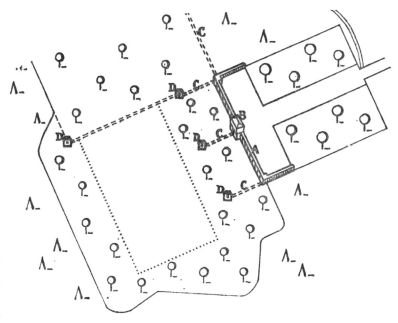

32 Hunting installation Rieseneck near Hummelshain in Thuringia. A wall, B shooting installation, C subterranean approaches, D former hunting installations

Spectacular Combats, Fox–tossing and other Macabre Shows in Castle Forecourts

"Now this is an amusement for great lords and ladies, as they watch for hours and with pleasure when animals are set against each other or tossed to death playfully by the gentlemen in attendance."

H. W. Döbel, Neu eröffnete Jäger–Practica, 1746

During the Rococo period the aristocracy found great pleasure and entertainment in animal displays which had little to do with real hunting and required little or no individual skill. Animal combats, for instance, and fox–tossing were very popular.

In these pompous entertainments in the forecourts of the castles in the residential towns the animals were degraded to fighting as mere performers, to amuse the court, after which they would be killed. These shows might well be compared to Roman Games, displaying as those did in late Antiquity, the parasitical character and way of life of contemporary society.

Döbel says of these entertainments: "The animals were brought in cages, any that were available, such as lions, tigers, aurochs (bison), buffalo, bear, wolf and many wild boar. There might also be a courageous stallion, mule or bull, and one after the other, which means all of them, are brought into the fighting arena. Then lighted squibs, consisting of fine powder and alcohol, or rockets are thrown, or tied to the bull's horns, and directed against other animals, to make them angry and ready to attack anything. Sometimes a few stuffed red scarecrows are lowered into the arena, and they, too, are attacked, especially by bears.

The animals attack each other. The bison is very strong, and, holding its head high, it throws off anything that comes against it. This animal is able to lift cattle and others completely off the ground, and throw them into the air. As for the wild boar, it can finish its opponent with one stroke.

Horse and mule have their hind and front legs shoed with iron. And even though the mule is considered usually to be a stupid beast, it is astonishing how it can defend itself, running, striking and biting, against bear, lion and other such animals.

Soon the animals are fatigued with fighting, and then hounds are brought into the arena to encourage them again to fight among themselves, and to run about …

When lion, tiger, horse and mule have not been too badly injured, they are put back into their cages. And so a *divertissement* comes to an end, an entertainment gentlemen and their ladies enjoy quite often at the great courts."

As late as 1693 at Berlin's town wall, where there was a coursing park built like an amphitheatre, "three beautiful lions, three African tigers, seven black bears, one polar bear, one large wild boar, a bison, and eight porcupines were brought for the general delight and special pleasure of the elector, the court and the public from far and wide." There were also "costumed" displays in the castle forecourts when animals were put into fancy dress before being tortured to death like living toys; solely for amusement.

Fox–tossing was a similar entertainment in the mid–eighteenth century. Small princely courts could not afford the display of expensive exotic animals but native foxes were always available for tossing.

For this the castle yard was surrounded by high sheeting or narrow–mesh net, fastened down firmly to the ground to make it impossible for the cunning foxes to escape, and so disappoint the noble lords. The ground of the courtyard was covered with fine sand or good turf, in case the amusing spectacle might have too quick an ending. It would never do if animals were allowed to fall, knock their heads on stone and break their necks, back, pelvis or antlers. They must not die in that way instead of being tossed!

The whole procedure was offensive to any sense of humane relationship with the animal. It was surrounded with much ceremony, pomp and circumstance. The writer Fleming has this to say: "When on a fixed day gentlemen and their ladies arrive at court, clad in green, decorated with gold and silver, they are taken to the appointed place to the sound of music. They are then shown into their seats, a lady and a gentleman in turn, and together they pull and toss up the fox on a narrow net."

The tossing nets would lie flat on the ground, and the animals were taken singly from their cages into which they had been put after being caught. Beaver, badger, otter, wild cat, marten, polecat and young wild boar were also used for tossing. It appears from contemporary sources that about 80 to 90 per cent of small predators were killed by tossing in the seventeenth and eighteenth centuries, not in open hunting grounds as is often stated in the literature on game killing.

Once the frightened foxes began running about the tossing nets, the noble assembly tossed them high into the air. If they fell back on the nets, they were tossed up again, and this went on until the fox broke its neck. Thus, according to Döbel, tossing the fox was regarded as a great amusement, especially if the two who did the tossing, got on well in working together. A good toss of the fox would be some 6—8 *ellen* (old German measure; about 3 to 4 metres). After this treatment the foxes staggered and crawled about, stunned. Quite a few died or were beaten to death, and the "game" went on to the last animal left.

At a fête in 1722 at the Dresden court 160 foxes were tossed. It was 414 in 1747 as well as 281 hares, 32 badgers and 6 wild cats. Four years after that at a court entertainment 687 animals were tossed to death to the macabre enjoyment of the illustrious company.

After the morte, according to Fleming, celebrations went on in the castle's banqueting hall. All huntsmen blew their horns when it pleased the Serene Highness to drink the health of all good huntsmen to much cheerful sound. A truly gruesome scene.

The French horn was a popular instrument in the hunting music of the eighteenth century. Apart from musicians at the court of Louis XIV, the bugle players from Bohemia who served the Imperial Count, František Anton von Sporck, were well known. These buglers, who were huntsmen, secured a high reputation for hunting music. At that time many pieces of hunting music were composed in Bohemia, specially fanfares and pieces for the French horn. A song composed by one, Haucke, in Bohemia in the mid-eighteenth century, was widely diffused in Europe as Count von Sporck's hunting song. There are sources which attribute only the words to Gottfried Benjamin Hanke (1724) and trace the tune to a popular song from Carinthia.

In the history of hunting music the "Lieutenant de Chasse de M. le Duc du Maine" is called "the father of music for the French horn". This Marquis Antoine de Dampierre, who was master of hounds of the Duc du Maine, in 1709, developed the French horn into a solo instrument for the concert music of court orchestras in all the princely capitals. After 1700 the trumpet makers of Nuremberg had begun copying the French horn and made it the leading fashionable instrument of hunting music. Many a hunting cantata and symphony were composed at that time which even now have a place in the repertoire of concerts. Johann Sebastian Bach, for example, composed the Hunting Cantata No. 208, "Was mir behagt, ist nur die muntre Jagd", which on 23 February 1716 was first performed as table music after a grand combat at the Jägerhof of Duke Christian of Saxony-Weissenfels. In Diana's aria, "Jagen ist die Lust der Götter" the French

horns play a major part. The vice-conductor of the Archbishop of Salzburg, Leopold Mozart, father of Wolfgang Amadeus, in 1755 composed the "Sinfonia di caccia" in D major, the so-called hunting symphony. In its first movement in particular it conveys a genuine hunting atmosphere. In 1765 Joseph Haydn was conductor to Prince Esterházy, and was known to be a passionate hunter himself. On the Esterházy estates he composed the Symphony No. 31 D major "Mit dem Horn Signal—auf dem Anstand", for string orchestra. Again and again typical hunting sounds were used in music for concert and opera. The French horn, early on used in hunting music, also came into its own as a solo instrument in the orchestra. Many hunting songs of the eighteenth century turned in time into popular folk songs. This was particularly so in the German-speaking countries where the songs express a love of hunting and the wide open spaces. All these songs now form part of hunting history.

33 Wolf trap. English wood engraving vignette of the 18th century.

Hunting Decrees for the Protection of Animals in Seventeenth and Eighteenth–Century Germany

"We herewith decree that from now on all animals, does, wild sows as well as hares and also birds, should be fully protected from 1 March to 24 August, and none of them should be shot."

Decree of King Frederick I. Berlin, 9. 11. 1705

Hunting in the sixteenth and seventeenth centuries did not take account of either sex or age of game, even though certain close seasons were fixed, mainly at the time of breeding and rut. The germ of conservation had been sown as early as the Middle Ages but hunting success and record–breaking quarry remained the dominant interest in most countries.

The reduction of game due to these circumstances in the seventeenth and eighteenth centuries firmly demanded conservation. Yet, measures to ensure it, were very often neglected or only taken limited notice of, due to the desire for excessive hunting. A few examples may show the character of decrees issued. An electorial decree for the Mark Brandenburg of 1. 2. 1622 states in paragraph 26 that no eggs must be taken from nests, or breeding birds disturbed. This was to include ducks and other fowl. Paragraph 30 of the same document fixes heavy fines for the illegal shooting of game, for example:

stag 500 thalers	wild boar 400	hare 50
wolf 50	fox 20	otter 10
bustard 50	swan 75	heron 40

On 12. 5. 1668 an order was made, stating that whosoever was not entitled to the shooting of large game, was not allowed to shoot bustards and swans. This order was confirmed again on 5. 11. 1683.

On 21. 3. 1670 an order was made against the taking of eggs of geese, duck and other birds, also prohibiting the destruction of nests. This order was repeated on 9. 6. 1677, 18. 3. 1680, 5. 4. 1698 and 10. 4. 1704, and read from the pulpit of every church in the electorate.

On 25. 8. 1686 a decree was issued for the protection of nightingales in the Mark Brandenburg, as all over the country this bird *(Luscinia megarhynchos)* had become rare. The decree was repeated on 25. 3. 1693. The town of Königsberg decreed on 17. 6. 1698 that no bird catcher should catch a nightingale nor risk keeping such a bird caged for his own advantage.

A police decree of the town of Magdeburg from the year 1688 "improved and extended on 20. 8. 1743, settled, among other things, a limit for the catching of larks in nets. The privilege of catching larks, granted as a special right in many towns, led to the catching of hundreds of thousands of singing birds for culinary purposes. The town of Lübeck decreed quite specially on 25. 5. 1698 that on Sundays, holidays or week days birds should only be shot in an orderly manner and professionally both inside the town and outside its gates. It was stated specifically that not only would children, servants and apprentices acting against the ruling be punished, but equally persons in charge of them.

In the seventeenth century the balance between male and female game was badly disturbed because of arbitrary shooting. In Saxony, for example, during an elector's splendid court hunts, the following game was killed:

Species of Game	1611–1650	1656–1680
red deer	14,656	27,755
stag	14,676	13,636
deer calf	3,410	4,258
roebuck	1,571	2,106
doe	7,680	14,665
fawn	719	93
wild boar	6,281	4,380
wild sow	8,947	10,966
young wild boar	12,323	6,652

With roe deer the proportion of male to female was particularly bad when for each buck seven does were shot. This meant that by the end of the seventeenth century roe deer was rare all over Germany. On 15. 6. 1693 a decree was issued in the Mark Brandenburg for the protection of roe deer which there, as everywhere else, had suffered greatly. This decree was repeated on 13. 3. 1713. In 1749 Westphalia, too, made it an offence to shoot a doe, while the buck could be shot all the year round.

With hunting and animal combats having become more sumptuous at the courts of Absolute monarchs, exotic animals and game of all kind were introduced to the native game parks. In 1680 the Elector of Brandenburg introduced to Berlin and Potsdam elks and stags from East Prussia. In 1707 and 1714 beavers were settled near Potsdam, Oranienburg and Liebenwalde. In

1717, 1727 and 1731 transports of bisons went from Lithuania to Dresden–Moritzburg. In July 1733 forty–nine bisons were settled in open ground near Liebenwerda. Orders were made to protect these very special animals:—

24. 5. 1681, in the Mark Brandenburg: "that elks, stags and other game settled there, should not be harmed";

8. 3. 1689 renewal of this decree, with the additional mention that some aurochs also have been released from game parks, to settle in open ground.

On 12. 10. 1703 Frederick I, King of Prussia, decreed that fallow deer should be protected everywhere and be allowed to roam freely. The king's father, the Elector Frederick William, had brought the animals "from far off countries and at great expense", and settled them in the game parks of Cölln on the Spree, Potsdam and Oranienburg. Through damaged fences the animals had escaped and had multiplied greatly in the open countryside. In 1703 more fallow bucks were released from the parks and the species spread slowly all over the Mark Brandenburg.

There are similar documents from Mecklenburg about the introduction of fallow deer, from the year 1770, also protecting this game.

There exist many decrees concerning the protection of beavers in Prussia, for example: a decree from 24. 1. 1714 concerned beavers released near Potsdam and Oranienburg.

Renewed and made more severe, on 24. 3. 1725, it states that beavers on the banks of the Elbe should be protected and not shot, fixing a fine of 200 *Reichsthalers* for offenders.

On 9. 11. 1705 an order was made in Prussia concerning the protection of game at rut and breeding time. It is stated that all over Germany game had been reduced and previous orders not been taken notice of. Animals therefore had not been protected as they should be but had been shot and killed at all times and without discrimination; an evil not to be tolerated any longer.

This decree, however, limited once again the full protection of snipe and duck for which the close season lasted only from 1 May to the beginning of July. It was repeated on 11. 3. 1713 and 8. 4. 1715.

On 10. 4. 1709 the King of Prussia ordered the magistrates of towns to guard against the town's tradesmen, particularly young unmarried lads possessing shotguns, and go hunting irresponsibly. Close seasons for all game, including the nesting time of birds, should be carefully observed. The government of the county of Lippe made an order on 8. 6. 1713, stating that "particularly in open country, in forests and woodlands birds' nests are ruined and taken away, together with the young birds. Also, birds are shot, thus damaging substantially the legitimate catching of birds which is part of fair hunting."

This latter statement makes it quite clear that birds were protected only in the interest of hunting, and that rules were made accordingly. Close seasons were reduced in order to assure good hunting. This was specially noticeable with regard to wild fowl. On 22. 12. 1723 a declaration stated that wild swan and duck should be protected while nesting, but wild goose, crane, heron, wood–pigeon, wolf, fox, marten, otter and lynx could be shot at any time.

Later hunting decrees, one, for instance, of 3. 10. 1743 limit close seasons further, at a time when with growing power the aristocratic landowners were able to insist on their own extensive rights to hunting.

In Mecklenburg on 18. 4. 1755 all close seasons and rules for the protection of game were cancelled. In contrast the development in the Free Towns of Germany was quite different, determined by the progressive spirit of their citizenry. The senate of the town of Lübeck decreed on 4. 5. 1782: "We, the Burgomaster of this town, have been displeased to receive several complaints and quite recently grievances have been made known to us by honourable citizens, regarding decrees given in the past about the shooting or catching of singing birds, not being heeded. Indeed, all kinds of idlers, some for sheer wantonness, others for their own evil greed, shoot and kill without any regard to protection, and with such unbridled audacity that by the continuance of these malpractices animals and birds will not multiply, and in time will disappear altogether."

With social changes applied to hunting laws, stocks of game were further reduced and by the mid–nineteenth century were at their lowest. Laws and police orders alone could not remedy this sorry state and guarantee the protection of animals. This becomes particularly clear in the war on predators which succeeded in the extermination of several species.

At the end of the nineteenth century representatives of animal protection and conservation began raising their warning voices against impending catastrophy.

The Hunting of Wild Animals is the Sport of Great Gentlemen

"All means should be employed in destroying dangerous, villainous and fierce beasts of prey, particularly wolves and lynxes. They should be caught in nets and hunted in every possible way."
Decree concerning the hunting of wolves in Thuringia, 1642

Hunting decrees published in the eighteenth century were aimed at the complete extermination of native beasts of prey. In several regions this lead to the destruction of all wild animals.

Among animals regarded then as beasts of prey were: bear, wolf, lynx, beaver, badger, fox, otter, wild cat, marten and polecat. Birds of prey at that time meant all types of eagle, the eagle-owl, all falcons, hawk, sparrow–hawk, kite, all kinds of owl and all raven–type birds.

"Ever since powder, lead, stalking and shooting on the wing began," said the writer Döbel, "the hunting of vermin has gone down, as it gives more pleasure to shoot than to find a dead animal in a trap." Döbel advocated the renewed use of traps, and described in detail 53 different methods of catching vermin.

"To achieve the complete extermination of all vermin" special monies were paid to foresters and other officials for the hunting and trapping of animals. A particularly good award was offered for producing the body of a wolf, namely 2 *thalers* and 12 *groschen.*

The policy of extensively hunting and killing vermin was also designed to appease the resentment and anger of the country people regarding the hunting habits of their overlords.

Vermin decreased spectacularly everywhere:

Between 1611 and 1717 the following were killed in Saxony: 709 bears, 6,937 wolves, 505 lynxes; in Thuringia, between 1643 and 1651: 80 wolves, seven lynxes, 179 otters, 3 wild cats; in Brandenburg–Prussia in 1700 some 4,300 wolves, 229 lynxes and 147 bears. Only some fifty years later the last bear was killed in Hither Pomerania, and in 1770 in Upper Silesia. In 1734 the last bear hunt in Saxony was held in the Vogtland district. In the Mark Brandenburg the last lynx was killed in the same year, and another about 1780 in the Thuringian Forest. In Saxony the last elk was killed in 1746, in Galicia in 1760 and in Silesia in 1776.

All species of European wild cattle met the same fate. The last aurochs were shot in 1627 in the forest of Jaktorow (60 kilometres from Warsaw). The last German bison, living in the wild, was killed in 1755 in the Forest of Tapiau (East Prussia). After that bisons found a last refuge in the forests of Bialowieźa (see page 217). The beaver *(Castor fiber)*, too, was exterminated in the heart of Europe, except for a few specimens on the central course of the Elbe. After 16. 12. 1729 here, too, the beaver could be shot by anybody. In 1787 the last beaver on the Oder was caught south of Görlitz. It is said that the last wild horse was shot in 1644 in East Prussia, and the last tarpan in 1879.

In 1607 on the river Gambia in West Africa a British commercial traveller shot the first elephant, and this was the beginning of a merciless hunt for all African Big Game. Animals on uninhabited islands were in special danger as the crews of sailing vessels killed them for food. Next to the giant tortoise, the great auk was in danger at that time. The bird did become extinct in 1790 in the Baltic, about 1800 in North America, and about 1834 in Great Britain. Around 1844 the last two great auks were killed on the south coast of Iceland.

The dodo *(Raphus cucullatus)*, a bird about the size of a turkey, inhabited the island of Mauritius near Madagascar, but was so completely exterminated that not even a body remains to show the bird ever existed. The last dodo was killed in 1693.

The fauna on the islands near Australia, New Zealand and the Caribbean, was also sadly diminished by ships' crews or impaired by the introduction of domestic animals. A classical example of this development is New Zealand where, after 1771, more than 35 mammals and 25 species of birds were exterminated by immigrants. In Australia, too, the native thylacine *(Thylacinus cyanocephalus)* became extinct through the introduction of dingos. The duck–bill, an egg–laying mammal, discovered in 1797, has only been saved from extinction at the very last moment, both in Australia and in Tasmania. There is a big money fine now or six months imprisonment for the killing of duck–bill in Australia. Also the ground parrot, native to New Zealand, became extinct through the introduction of wild pig, dog and cat. The kiwi, the bird unable to fly, of New Zealand, is in danger too. Its nests and eggs are being destroyed by animals introduced to the country. The furry animals are perhaps the hardest hit species in all the world, as their soft skins are worth their weight in gold.

153

130 Parforce *hunting horns of the 18th century. Deutsches Jagdmuseum, Munich*

131 *Hunting signals for the* parforce *hunt. From: Fleming,* Der vollkommene Teutsche Jäger, *1719.*

132   J. E. Ridinger: Cutting up of the stag and handing the foreleg to the Master of the Hunt. Etching. Staatliche Museen, Kupferstichkabinett and Collection of Drawings, Berlin

133   J. E. Ridinger: Parforce hunt for a stag, and how it is killed. Copperplate. Staatliche Kunstsammlungen, Kupferstich-Kabinett, Dresden

134 *Representation of a "Lauff-Schiessen" in the boar park at Moritzburg on 12. 1. 1656. Barockmuseum, Moritzburg*

156

135 Jean-Baptiste Oudry: Stag hunt among the cliffs of Franchard.
Tapestry from the series "Hunts of Louis XV" (section), 1738. Palazzo Pitti,
Florence

136 Jean-Baptiste Oudry: Assembling the pack. Tapestry from the series
"Hunts of Louis XV". 1746. Palazzo Pitti, Florence

137 H. Schnee and C. I. Arnold: Arrival of the Emperor William I for the "Rote Jagd" in the Grunewald, 1887. Staatliche Schlösser und Gärten, Jagdschloss Grunewald, Berlin (West)

138 G. A. Eger: Hunting at the Dianaburg about 1750. Jagdmuseum, Kranichstein (German Federal Republic)

139 "The hay barn or feeding of
red deer in winter." Etching by
J. E. Ridinger. Staatliche Museen,
Kupferstichkabinett and Collection
of Drawings, Berlin

Die Heu Schuppen oder Winter Fütterung vor das Roth Wildpreth.

140 "How big game is hunted by
stalking." Etching by J. E. Ridinger.
Staatliche Museen,
Kupferstichkabinett und
Collection of Drawings, Berlin

Wie das hohe Wild mit beschleichen auf der Weyde gepürschet wird.

141 Court hunt on 8. 10. 1748 in Leonberg (Württemberg). Coloured copperplate.
Deutsches Jagdmuseum, Munich

142   Six-in-hand stag carriage of Landgrave Ludwig VIII of Hesse
(1691—1768). Painting by an unknown artist. Jagdmuseum,
Kranichstein (German Federal Republic)

143   W. F. V. Roye: Menagerie of the Elector Frederick III of
Brandenburg. 1697. Represented are: one snowy owl, two Axis
stags, two cassowaries, one bee-eater and a crested goose.
Staatliche Schlösser und Gärten, Jagdschloss Grunewald,
Berlin (West)

*144 "Coursing in the Altmarkt at Dresden." Sheet 2:
Coursing wild boar, 17th century. Sächsische
Landesbibliothek, Manuscript Collection, Dresden*

145 "*Coursing in the Altmarkt at Dresden.*" *Detail of sheet 4: Tossing the fox. Sächsische Landesbibliothek, Manuscript Collection, Dresden*

Wolfs Jagt

65

Wie man die Wolf mit Hetzhün
den jagen vnd fangen soll .

Das · 10 · Capittel

Wolfs Jagt

68

Diß waß weiß vnd gestalt man die
Wolfs fallen richten vnd stellen soll ,

Das · 17 · Capittel

146/147   *"How wolves are coursed and caught with hounds, and how to set a wolf
trap properly." Hunting manual of 1580. Sächsische Landesbibliothek,
Manuscript Collection, Dresden*

Traps, Trappers and Leather Hunters

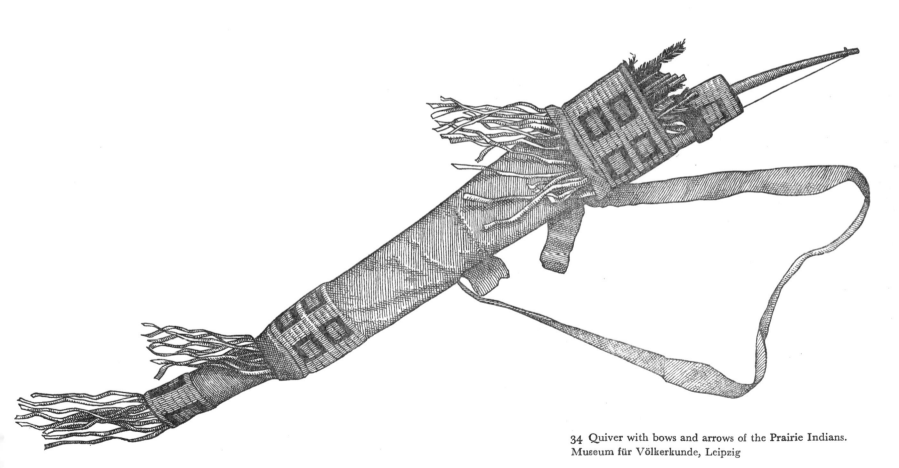

34 Quiver with bows and arrows of the Prairie Indians.
Museum für Völkerkunde, Leipzig

"Soft Gold" from the Siberian Taiga

"The pelts of beavers are highly valued and all Russians have their clothes trimmed with fur ..."

S. von Herberstein, Moscoviter wunderbare Historie, 1563

In the trade balance of the eastern European countries income from their hunting economy and from timber formed a substantial part of all earnings. Visby, on the island of Gothland, and Novgorod were established trading centres on the Baltic as early as the twelfth century, serving as entrepôts for the trade in Russian and Siberian furs and skins. The local merchant family of Stroganov

35   Merchant-men in the North-East Passage. Woodcut

held a monopoly for the trading in salt and skins ever since the fourteenth century.

Through the search for a north-east passage to China and Japan, the trapping of fur animals and the catching of fish on the coasts of the White Sea became increasingly important in trade relations. The Moscovy Company (sometimes called the Russia Company), founded in 1554 in London and Boston, created a focal point for the trade with its settlement in Archangel. It handled trade in Russian and Siberian skins of ermin, sable, white fox and walrus.

We know from reports of an Arab traveller, Ibn Fadlan, of the great wealth of fur animals in the Urals and the Taiga regions. The trading for peltry in the ancient country of Perm was very important to Arabian traders, as furs and trimmings of fur belonged to the clothing of the ruling classes at the court of the khalifs. Top prices were paid for these luxury goods, and the Fur Fairs in the town of Bulgar on the Kama river were a popular place for traders to meet.

In the winter of 921/22 Khalif Muktadir (908—932) sent a trading expedition to the place, of which Ibn Fadlan was a member, and he wrote about the hunting peoples of the Jura tribe:

"The inhabitants of Bulgar make expeditions into the countryside, to bring back clothing, salt and other things with which they trade. To transport these goods, they make small carts which are drawn by dogs. Due to much snow falling in that country, no other animals can travel there. The people tie the bones of cattle to the soles of their feet, and everyone carries two sticks with points in their hands. In that way they stem themselves against the snow and glide on its surface ... They buy from and sell to the natives, making themselves understood by signs, and in that manner bring back fine sable furs."

Through the use of dog sledges and primitive snow-shoes hunting fur animals was possible in the Arctic as early as the tenth century.

In the sixteenth century the Austrian ambassador to the Russian Imperial Court, Graf S. von Herberstein, reported on the travel possibilities in the Siberian Taiga. In 1581 cossacks and fur trappers, let by the hetman, Yermak, to the vast plains of Siberia, conquered regions east of the Urals for the Russian Tsar. In 1610 the Yenisei river was crossed, and the mouth of the Lena reached in 1637. The party obtained rich booty of furs, sable, silver, blue and white fox, and many others. These precious furs, the "soft gold" of the Taiga, played the same devastating part in Siberia, as did gold and silver in the conquest of the New World.

The riches of the Moscovite Empire consisted to a great extent in its wealth of furs, the sound foundation of the country's economy and finances. In the Siberian chancellery in Moscow careful accounts were kept about the furs to be delivered by the voivodes of Siberia. In 1587, for example, 200,000 furs of sable, 10,000 of silver fox and 500,000 of squirrel were sent as their tribute to Moscow. In the mid–seventeenth century every subject of the Tsar in Siberia (excluding the clergy) had the duty of supplying a pro–capita tax of—when reaching the tenth year of life: 2 sable furs; at reaching the eleventh: 3 sable furs; at reaching the twelfth: 4 sable furs and so on. On reaching the age of twenty, the number of sable furs to be supplied annually was twelve, and it remained that figure until the age of fifty, when the numbers were reduced again.

In 1692* a traveller to Russia, Georg Adam Schleissing, wrote in his book, *Seweria* (Siberia) about the trapping of sable: "People who are in disgrace, and banned to Siberia, are given the knout before they leave Moscow. This knout is square and sharp, and applied to the naked back, it cruelly injures flesh and skin. Then the poor wretches are sent like cattle to the vastnesses of Siberia where they have to trap sable ...

It is well at the same time to remember that there is an abundance of sable and other game in those vast regions, so that even an inexperienced hunter, who is not accustomed to bow and arrow, can easily shoot the numbers requested of him. They do not shoot with pointed arrows, so as not to damage the precious skin. Instead of a point, the arrow is fitted with a blunt head. In that way they shoot the sable off the tree, and when the animal is stunned, they run and beat it to death."

A good huntsman killed on an average sixty to eighty sables during one winter. He followed the sable's trail on snow–shoes to the layer in a hollow tree, and would chase the animal from it and kill it. A sable's home ground might be one to two square kilometres in size, and it might be quite difficult to find the animal's habitat. The sable's hole or nest in a hollow tree was, when found, surrounded by nets, while the hunter tried to smoke out the animal. Sometimes the whole tree was cut down. There is a vivid report by Krashennikov about catching sables east of Lake Baikal on the river Vitim, where, as early as the eighteenth century, hunting parties of up to forty people assembled.

* An unknown writer dedicated to the burgomaster of the town of Stralsund, as early as 1690, a small book, printed in Stettin, *Neu-entdecktes Sibyria oder Sieveria, worinn die Zobel gefangen werden.* The hunting for sable is described here in the very same way.

36 Sable hunting with the Chanti and Mansi. From a 19th century drawing

37 Herberstein and his companions in sledges and on snow-shoes. Woodcut after Hirschvogel. From: S. von Herberstein, *Moskowia*, Vienna, 1597.

Sables are still caught by surrounding their lairs with nets and then smoking them out. A hunting tale by W. Bondarenko describes this procedure with the Nanai hunting tribes on the lower course of the river Amur: "I cannot but admire the power of observation of the hunter. Incredible, what he does find out ... In the end the long pursuit begins. The sable's trail is leading us to a clearing. A last climb. Again my heart beats wildly, and sweat streams from every pore. In the end I can see that the sable's trail finishes at a lonely pine tree. We have reached the animal's lair. As I have followed the long trail of the robber, I would naturally like to see the animal now. From a bag which looks like a cartridge pouch, the hunter pulls a long net, very like a stocking. There are a few wooden rings with the net, each the diameter of a small bowl. Suanka uses the first ring quickly to bar the entrance to the hole.

'I wonder whether you are asleep? We've come to put an end to you. Get up!', shouts the hunter, and moves his long stick about the entrance to the hole. 'You don't want to come out? Just you wait', and he pulls from his pocket some birch bark and dry moss. Then we collect more moss from the trees around, break down a few branches, and Suanka lights a fire right at the entrance to the hole. After a few minutes we can hear the sable sneeze again and again. Soon after the long body of the small animal shoots out like a flash from the hole, and past my feet. The sable has knocked over the ring, and now kicks about in the net which closes firmly around the animal. Neither its sharp claws nor its strong teeth can help. The hunter seizes the sable with one hand behind the neck and the other under its forefoot. In a moment he presents the dead animal. 'See, that's what a sable looks like.'"

The Tungusians, the hunting peoples of the Taiga, used a great variety of snares and traps in the killing of animals. All skins to be delivered, had first to be shown to the customs officer who retained one in every twenty as a free contribution to the Tsar. The fur merchant, too, had to give up every tenth skin to the ruler. In that way the Lord High Treasurer received annually sable skins worth some 200,000 rubles. They were used in the service of Russian diplomacy. Precious furs were given as valuable diplomatic gifts to foreign ambassadors. The writer of *Moscoviter wunderbarer Historie*, 1563, reports that "everyone was given a golden robe lined with sable. Also the prince gave each of us 42 skins of sable, 300 ermine and 1,500 vixen."

When in 1595 Tsar Boris Godunov sent the ambassador, Vel Yeminov to the emperor in Vienna, he gave him these furs to take: 40,360 sable, 20,040 marten, 337, 235 squirrel, 3,000 beaver, 120 silver fox and 1,000 wolf as well as 75 elk.

In the late sixteenth century the wearing of sumptuous furs belonged to the fashion of the courts, particularly in the countries of Eastern Europe. King Sigismund of Poland, for example, wore a coat of sable, and an enormously high cap made from the skins of a marten.

Next to sable and black fox as well as "grey furs" which were of the same colour summer and winter, were much in demand.

At the end of the eighteenth century prices in Siberia were:

1 pound silver		= 16 rubles
black fox	per skin	= up to 100 rubles
blue fox	per skin	= 1—3 rubles
red fox	per skin	= 0.8—1 ruble
wolf	per skin	= 2 rubles
sable	per skin	= 2.5—10 rubles
otter	per skin	= 20—80 rubles
American beaver	per skin	= 5—9 rubles
1 pound walrus teeth		= 5—10 rubles

Fur hunting activities remained an important factor in the trade balance of tsarist Russia, particularly in her trade with China. In 1777 from the trading centre of Kiakhta 1.3 million rubles worth of furs were exported to China. Smuggling across the border of furs and the teeth of walrus and mammoth was estimated in the same year to be worth about 8 million rubles. In 1800 ten million skins of squirrels were sent to China alone. This speculative trade led to ruthless exploitation and rapid reduction of animal stocks. In Siberia on an average the following animals were caught annually:—

about 1600	some	200,000 sable	1928	some	1,100 sable
1630–1640	some	130,000 sable	1948	some	33,800 sable
about 1900	some	48,000 sable	1963	some	184,800 sable
about 1963*	some	22,000 sable	1968	some	180,000 sable
1923	some	16,000 sable			

This list shows clearly the reduction in game, and the slow rise through careful conservation.

Now, that is to say in the early seventies, the number of sables in the Soviet Union is given as about 800,000 animals, and some 200,000 skins of sable are sold annually in the fur trade. This includes 6,000 skins from fur farms. Today the sable lives mainly in sixty–seven sable conservation areas in the Sayan mountains on the Kamchatka peninsula and in the region of Lake Baikal. In the sable reservation in the Barguzin Nature Conservation Park on the eastern shore of Lake Baikal stocks of sable have multiplied tenfold, thanks to intensive protective measures. At the moment one of the largest National Parks in the Soviet Union (11,200 square kilometres) is being made at Lake Baikal. Here tourists from all over the world will be able to admire Siberia's beautiful natural scenery.

---

* Between 1913 and 1916 hunting the sable was prohibited in Russia.

Penetration of the northeastern Taiga of Siberia has led to the discovery of hunting grounds there, and a new epoch in the systematic and scientific exploration of the world.

Not only hunters and trappers entered these virgin forests, but specially equipped and organised scientific and hunting expeditions were sent to the region. Scientists and naval officers took part in these.

Commissioned by the Senate of the Russian Academy of Science in St Petersburg, geographical, geological and particularly knowledge of flora and fauna were collected on these expeditions. Anthropological reports, too, were made, giving, among other things, many interesting details about hunting.

One of the most successful expeditions in the history of world exploration was the Great Northern Expedition of 1734—1743. Tsar Peter the Great (Peter I Alexandrcievich, 1672—1725) ordered Vitus Bering (1680—1741), navigator and explorer of Asia, further to investigate the coasts of Siberia, and find out whether there was a possible land connection between Asia and America. In 1728 Bering sailed along the coast of Kamchatka and discovered the sea, called after him Bering Strait, a water–way to the Pacific Ocean. To continue this early exploration Bering fitted out the Great Northern Expedition in 1733. Among its 510 members was the German naturalist, scientist and ship's doctor, Georg Wilhelm Steller (1709—1746). His report of the great expedition provides clear information about the rich fauna of this unknown territory, also about the relationship of people and the animals around them.

On 5 November 1741 the expedition vessel, "St Paul", commanded by Bering, was wrecked on the rocky cliffs of an island — 85 kilometres long and 40 kilometres wide — in the Bering Strait. This island, Avatcha, belonged to the Aleutian Islands chain, and was part of the Komandorski Islands, 200 kilometres east of Kamchatka. Later on it became known as Bering Island, and here Bering died in 1741.

The ship–wrecked company, suffering from scurvy, spent the winter of 1741/42 on the island. Steller reports that tens of thousands of white and blue foxes lived on the cliffs, and that there were also many sea–otters. The ship–wrecked sailors killed the animals to eat the flesh of the sea–otters, but carefully stretched the skins to dry. There were very many foxes and they were exceedingly troublesome, Steller wrote: "When we skinned an animal, it happened quite often that while doing this, we killed two or three foxes with our knives, as they tried to tear the meat from under our hands ...

As they did not leave us in peace, either day or night, we became so exasperated that we killed young and old, and caused them much suffering. When we woke up in the morning, there were always two or three at our feet which we had killed during the night. I alone may well have murdered more than two hundred while on the island.

On the third day after my arrival I killed over seventy with an axe, within three hours. From their skins we made the roof of our hut. They were such greedy eaters that one could hold a piece of meat in one hand, and an axe or stick in the other with which to kill them. Some third of all the foxes were of the valuable 'blue' variety."

The fox they dealt with was the short–eared Arctic fox *(Alopex lagopus)*, also called ice–, snow– or white fox. Its long thick winter coat is called white fox in the fur trade. Its summer coat is brownish–grey on the back and white under the belly.

The blue fox, however, is a blackish variety of the Arctic fox, with a beautiful blue–black long–haired winter coat. Blue foxes are now rare in the wild, but their number has rapidly increased in the twentieth century through planned farming.

The silver fox is a colour variant of the red fox *(Vulpes vulpes)* and there is also the North American grey fox *(Urocyon cinereo-argentatus)*. The Arctic fox has become rare on Bering Island because of excessive hunting for its precious fur.

In 1741 on the island Steller observed for the first time giant sea–cows—manatees—7 to 8 metres long. With thick wrinkled skin, these animals *(Rhytina stelleri)* belong to the Sirenia order, and were eventually named after their discoverer. Only a few years after being sighted, they were completely exterminated. The defenceless creatures were cruelly hunted by natives and seafarers, first for their tasty meat, also for their blubber which was boiled down into oil and their thick skins were used for building boats. Only few skeletons of Steller's sea–cow are now in the great natural history museums of the world. No living sea–cow has been seen after 1854. Here again indiscriminate hunting led to the end of a species. In the Soviet paper for the protection of wildlife, *Priroda*, there appeared an article in 1963 whose writer expressed

38 Waxwell, a member of the Great Northern Expedition, drew this Steller's sea cow in 1742.

the opinion that in some shallow waters off the coasts of Kamchatka and Tchukotka small herds of sea–cows were still about. It appears, however, that this is not so, as the Institute for Research in the Pacific in Vladivostok does not claim scientifically proved sightings.

During the last few years a completely unknown species of game arrived from the East Asian forests in single specimens in Western Europe. It was the racoon dog *(Nyctereutes procynoides)*. Because of its silvery greyish–black coat, it is sometimes called the Japanese or sea fox. The animal must not be confused with the true racoon *(Procyon lotor)* which is native to North America, and has also appeared in several regions of Central Europe. These animals are escapees from fur farms, but continue to multiply in the wild. The stock of racoons in the forests around Berlin is estimated, for example, at more than three hundred. In the state of Hesse in the Federal German Republic more than 40,000 racoons are said to live in the wild. The home of the racoon dog is Southeast Asia where there are largish stocks in Korea, Eastern China and Japan. According to Nowack, stocks are estimated to be at least one million animals in the wild where leafy or mixed woods exist at a height of about 200 to 700 metres. These are the animals' natural habitat. With a brood of nine young ones on average, the existence of the racoon dog is assured.

From 1928 to 1952 the Soviet Union settled some 9,000 animals from the natural stock of the Manchurian–Chinese fauna in different parts of the countryside. It has also been tried to rear the racoon dog in fur farms, but this has not been successful. At present stocks in the European part of the Soviet Union have multiplied sufficiently for some 60,000 animals to be shot annually between 1960 and 1965. During the last few decades the racoon dog has advanced further into Central and Western Europe. The first racoon dogs were seen in 1935 in Finland, in Sweden in 1945/46, in 1951/52 in Rumania, in Poland in 1955, in 1959 in Czechoslovakia, in Hungary in 1961/62, in the German Democratic Republic in 1963/64 and in Austria in 1969/70. Also in the German Federal Republic and in the Netherlands the first racoon dogs have been shot. In 1970 two hundred and twenty–two racoon dogs were killed in hunting grounds in Poland. As during the night the racoon dog causes a fair amount of damage among smaller game, it has been declared fair game, in spite of its being still rare in the mixed forests of Europe. So far no spread of the animal north to the Siberian coniferous regions of the Taiga nor to the North American or Canadian forests has been observed.

Rangers, Trappers and Deer Slayers

"I'm not a trapper," replied the young man proudly. "I live by my gun, and, as far as that is concerned, I will challenge anybody between the Hudson and the St Lawrence, I have never sold a skin which did not have a hole in the head besides the ones nature created for seeing and breathing."

J. F. Cooper, The Deerslayer, 1841

Fenimore Cooper's bestseller, *The Deerslayer*, published in 1841, presents a romanticised picture of the life and struggle of the white ranger *(coureurs du bois)* among the hunting tribes of the North American Indians. Trapper Harry Hurry and the hunter of scalps, Hutter, embody the egoistic type of pioneer settler who, for monetary gains, as trapper and fur hunter, mercilessly reduced the game stocks of the North American forests. Quite different is the Deerslayer himself. In 1740 at Lake Otsego he mastered fur hunting like an art. In strong contrast to the lawless crowd of hunters, he expressed his disgust at the reckless slaughter of game. Cooper's *Deerslayer* together with the hunter, Daniel Boone, became world famous as the prototypes of the rangers of North America. Business transactions with the flesh of game and with furs, however, had begun two hundred and fifty years before the publication of Cooper's book.

In 1497/98 John Cabot discovered rich fishing grounds around the coasts of Newfoundland and Labrador. From 1501 the Portuguese–Bristol Trading Company was first in organising hunting and fishing on the Canadian coasts. The company concerned itself with the catching of cod (then called *bacalao*), whaling and fur trade on a largish scale. At the same time Basque and Breton fishermen frequented the good fishing grounds.

With the discovery of the StLawrence in 1534 by the Frenchman, Jacques Cartier, and the founding of New France, ships returning from there, brought home precious furs of beaver, otter and sable.

In the early sixteenth century Renaissance fashion created a large demand for furs in Europe. Fur represented a special ornament in the dress of Italian and French noblemen. Apart from warm fur linings, marten, lynx and sable were used for trimmings. With a constantly rising demand for quality furs, prices, too, rose steeply, and great gains could be made by fur hunting.

The colonisation of Canada by the French, particularly through their governor, Samuel de Champlain, brought about the opening up for commerce of the rich hunting grounds of the Great Lakes.

The towns Quebec—founded in 1608—Montreal—1641—and Ottawa, as well as the harbour of Port Royal, became important entrepôts for this trade. The first noteable trading company was the "Compagnie des Marchands de Rouen" whose ten to eighteen ton barges undertook the trading in furs with the Algonquian Indians. When in 1612 the Dutch also began trading in furs with the Iroquois, from their newly founded settlement of New Amsterdam on Manhattan Island—now New York—a fierce competition developed.

In the sixteenth and seventeenth centuries French and Dutch trading companies exercised a monopoly in the North American fur trade. Furs were sent to Europe via Bruges and Antwerp. The English influence developed only later, and a merciless struggle for expansion began. The business with precious furs started a new epoch in the history of hunting, as French rangers—*coureurs du bois*—roamed the Canadian forests, untiringly, enduring great hardships and dangers in the pursuit of fur animals.

For some 3,000 francs a trader bought from the French government a licence, *congé* for fur hunting and trading with the Indians. As a rule, he organised a group of six rangers whom he supplied with goods to the value of 5,000 francs. After a year the rangers returned with two heavily laden canoes, bringing back some 40,000 skins of beavers. These were bought in the offices of the company, so that an average profit of 32,000 francs was made from each *congé*. This was divided, giving the trader 40 per cent and 10 per cent to each ranger. The rangers obtained annually some 6,000 to 7,000 beaver skins each, or traded them in exchange from Indian hunters.

At that time beaver skins were used mainly for the making of felt hats, and not so much for clothing. Skins were therefore divided into parchment and coat beavers.

The offices of the French company bought the skins by the pound, and paid on average:

white beaver skins	18 francs
black beaver skins (Castor de Muscovie)	8 francs
parchment beaver (Castor gras)	$4^1/_2$—6 francs
Castor demi gras	3—$4^1/_2$ francs
Castor sec	$2^1/_2$ francs

Quality and prices fluctuated greatly, and English trading offices in Boston and New York paid the best prices. Speculation, illicit trade and bitter competition were the marks of the fur trade during the following decades.

With the founding of the British Hudson's Bay Company a new phase in fur trading began in North America.

Trapping Fur Animals—"pro pelle cutem"

With a capital of 105 shares at one hundred pounds sterling each, the Hudson's Bay Company began a profitable trade in peltry on a grand scale. Many fur trading forts secured this trade against French competition. Through cheap British ready–made goods and West Indian rum, the Company could obtain large quantities of fur at the market in Albany. This put them into fierce competition with the "Compagnie du Nord" of Cauada.

Between 1689 and 1713 there were constant arguments between the companies when British and French campaigns and raiding expeditions hampered the trade in furs. Through all this the Hudson's Bay Company suffered the tremendous loss of £ 118,014 in the years between 1684 and 1688. It took two years to make up the loss by increased trapping and enlarging the hunting grounds. With this intensive exploitation the capital of the company trebled, so that every shareholder could add three new ones to his existing shares; receiving in addition a dividend of 25 per cent on the newly acquired capital.

"The Compagnie de l'Occident" which dominated the export of furs from Canada, paid a dividend of 40 per cent annually to its shareholders. At the Bank of Louisiana the 500 franc shares of this company were traded in 1719 at a rate of 2,000 francs.

This profitable business could be carried on only because precious furs were bartered against cheap goods.

In 1713 a boat from France brought goods valued at 8,000 francs to Hudson Bay, returning home with bartered goods worth 120,000 francs.

The Hudson's Bay Company, too, took a successful part in these lucrative dealings. Their commissioners received, for example, in 1740 at the exchange for colonial products in London the sum of £ 60,000 for skins sold. The outlay in European goods for barter had only been £ 3,800. The trade in furs became the trade of the century. The game–rich forests of the North American vastnesses acted like a magnet. Adventurers, soldiers, refugees from all over the world were drawn to these parts, all of them rough and hard fellows. As hunters and trappers they were keen to take their share of the general speculative boom. These "greenhorns" knew how to use a revolver, but they hardly knew what fair hunting meant.

After the Peace Treaty of Utrecht of 1713 which lost France the military supremacy over North America, the fur trade flourished greatly.

According to Seton–Thompson, there were said to be 60 million beavers in North America, an evaluation which might be doubted.

"The beaver has done more for the making accessible of Canada than anything else. Hunting the beaver brought the first pioneers to the country, and colonists followed in their wake."

Seton–Thompson, 1953

On 2 May 1670 a British trade expedition landed in Hudson Bay to exploit the country's abundance in fur animals. They returned with valuable furs which were sold at a sizeable profit in London.

In 1670 King Charles II issued a charter for the new trading company which was entered under the name of "The Governor and Company of Adventurers of England trading into Hudson's Bay". The shorter form "Hudson's Bay Company" was increasingly used in the centuries to follow.

Hudson's Bay Company
INCORPORATED 2ND MAY 1670

39   Coat-of-arms and seal of Hudson's Bay Company.

In the older hunting grounds stocks of game had already been exterminated. But in the search for new grounds, and to find the north–west passage to the Pacific, trappers and rangers advanced after 1720 into unexplored northwestern territory of the American continent. There they found rich quarry. The trading statistics of the Hudson's Bay Company registered everything trapped or hunted. In 145 years (between 1766 and 1910) more than 9.6 million beavers were killed by the company's hunters and trappers. In the whole of North America, including Canada, in the same years 16.5 million beavers and 14.1 million sable were killed, to be sold in the European market. According to other sources, the annual yield of beavers in North America in the seventeenth and eighteenth centuries amounted to some five hundred thousand.

For every beaver skin, the trapper or Indian, on handing it into the office of the trading company, did not receive money, but a small wooden disc (a metal one after 1854) as a token of the deal. All other furs were converted into the value for beavers. Three sable furs, for example, two furs of otter or four foxes counted as one beaver. Only a bear skin counted for two beavers. In the company's store the tokens had to be exchanged against goods, the value of which was again marked against beaver furs. The following is an example:

Kind of goods	Quantity	Number of beaver 1733	furs to be paid 1863
gun	1	12	20
flint	20	1	2
glass beads	1 lb	2	6
axe	2	1	6
brass kettle	1	1	16
woollen blanket	1	6	10
trousers	1 pair	3	9
shirts	1	1	3
red paint	2 ounces	1	2

All goods, including furs, were put together into bundles of ninety pounds each, and transported mainly by water. The company had its own ships. The boatmen or *voyageurs* who navigated the toboggans overland and the *pirogues*, received as daily food ration each: eight pounds of buffalo meat. To ensure this supply of meat the company established a hunting station in Fort Edmonton in the southern part of Saskatchewan. Pemmican was also produced here, a preparation of food, as made by the Indians, containing a large amount of nutriment in small volume. Pemmican keeps for a long time unharmed, and each hunter or *voyageur* was given three pounds a day. It consisted of the ground meat of buffalo and liquid fat mixed with berries or raisins. The preparation was dried, and packed into sacks.

The standard hunting equipment of a trapper at the beginning of the nineteenth century consisted of a gun, hunting knife, axe, tools, some 500 to 600 traps and provision for one hunting season. This was made up of one barrel of flour, a quarter barrel of salted pork (50 pounds), twelve pounds of candles, thirty pounds of dripping, ten pounds of butter, some tea, salt, baking powder and beans. The trapper also took tenting equipment and woollen blankets. The whole outfit (without weapons) cost between 500 and 600 dollars. The trapper could obtain this money as a loan from the company, and through this truck–system he became completely dependent on the company.

The hunting season began in October, so that the trapper could be put into arranged places in the apportioned hunting grounds. To inspect the traps regularly, he often had to walk some 50 to 80 kilometres on snow–shoes per day, with only his dogs for company. They drew his toboggan. A skilled trapper would skin a sable in ten minutes and three to four foxes in an hour. The skins were dried on willow frames in the open air. At the end of April the trapper returned to the trading station, laden with furs. The rich quarry achieved then is convincingly documented in the statistics of the London Fur Exchange where North American beaver and sable were sold mainly.

In the mid–nineteenth century the catching of game in North America —as elsewhere—declined steeply. Only the yields of mink, musk, opossum and skunk rose quickly. About 1900 the stock of beavers in the United States became practically extinct, according to Seton-Thompson. Only in Canada a few beavers were living in the wild. In 1887 a protection order was made, stating that beavers were to enjoy a five–year close season. This order was extended to 1909. Not before 1925 was a general order made, prohibiting the trapping of beavers. Thanks to these measures the stock of Canadian beavers had risen in 1972 to some two million animals.

For the Hudson's Bay Company another "golden boom" began with the settling of the prairie. The building of the Canadian–Pacific Railway made new towns spring up everywhere, towns which urgently needed land for building. The company sold land, and prices rose steeply. An acre (0.4 ha.) cost 1.5 dollars in 1889; in 1906 it was 7 dollars and as much as 12.6 dollars in 1909. In Winnipeg, for example, a building site of 100 dollars value, rose to as much as 5,000 and eventually 10,000 dollars.

The sale of prairie land which once maintained large herds of bison, now made dividends rise to 30 to 40 per cent annually.

Pro pelle cutem proved to be a fitting motto. It was the inscription on the coat–of–arms and on the seal of Hudson's Bay Company: "I risk my skin for a hide."

Indian Buffalo Hunting

"I see yellow buffaloes
I smell the dust they raise
with their pink nostrils
on the sandy path.
Do not now desert me my good bow,
fly my good arrow, fly!"

Hunting Magic of the Blackfeet Indians

There are surely few who in their young days have not read tales of the wild romantic hunts of the prairie Indians in pursuit of the North American bison, better known as the buffalo of the Indians.

Many books about Red Indians, stories about the Wild West, tales of adventure and of hunting in many languages have captured the world's imagination, and, indeed, the Red Indian hunting for buffalo—the silent hunt—is a most interesting aspect of the general history of hunting. It is unique for having ensured the well–being of a whole population which depended almost entirely on the existence of one particular kind of game. The North American bison *(Bison bison)* supplied all essential products for the economy and culture of the prairie Indians. This economy, become legend, did, in spite of large herds of buffalo, at times lead to periods of starvation among the Indians. The writer Tanner remarked that "this threatening fear of being starved to death which might be brought on by misfortune in hunting, bad hunting weather and the inability of certain Indians to hunt successfully, led to the unconditional sharing of all quarry." Between 1789 and 1819 Tanner lived among the Ojibwa Indians in the Middle West. These sub–Arctic hunters as well as the Kutenai Indians of British Colombia lived in the spring by trapping beavers, catching fish and selling winter skins to the fur com-

pany. In summer they lived by hunting buffalo and gathering and drying bilberries. In autumn and winter they hunted bear, elk and buffalo while also trapping small game; marten, mountain–hare and sable.

The dominant feature, however, with all prairie Indians, was hunting the buffalo. In the vast grasslands of the prairie, stretching over some four million square kilometres, from the slopes of the Rocky Mountains to the plateau of the Appalachians, some four million buffalo fed only two hundred years ago. In these plains, covered with luxuriant, short buffalo grass *(Buchloe dactyloides)*, great buffalo hunts were carried out each year by Indian tribes.

There were three types of hunting methods, clearly recognisable in the drawings made by G. Catlin in 1841:

1) The Great Summer Hunt

The whole tribe took part in this collective sacred hunt, carried out on firmly established ceremonial. The hunt began with the Buffalo Dance, carefully supervised by the Buffalo Police, who punished each mistake by a stroke of the whip. Everybody had to submit to the appointed leader of the hunt. Large fires were kindled in the prairie to encircle the buffalo herds, and the hunters killed the animals with bow and arrow. The silent approach of the Indians was often made more effective by the hunters disguising themselves as coyotes (prairie wolf). Similar methods were used by the Indians in stag hunts. Each hunter marked the animal he had killed with his own identification disc, and received the skin as reward. The buffalo meat was distributed, and families whose hunters had not been successful in the hunt, still received their share.

2) Mounted Buffalo Hunt

With the Indian's use of the horse—the horse came to the prairies in 1700 via New–Mexico and Texas—methods of hunting the buffalo changed. Now most Indians, above all the Blackfeet, coursed the buffalo on their hardy horses, shooting with bow and arrow from the saddle of a galloping horse. There are also hunting scenes where the hunter jumps from his horse on to the withers of the buffalo, to finish the animal with his tomahawk. It was important with this type of hunting that a single animal should be separated from a large herd. No hunting success was assured without this because of the constant danger of the hunter being overrun by the throng of animals.

3) Winter Hunt

In contrast to collective hunting in summer and autumn, the buffalo was hunted in winter mainly by individual hunters. Every year the prairie buffalos retreated into the northern regions of the plains, some 400 to 600 kilometres away. There the hunters pursued them on snow–shoes. As the animals could move only very slowly in deep snow, they were killed with ease by the Indians.

Common to all three kinds of hunting was the fact that the hunter had to tackle the animal from close quarters. Only with the appearance of the repeater gun, after 1860, did buffalo hunting change completely.

41   G. Catlin: Indians draped in coyote skins, hunting buffalo. 1830. From: *Die Indianer Nordamerikas*, Brussels, 1848.

42 Mounted buffalo hunt. 1830. From: *Die Indianer Nordamerikas*, Brussels, 1848.

Until then the buffalo had remained the mainstay of the prairie Indians who used every part of the animal, and no large quarry was needed to secure the tribe's provision. Herds of buffalo and Indians formed a unity, and became the symbol of a sound relationship of man and nature. Luck of the hunt and its success solely decided the well–being of the Indian.

This legend is told of the Kiowa Indians: "Here are the buffaloes. They are to provide you with clothing and food. But if one day you see the buffaloes disappear from the face of the earth, you will know that your end, too, has come."

43 G. Catlin: Winter hunt of the Prairie Indians on snow-shoes. From: *Die Indianer Nordamerikas*, Brussels, 1848.

All Indians felt a close kinship to the animal, not just the hunting tribes. In the Indian's imagination animal and hunting magic became reality. They believed that if man worshipped wild animals, and wore part of them as ornament, the attributes of the animal would be transferred to him. "The skin of a puma gives strength and valour to the man who wears it, the skin of a fox supplies cunning, while a snake skin allows the owner to move among enemies, unseen. An eagle's feathers give speed, and make a man free from fear in an attack," say the Arauca Indians. Through dances and prayers man tried to curry favour with wild animals. The best known ceremony is the Buffalo Dance of the Mandan Indians, described in detail by Catlin. This dance, enacted in the village, and often lasting several days and nights, was to attract by magic the roaming herds of buffalo. The dance was carried out according to strict ritual until the moment when scouts spotted buffaloes out in the prairie. Then the hunt began, and the whole village would again have meat to eat.

Up to this day Indians living in reservations show similar dances, and not only as tourist attractions. An example is the Dance of the Hunters of Wild Game, with the Zia Pueblo Indians of New Mexico, or the Stag Dance of the Santa Clara Pueblo.

In the whole of American Indian culture the animal living in the wild as a brother of man, took a special place, and was respected, even venerated. In 1723 the Canadian Abnaki hunters spoke thus to the bear they had killed: "Do not be angry with us because we had to kill you. You are wise, and you do see that our children are hungry. They love you, and invite you to enter their body. Is it not glory to be eaten by the chieftain's children?" That kind of poetic language expresses the Indian's relationship with the animal.

The white man's relationship with the Big Game of the prairie was entirely different. It is a well known fact that when the devastating struggle of the white man against the Red Indians began, the buffalo was systematically destroyed from the eighteenth century onwards. It was a means of destroying the Indian's very basic condition of life. Death then came to the prairie.

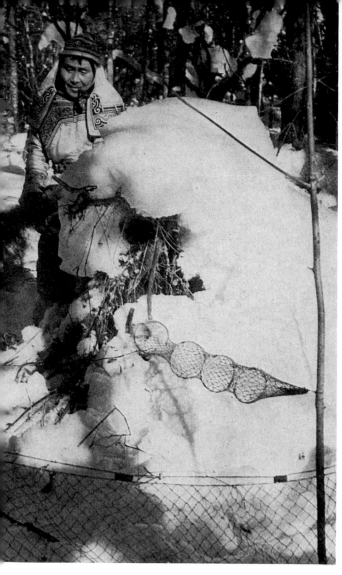

148 The huntsman, Didu Kjalundsuga, from the Khabarovsk
region on the Amur, smoking out sable. U.S.S.R., 1973

149 Giljak hunters in winter clothing. From L. Schrenk: Reisen
und Forschungen im Amur, St Petersburg, 1881.

150 Yerkov trap of the Yakuts for trapping fur animals. Museum
für Völkerkunde, Leipzig

178

151/152 Pews of the Novgorod Travellers. These four reliefs from the pews of the "Russia Travellers" are described in the literature on art as "scenes from squirrel hunting", but, undoubtedly what is being represented is the hunting of sable. 14th century. Nicolaikirche, Stralsund

153 L. Cranach the Younger: Joachim II Hector, Elector of Brandenburg. About 1555. Staatliche Schlösser und Gärten, Jagdschloss Grunewald, Berlin (West)

154 *Hunting with traps in present-day Canada.*

155 *Bison herd in Wind-Cave National Park.*

156 *Hunting the bison. Coloured aquatint engraving by C. Vogel from a drawing by K. Bodmer for:* Reise in das Innere Nordamerikas 1832—1834 *by Maximilian, Prince von Wied. Coblenz, 1839—1842*

157 *G. Catlin: Summer hunt of the Prairie Indians. 1830. National Collection of Fine Arts, Smithsonian Institution, Washington*

158   A hunter of sable at the Sea of Okhotsk. Ivan Panishev (in the region of Magadan) specialized in hunting sable, fox and ermine U.S.S.R., 1966

159   The hunter, Vladimir Rusavin from the Fur Animal Co-operative Bratsk, hunting sable at the Angara. U.S.S.R., 1971

*160   Storehouse of the Hudson's Bay Company. From:
E. Brass,* Aus dem Reich der Pelze, *Berlin, 1925.*

161   The buying of furs in North America. From: E. Brass,
Aus dem Reich der Pelze, *Berlin, 1925.*

162   A saleroom for furs in Alaska. From: E. Brass,
Aus dem Reich der Pelze, *Berlin, 1925.*

163   Racoon dog in the wild

164 *Indians hunting bison. From: T. de Bry,* Historia Americae sive Novi Orbis, *1595.*

165 *Heaps of bones of dead bison at the railway station. From: P. Frank,* Schlacht am Little Bighorn.

166 *Shooting buffalo—indiscriminately—from the Kansas-Pacific Railway. From R. J. Dodge,* The Hunting Grounds of the Far West. *London*

167 *Mountains of hides of dead buffalo at the railway station. From: P. Frank,* Schlacht am Little Bighorn.

Beefsteak and Leather Hunters, Extermination and Conservation of the Animal World in the U.S.A.

"Never before in the history of mankind have so many large animals of one species been exterminated in such a short time."

Theodore Roosevelt (1858—1909)

Every housewife nowadays is familiar with the many excellent dishes which may be prepared with first-class steak, let alone the less luxurious pleasures of corned beef or mince. Beefsteak *à l'américaine* has made its triumphant way through the kitchens of the world, and a tender piece of ox tongue is a gastronomic delight.

Today these treats come from the loins of cattle exported in vast numbers from American slaughter houses, when only a hundred years ago the game of the prairie supplied plenty of meat. The numerous herds of buffalo amounted to some sixty million animals about the year 1800. With a life weight of 700 to 900 kilogrammes per animal these wild herds represented an almost inconceivable reserve of meat which might well have contributed to world nutrition. However, in 1691 the white man began to hunt the mighty wild cattle, but he did not, like the Indian, use the whole animal. "We used to take, as usual, only the tongue, the marrow bones and the loin steak, leaving behind the rest," a hunter, called Streberg, wrote in 1858, about his own hunting of the American buffalo. Apart from the tongue, the skins were used, and the remainder left lying in the prairie. Huge heaps of bleached bones showed the trail of the buffalo hunters.

"Colonel" William Frederick Cody—Buffalo Bill—a legend even in his own lifetime, signed a contract in 1860 as a hunter of buffalo for the Kansas Pacific Railroad Company, according to which he had to supply every day 10 to 12 ham parts of buffalo, to provide food for the workmen's camps. Inside a year and a half Cody shot more than 4,280 buffaloes. "A hunter shot in just an hour, from one and the same spot 63 buffaloes, with 115 shots.

Another shot 91 in the same way. In less than three quarters of an hour another hunter shot 212 animals which all lay in a semicircle of hardly 200 metres diameter," says a report by Hornaday.

This was easy hunting, carried out with no undue effort. The leader of the herd was shot first, and after that it was simple to shoot animal after animal, aiming mainly at their spines. With the new Winchester repeater it was not a great feat to accomplish. Through the building of the Transcontinental Railway (1860) the grazing grounds of the buffalo were several times traversed, and herds became divided into a northern and southern one. From the Pacific Railway people were able to shoot at the buffalo arbitrarily from the carriage windows, and a period of cruel murder began. The dirty business of leather hunters was encouraged quite specially by the big ranchers of Texas who, through this massacre, obtained grazing grounds for their own Long-horn cattle, the very grazing grounds until then of large herds of buffalo. In that way the southern states supported, by all political means available, the extermination of the buffalo, and at the same time the Indian of the prairie. This was all done for profit and new income from raising cattle. In place of the herds of buffalo more than 6 million Long-Horn cattle grazed in Texas alone, as early as 1865. General Philip Henry Sheridan, a typical representative of Southern interests, wrote: "The buffalo hunters have contributed more to solving the Indian problem than the whole American army has done in thirty years. The extermination of the buffalo is the only way of laying a solid foundation for permanent peace, and to further at the same time the progress of civilisation." Thus, in the name of progress one of the biggest campaigns in the history of mankind for the extermination of a species was carried out. Marie Sandoz and the scientific director of the Gateskill Game Farm in the state of New York, Dr. H. Heck, have in recent years assembled the history of the extermination of the buffalo. It is a sad tale of ruthless hunting which made the stocks of wild cattle shrink to almost nothing in the space of a few years. It was only possible to save the prairie and wood buffalo at the very last moment. All the harassing documents and facts certainly illustrate the most deplorable chapter in the history of hunting.

Owners of the Red-River-Half-Breeds helped to intensify the murder of the buffalo in a most spectacular way in the region of the northern Mississippi. Detailed statements are available for the years 1820—1840. Every autumn whole expeditions were equipped, consisting of 600 to 1,100 wagons and several hundred people. These groups, in the years mentioned, killed 652,275 buffaloes. Another example: as early as 1840, the American Fur Company sent 67,000 skins to St Louis, and raised this number to 110,000 in 1848. Between 1872 and 1874, 5,373,730 buffaloes from the two herds were killed.

The slaughter of the northern herd accelerated after 1880. In 1876, for example, 80,000 skins were dispatched from Fort Brenton. In 1881 the Northern Pacific Railway alone loaded 50,000 skins; in 1882 the number had risen to 200,000, falling to 40,000 in 1883, a sure sign that the herd was shrinking. In the autumn of 1883 the northern herd consisted practically only of a small group of some 10,000 animals in North Dakota. From September to November of that year it was completely killed off. According to Heck, this was the last big herd living in the wild in the United States.

The following table gives a clear picture of the extermination of the buffalo in North America, and its eventual protection:

about 1750	Some 40 million buffaloes grazed in the North American prairies of the Indians
1800	The last buffalo bull was shot in Pennsylvania on 19. 1. 1801.
1830	The last buffaloes east of the Mississippi were killed in the states of Indiana and Wisconsin.
about 1840	West of the Mississippi there are still herds of some 60 million buffaloes*
1860—1869	Through the building of the Pacific Railway stocks of buffalo in Texas and Arkansas were divided into a southern and northern herd.
1871—1874	Extermination of the southern herd (3,158,820 buffaloes were shot).
1877—1878	Only few animals live in the state of Kansas. The last four buffaloes from the southern herd were settled in the Buffalo–Springs National Park in Texas.
1872—1883	Extermination of the northern herd.
1884	The last buffalo herd, living in the wild in North Dakota was shot.
1889	In the whole world there are now only 1,091 buffa-

* The number of 60 million buffaloes is doubtful, as within 50 years by hunting alone the enormous stock of these animals could not be exterminated (every year more than 2 million animals would have had to be shot, considering their natural increase). But if these figures are right, epidemic diseases (infectious and parasitical) appear to have been brought in with the Long-Horn herds of cattle, so that the devastating decrease of the buffalo could happen at all.

Research has revealed also that buffaloes quickly contract anthrax—splenic fever—, and die after two or three days. As the spores of splenic fever remain live for up to 80 years in an animal's carcass, all dead animals are nowadays burnt, and not just buried, while in the late nineteenth century the remains of animals lay for months in the prairie. Now stocks of buffalo are vaccinated annually against splenic fever, with serum injected into the nape of the neck. This is the only way to save wild cattle in North American and Canadian games reserves and National Parks, and to keep them in largish herds in the prairie.

loes: 550 of these in Canada, 285 in the U.S.A., and 256 single specimens in Zoological Gardens.

1893	The Wood–Buffalo Park of Canada is founded, as the first buffalo conservation area, with a herd of some 500 animals.
1900	The Canadian government buys 700 buffaloes, to found a game reserve at Lamont near Edmonton. Later on these animals are transferred to Wainwright.
1905	On 1. 12. 1905 at Bronx Zoo in New York the American Society for the Protection of the Buffalo is founded.
1907	The American government, under President Theodore Roosevelt, founds the Wichita Reserve in the state of Oklahoma, and there settled the first 15 buffaloes.
1915	A conservation area for the wood–buffalo is established in the Wood–Buffalo Park in Canada. With its 45,000 square kilometres it is the biggest game reserve in the world.
1929	The world stocks of buffalo have risen again to 18,494 animals.
1933	World stocks now amount to 21,701 buffaloes, of which there are 17,043 in Canada, 4,450 in the U.S.A. and 208 in Zoological Gardens.
1974	Stocks of buffalo in North America alone are estimated at 25,000 animals living in the wild.

The prong–horned antelope (*Antilocapra americana*), native to North America's western prairies, met a fate similar to that of the buffalo. About 1800 herds of 30 to 40 million animals were accounted for, about 1900 there remained hardly 20,000 animals. Here, too, shooting and the destruction of the flora of the grasslands—used as grazing for Long–Horn cattle or turned into wheat–growing areas—decided the decline of the prong–horned antelope. Through conservation measures the stock of the prong–horned antelope has again risen to 400,000 animals.

These examples from the United States show that through timely protective measures game in wide open conservation areas can be saved. There are at present 36 National Parks in America, 33 National Monuments and 163 state–owned parks. On the Yellowstone river in the Rocky Mountains the first National Park in the world was founded in 1872. In 1864 the state of California had already declared the Yosemite Valley in the Sierra Nevada a conservation area. The National Park Service in Washington, founded in 1916, is responsible for all government–owned conservation areas.

Nowadays it becomes necessary to impress the public through vigorous publicity and education with the need for the preservation of fauna and flora even in the National Parks themselves. Hunting in the American nature reserves is strictly regulated by law and controlled by the government.

Hunting and Game in the Nineteenth Century

44   Engraved lock plate of a "Bock" double-barrelled gun from Suhl (Thuringia).

Hunting, Game and Revolutions

"Hunting privileges on ground, not owned, hunting services, compulsory labour and similar duties, are annulled without compensation. Everybody is entitled to hunt on his own property."

National Assembly at Frankfort, 91st session on 5.10.1848

With the great French Revolution (1789–1794) a new epoch began in the history of the world which, among other things, brought about many changes in hunting.

Through the disappearance of feudalistic and absolute rule and the abolition of serfdom in France, all hunting privileges of the feudal nobility disappeared also.

The climax of poverty and misery of large sections of the population was reached in 1788. Caused by bad harvests, the whole country was swept by famine, revolts and risings of the peasants. While the people suffered starvation, the large stocks of game in the royal reserves existed solely for the pleasure and entertainment of the court nobility. If at the time of King Louis XV (1715–1774) mounted coursing was carried out mainly in the forests around Fontainebleau, Louis XVI (1774–1792) again hunted in grand style all over the country. Apart from the reserves with large stocks of game, many menageries and animal enclosures were kept in the park of Versailles for the amusement of the court.

When on 14.7.1789 in Paris masses stormed the Bastille, the symbol of despotism, workers and peasants rose at the same time in provincial towns and villages. Their call of *Vive la Liberté* quickly spread in France and beyond its frontiers. Armed peasants stormed the castles and estates of the Champagne and in all other provinces, particularly in the Franche–Comté. They burnt hunt registers, containing the feudal documents concerning compulsory hunting services, and other oppressive measures. The people forced their masters to sign papers, annulling all feudal rights.

They divided their masters' fields, woodlands and meadows among themselves. While abolishing feudal taxes and privileges, armed peasants destroyed the packs in many hunting boxes, and let the game out of the reserves for everybody to hunt to his heart's delight. "The peasants were convinced that the Revolution was to bring about the equality of all property and provide an equal standard of living for everybody. They turned mainly against the landowners," states the *Courrier français* of the period. Great fear of these peasant revolts forced the National Assembly on 4.8.1789 to announce the abolition of all feudal privileges in France, in order "to destroy the feudal system completely".

These orders validated emphatically the abolition of hunting privileges, compulsory labour and everything connected with these.

Immediately after 8 August the peasants everywhere in France began hunting their master's game. Having been onlookers only for so many years, as the game destroyed their harvest, they now killed these thieves without waiting for permission to do so. When during the night of 4 August the nobility renounced all hunting privileges, the privilege to hunt should have been given to all citizens. However, the advocates in the Citizen's Assembly restricted these radical demands, in favour of free competition (abolition of feudal privileges by redemption). The circle of people who wanted to enjoy hunting, was limited to the people who owned the land.

Only they had the right to hunt and kill game. The right to keep animals in enclosures however was abolished. This decree of the National Assembly was confirmed only on 30.4.1790 by Louis XVI, "by God's grace and elected by constitutional law, King of the French". This law, abolishing all feudal hunting privileges in France, stated that "all persons are prohibited to hunt on someone else's property without the owner's consent, at whatever time and in whatever way".

Under threat of money fine and duty of compensation, it was prohibited also to hunt in unfenced fields before 1 September. However, article 15 of the law allowed owners and tenants at all times to chase or destroy game in the fields by traps or other means. Only in the royal hunting grounds of Versailles, Marly, Rambouillet, St Cloud, St Germain, Fontainebleau, Compiègne, Meudon, Vincennes and Villeneuve–Le–Roi, all hunting and destroying of game was prohibited. These areas, including the adjoining land–marches and forests continued to be reserved for the royal household and "the personal pleasure" of the king. (from Finbert 1960).

The resolutions passed by the French National Assembly, together with the Declaration of Human Rights of 26.8.1789, greatly influenced revolutionary thought and the social conscience of all peoples in the nineteenth century. These sacred and inviolable rights of the freedom of the individual, of speech and expression, as well as the right to resist oppression, were not taken as a merely personal thing, but solidarity was extended to the world of animals.

The all overriding call for liberation extended to the demand for game in the royal parks and menageries to be set free, and no longer be kept in captivity for the sole enjoyment of the court.

When on 5 October 1789 huge crowds marched from Paris to Versailles, the people forced the king to confirm the resolutions of the National Assembly. They also asked for the king to take up residence in Paris, and then set free all animals from the crowded "Ménagerie Royale de Versailles".

The animals were set free by the will of the people, to live in the open as nature intended them to do. Only beasts of prey, including a lion, a rhinoceros and a buffalo remained in their cages, as they were considered too dangerous to be let out. The other exotic animals, among them a dromedary and five different kinds of monkeys were taken in triumphant procession from Versailles to Paris, with drums beating and banners waving in the air. In Paris the animals were given new and bigger enclosures, thus starting the first public Zoological Garden in the world, right in the heart of Paris. The beginning of the 6 ha. big park was the "Jardin Royal des Plantes Médicinales", established in 1650 for King Louis XIII. With the help of Georges Louis Buffon, the famous naturalist, who had been director of the "Jardin du Roi", the park was extended to become a zoological garden. Here the animals from Versailles found a new home in 1792. In 1802 a new elephant house was opened, big enough to let the animals move about freely. Only a moat separated them from the public, a principle met again in modern zoos.

In 1793 the Chamber of Deputies made in the name of the Revolution, Bernardin de Saint Pierre the new director of the "Jardin des Plantes" and the "Musée d'Histoire Naturelle". The establishing of the Paris Zoo on 21. 1. 1793 falls into that period. "Liberty, Equality and Fraternity" had become the ideal of the young republic. In June 1793 the National Convention demanded that all land, without exception, should belong to the people who lived on it. In that way article 4 of the old administrative regulation for forests, hunting and waters, of 1669, was finally abolished. This left the nobility no longer free, as had been the case before, to deal with forests and woodlands in whatever way it pleased them and was to their own advantage.

Under the revolutionary Jacobite dictatorship the yoke of feudal ownership was lifted by a decree of 17. 7. 1793 which confirmed the definite termination of all feudal privileges in the whole of France. All documents concerning feudal hunting laws and rulings were to be destroyed, under threat of punishment. These new regulations changed the law in the interest of peasants without, however, ending poverty or dissatisfaction among the landless people of the countryside.

News of the victory of the French Revolution spread like wildfire through Europe, inspiring the masses in Belgium, Spain, Austria, Bohemia, Russia and Italy, and leading to spontaneous risings, particularly in the Netherlands, Hungary, Western Germany and the Electorate of Saxony. In the summer of 1790 villages in this region experienced open revolt. In eighty-six villages the subjects of the manorial estates refused compulsory services to their overlords. By mid-August the risings had spread practically through the whole country. The army ended the rebellion by force.

45 Carl Stülpner, folk hero and poacher in the Erzgebirge. Lithograph by C.G. Rudolph, 1835.

The fight of the countryfolk was aimed mainly at feudal hunting privileges. The wrath of peasants and labourers had come to boiling point through watching the enormous stocks of game and the ruthless and brutal behaviour of the huntsmen. In spite of poor harvests and famines, the lordly huntsmen bought up grain and potatoes wherever they could find them, in order to feed their game stocks. In 1770 in Saxony, for example, a *Scheffel* (old German grain measure, about one and a half bushels) of grain cost one *thaler* and twelve *groschen*. In the summer of 1771 it had risen to ten *thalers* and to thirteen in 1773. These social abuses helped to prepare the ground for revolutionary risings all over Germany.

46 Peasants burn their masters' deeds, concerning feudal taxes and services. 1848.

The ending of hunting privileges in France contributed to making the country people in Saxony rise in the early summer of 1790, "to march into the forests, chase the game and shoot it. Insolence and wickedness has gone so far," states a report of the government of Saxony, "that the whole thing is more like a riot, and was repeated several times." Though the rebellious peasants lacked in hunting experience, they did manage to do "some proper coursing".

In a pamphlet of 8 June 1790* the *Kleinwolmsdorfer Kampfschrift*, directed against "huntsmen, slave drivers, henchman and many others", the peasants gave vent to their feelings.

"As we ourselves and others in parts where hunting takes place, are roughly treated and suppressed, we shall with all the reason we have and with power, poor people that we are in a poor country ... see to it that you knackers and slave drivers are shot through your foul bodies, with powder and lead. Your tongues will be cut out from your mouths, and you, huntsmen, too, will get no mercy. Fire will be set to your tongues and your eyes. Spit and hayfork will pierce your bodies, and we'll splinter your heads with pitch fork, axe and dung hook. The first pole in sight shall smash your legs. And remember, you have deserved all you get, and for a long time, for your 'yes' is 'no', and your 'no' you make into a 'yes' ... You, huntsmen will become the bloody sacrifice for many others. And we, the poor, will harvest corn and potatoes, so that other poor people, like ourselves and our children, will have enough to eat, and still their hunger. The first huntsman to turn up, is to get the first bullet, spit or pole. All these things will be there to serve the huntsmen.

Amen, which means that's the way it will be."

A German poet, J. G. Wolf, from Niederposta near Dresden, wrote rhyming lines, expressing similar sentiments, standing up for the rights of the ordinary man to hunt without hindrance, and for the farmer to raise his animals and tend his crops without interference. "Don't we all spring from Adam?" he asked, "and therefore belong to the oldest nobility there is."

The demand for the ancient right of free hunting for everybody is expressed in many petitions by peasants in Saxony, from the year 1790. Risings and unrest in the early summer of that year became the prelude to an extensive movement of the people in the Electorate, alerted by the French Revolution. This reached its climax between 23 and 26 August 1790, but with the general defeat of the risings, every peasant had to promise solemnly again to perform compulsory services as before. One hundred and fifty-

* From files kept in the State Archives Dresden: Loc 1095 Vol. I and II; Loc. 5433 Vol. I; Loc. 6048; Amtsgericht, Dresden No. 747, 756/57, 928. Cited from R. Limpach, 1958.

eight leaders of the peasants received harsh sentences of imprisonment in fortresses, for the part they had played in the rebellion. It was not until 1830 that compulsory labour was abolished in Saxony.

In 1848 revolutions broke out in wide parts of Europe. The March Revolution of 1848 shook the foundations of ancient rights and privileges clung to for centuries by the feudal lords of the manor all over Germany.

In Baden, Württemberg, Saxony and Mecklenburg—peasants and labourers stormed their master's castles, just as their ancestors had done in 1525. These risings contributed much to the abolishment of all hunting privileges, enjoyed by the German nobility. On 7 and 8 March 1848 peasants in Baden, for example, forced Baron von Adelsheim to sign a document of renunciation,

cancelling all his feudal rights. Hunting and fishing everywhere was to be leased, and the monies obtained were to go into community funds. In the Duchy of Nassau 30,000 landless peasants stormed the castle, shouting: "Smoke out the burrow, and the badgers will come out." The Chronicle of Nassau of 1848 states: "Who was it then that prepared the revolution in Nassau? The stags did it, the stags which fed in the cornfields at night. They were the true culprits, the ones who incited the wrath. These very stags put liberal ideas into the heads of the peasants." Ducal foresters were driven away, and hunting went on in all forests.

On 22 May 1848, in Mecklenburg, labourers, armed with hayforks and scythes went to the castle of Torgelow near Waren (Müritz), and burnt it down. The local paper, *Blätter für freies Volkstum* stated at the time: "The stag counts for more than a

47 Satirical pamphlet on the Prussian hunting laws, designed against the peasants. Berlin pamphlet, before 1848. Pen lithograph. Staatliche Museen, Stiftung Preussischer Kulturbesitz, Berlin (West)

human being. Human rights are disregarded by the shameless lust for murder, while the rights of hare and stag are proclaimed with lordly arrogance, the firing of shots and such noise. There is no stronger witness to our oppression and the brutality of our masters than the hunting laws and their murderous execution."

In many legislative proposals—founded on the resolutions of the 91st session of the National Assembly in Frankfort on the Main, of 5. 10. 1848, an alteration concerning general hunting laws was prepared. The basis of these alterations was to be: "All hunting rights on ground not owned, are to be cancelled without compensation, and must not be introduced again in the future as prerogative rights." This lead to new hunting laws being issued on 31. 10. 1848 in Prussia; 24. 9. 1848 in the Duchy of Saxe–Altenburg; 16. 8. 1849 in Mecklenburg–Schwerin; and 30. 3. 1850 in Bavaria.

While at that time feudal hunting rights were abolished in Prussia and Austria without compensation, in Saxony, Württemberg and Hanover compensation was paid to the landowners. In fact, all over Germany hunting restrictions were lifted. Everybody could now hunt or trap game. There were no close seasons nor rules for the protection of game. The Austrian district of Carinthia was an exception. As early as 1798 the first hunting association in any German–speaking country was founded there, the "Klagenfurter Jagdgesellschaft". The society aimed at educating huntsmen to be at one and the same time keepers and protectors of nature and her creatures. In fact, the society was to teach proper huntsmanship.

After centuries of oppression, with compulsory labour and great damage done to harvests by game, the anger of labourers and peasants is easily understood, even more so after the bitter years of famine of 1846 and 1847. Every single man wanted to go hunting and kill the hated game of the overlords. Within a few weeks hunting grounds were completely emptied. In large parts of Thuringia, for example, red deer became practically extinct, and the same happened to roe deer in the countryside around Münster.

This reckless killing led to a low ebb in hunting economy which took years to recover. The hunting laws of 1848 lacked consideration for fair hunting, only slightly helped by experienced huntsmen promoting the hunt for small game. One of them, Carl Emil Diezel, published a hunting textbook in 1849 which went into many editions, and is still popular in Germany. Although much reduced, stocks of game did recover. Yet, a counter–revolution was on the way, and was to take in the management of hunting.

On 7 March 1850 Prussia issued the *Jagdpolizeigesetz*, re–establishing law and order by force of police. According to this new law the right to hunt was not granted to every owner of land, but a person had to own at least 75 hectares (1 ha = 10.000 square metres) contiguous land. This qualifying clause meant that all townspeople, small farmers and labourers were again excluded from hunting. The big landowner became once more the sole master of hunting and of game. Only now, next to the nobility, the growing middle class also owned land for agricultural use, forests and hunting grounds.

The smallest area for hunting was fixed at different levels in the various German regions. It was 75 hectares in Prussia, 82 in the Bavarian plains, 136 in the mountainous parts, 15.7 in Württemberg, and in Anhalt even 250 hectares. Oldenburg alone gave the right to hunt even to the smallest landowner.

Only a few years after the Revolution of 1848 things were the same as before, and basically nothing had changed. Forests belonging to the princes or to the state became the favourite hunting grounds of princes, the court nobility and the new rising middle-class.

Poets and patriots in many countries raised their voices against this abuse, advocating a fairer pursuit of hunting.

168 *The Slovak rebel, Janosik, and companions in the forest. Slovak painting behind glass, first half of 19th century. Schweizerisches Museum für Volkskunst, Basle*

169 *Rebel poachers became folk heroes.* Der Bayerische Hiesel *(Matthias Klostermayer). Picture sheet, Augsburg, second half of 18th century. Tobler collection, Switzerland*

170 *Feeding of wild boar in the Animal Park at Moritzburg, about 1848.*

171 *J. L. Appold: Hunting law. Steel engraving, 1854, from a painting by Karl W. Hübner (1845).*

172 F. Krüger: Search for hare and fowl in the autumn. Mid-19th century.
Staatliche Galerie, Georgium Castle, Dessau (German Democratic Republic)

173   G. Courbet: Morte of a stag hunt in winter. 1867. Musée des Beaux Arts, Besançon

174 Folk-art room decoration: *"Funeral of a huntsman". Coloured lithograph, first half of 19th century. Pieske collection, Frankfort (Main)*

175 *J. P. Hackert: Ferdinand IV, King of Sicily, boar hunting. Galleria di Capodimonte, Naples*

UN CHASSEUR QUI A DE L'AMOUR-PROPRE.

— V'la vot'affaire... faut y joindre une belle oie?.. j'ai aussi un superbe bouzard!..

QUAND ON A DU GUIGNON.

— Dire que je n'ai pas pu tirer seulement un coup de fusil depuis c'matin!
— Oh! moi c'est différent..... j'ai tué mon chien!..

— Je vois remuer quelque chose au sommet de cet arbre..... ne serait-ce pas notre lapin qui aurait grimpé la-haut!

176/177 H. Daumier: The instinct to hunt and shoot.
Lithograph. Staatliche Museen, Kupferstichkabinett
and Collection of Drawings, Berlin

178 H. Daumier: Bad Luck. Lithograph. Staatliche Museen,
Kupferstichkabinett and Collection of Drawings, Berlin

179 G. Courbet: Eagle owl feeding on roe. Staatliche Museen, National-Galerie, Berlin (lost during war)

Illustration on the following page:

180 Mounted hunt in the Nuremberg Volkspark.

Huntsmen, Artists and Patriots

"Hunting with gun and hounds is fine in itself.
But, let us suppose, you are not born to the hunt,
yet you love nature and freedom. Then you are bound
to envy us our hunting."

Ivan Turgenev, "Notes of a Huntsman", 1852
From the tale Forest and Steppe

Social and political upheavals were naturally reflected in the awareness of artists and writers of the time. Classicism, the Romantic movement and Realism, the three main artistic movements of the period, all concerned themselves with hunting in some way or other.

In Paris Honoré Daumier (1808—1879) and Gustave Courbet (1819—1877) were among the most important artists of the nineteenth century. Armed with gun and drawing pencil these radical artists and huntsmen experienced the revolutions of 1848 and 1871.

After the July Revolution of 1830 Honoré Daumier made his name as a caricaturist with his many satirical drawings. His lithographs are a powerful accusation of the monarchy, reactionary forces and the world of the *petit bourgeois*, and his humanity and closeness to the people found ample expression in his work. He made more than four thousand lithographs, one thousand woodcuts and hundreds of drawings and paintings. In many of these the subject of hunting is well represented, particularly so in the caricatures.

Daumier's friend, Gustave Courbet, was among the most important representatives of French Realism. As a passionate hunter and lover of nature, he painted masterfully many colourful pictures of hunting and the countryside, with the aim of showing the beauties hidden in nature. To him beauty was at the same time truth, and he did see beauty even in functional things. His hunting scenes and landscapes are vigorous, and rightly he is considered the last in the great epoch of hunting paintings.

As a genuine Realist he no longer created landscapes where hunters and game only served as "stage properties" but quite deliberately put whole hunting scenes in the foreground of his paintings. His most famous picture is of a stag hunt in winter. Resolved not to compromise with the "respectable", Courbet's "realism" marked a revolution in art. In 1871 he joined the Commune, and consciously put his work into the service of the political ideas of his time. He became the model for the politically "engaged" artist.

After the victory of the counter-revolution, Courbet, too, had to appear before a military tribunal on 7. 6. 1871. Because of his supposed part in the destruction of the Vendôme Column—his innocence was proved only in 1951—he was sentenced to six months imprisonment at Sainte Pélagie. During his time there he painted some of his finest still lifes.

After his release the state again took up the process against him, so that on 23. 7. 1873 he fled to Switzerland, where he died at Vevey in 1877.

In 1874 he was sentenced—in his absence—to have the Vendôme Column restored at his expense. As Courbet could not raise the 323,000 francs required, his studio with many important works had to be auctioned, so that some of his pictures are privately owned, but many can be seen in the great collections of the world, the Louvre, for example, the Musée des Beaux Arts at Lyons, the museum at Besançon, the Museum of Fine Arts at Boston and the Wallraf-Richartz Museum in Cologne.

Poland struggled for independence from tsarist Russia and Prussian tutilage in the Grand Duchy of Posen. The national liberation movement, led by the Polish gentry, reached its first height in the risings of 1830/31. Patriots, organised mainly in the Polish Democratic Association, were close to Polish men of literature. The poet Adam Mickiewicz (1798—1855) belonged to the representatives of the new Polish Romantic Movement.

Under the influence of the defeat of the November risings of 1830/31 Mickiewicz wrote *Pan Tadeusz*, the Polish national epic (1834). In this genuine masterpiece he created a picture of life in rural Lithuania, about 1812, with hunting as a main theme. When the Crimean War broke out in 1855, Mickiewicz went from exile in Paris to Turkey, there to establish a Polish legion against tsarist Russia. A painting showing him with hounds, was made during that time.

In tsarist Russia, too, a new form of the artistic representation of hunting was developing. Portrayal of the true experience of hunting was combined with a desire to show the beauty of nature.

Alexander Pushkin (1799—1837), Russia's greatest poet has, though himself not a passionate hunter, written most vividly about hunting. In poems and short stories he represents hunting as a social function and close to the people. There were other Russian patriotic writers who described with passion the miserable life of the serf during a hunt. Serfdom was abolished in Russia only in 1861.

The works of Nikolai Nekrasov (1821—1879), too, belong to the Russian Realist school, and give strong expression to national aspirations and tendencies of contemporary life. Hunting plays an important part, and in a poem of 1874 he called his gun dog, his hunting knife and an accurate gun, his best friends. There are other poems which in poetic language describe Nekrasov's many hunting adventures.

The writer, Sergei Aksakov (1791—1859) in his *Family Chronicle* (1858) and its continuation, *Years of Childhood* (1858) supplies masterly portrayals of the patriarchal life of the Russian gentry, as well as describing himself as a hunter and angler.

48   Illustration for *Pan Tadeusz*. 1834

The prose of Ivan Turgenev (1818—1883) has many descriptions of compulsory labour and other forms of oppression and exploitation of the Russian peasantry. His *Annals of a Sportsman* (1852) which made him famous, is a strong accusation of *corvé* and serfdom in general. Turgenev's open social criticism led to the poet being banished to his estates. When in 1869 a French paper asked Turgenev about his favourite hobby, he answered without hesitation: "Hunting." Apart from emotive fiction, Turgenev published a hunting textbook.

In his great novel, *War and Peace*, Tolstoi gives a vivid description of the coursing of wolves, and Polish and Russian politically committed writers in general expressed their criticism of society, in particular criticism of the ways of hunting.

Nineteenth-century Polish and Russian painters also contributed their share to the subject, in drawings, water colours and paintings. Mention must be made of the Polish landscapists and painters of historical pictures—Juliusz Kossak, Julian Falat, Josef Chelmonski, Josef Szermentowski, to name only some of them. The Polish Romantics saw hunting as an activity closely related to the life of the people, and the artist presented it in that way. Keepers of hounds, beaters, and hunting lads were an integral part of the whole painting, so that next to the noble lord and his guests, the common man was well represented. This deliberate inclusion of huntsmen and peasants in the work of the Romantics, reflected the very spirit of contemporary Poland.

The Russian painters who are typical representatives of Realism are R. W. Lebedjev, L. O. Pasternak, I. L. Repin, F. Rubov, Samokish and A. S. Stepanov. They all have depicted impressive hunting scenes in their paintings and pastels.

In Germany Wilhelm Leibl (1844—1900) is a representative of Realism in painting. He was influenced by Courbet. In 1876 he painted his famous picture "The Hunter". Max Liebermann, too, a German artist from the beginning at variance with the academic trends of his period, made some graphics on the subject of hunting, which excel through their simplicity and freedom of style.

In the early nineteenth century Germany experienced a revival of humanistic ideas, which showed in the work of Classic and Romantic writers alike. A progressive middle-class culture developed in the wake of the French Revolution, and in sharp contrast to stubborn reactionary thought in the period of the Restoration. This is shown in the work of contemporary writers, and musicians, whose compositions frequently went back to the grass roots, to oral tradition, popular ballads and songs. In turn many of their poems and songs became folksongs, a great number in praise of nature and the joys of the hunt. Some still have a place in the international repertoire. Goethe, himself a keen hunter, wrote many a poem in a small hunting box near Ilmenau in the Thuringian Forest. The German poets, Schiller and Eichendorff, wrote well known hunting songs, and the climax came with Carl Maria von Weber's romantic opera, "Der Freischütz", greatly acclaimed at its first performance in Berlin, on 18 June 1821. In London alone, it was staged at three different theatres at the same time. "The Hunters' Chorus" of the third act, with its hunting sounds and popular tunes, has remained a favourite to this day.

By the end of the nineteenth century hunting had definitely ceased to be the privilege of the well-born and wealthy. It had become more and more the enjoyment of many and different people.

Foxhunting in Britain

"Foxhunting during the eighteenth and nineteenth century was the democratic sport; shooting the snob sport, as many stories testify."

C. C. Trench, A History of Horsemanship

In the early eighteenth century in Britain—as elsewhere in Europe—Versailles had become the prototype for the building of great houses and the layout of gardens. True to this vogue for French taste castles and parks all over Great Britain followed the formal Baroque of France, and became regular and richly ornamented, genuine representatives of the Rococo.

Hunting, too, was carried out on the model of the French *par-force* hunt, both for red deer and hare. Since the Norman conquest in 1066 coursing game with hounds had become popular. Twici, a huntsman at the court of Edward II (1307—1327) described the sport vividly in a textbook on hunting. Mounted hunting took pride of place in Great Britain until well into the seventeenth century. As large stags had become extinct in open ground, game was kept in the parks, and let out for coursing.

Following the social tensions and conflicts between Britain and France in the mid–eighteenth century, a strong movement began in England against anything French. Among other things it was directed against the regularity of French architecture and garden layout, as well as the French type of coursing. William Kent (1684—1748), painter and landscape gardener, was one of the first to point out that nature abhorrs straight lines. The French formal garden was replaced by the English park and Stowe House, the magnificent mansion of the Dukes of Buckingham, and its gardens was a fine example of the new style. So were Kensington Gardens, also made by Kent. The grandest are perhaps the gardens of Blenheim Palace, laid out by "Capability" Brown.

There are many descriptions of the "English park", one of them says:

"Trees are planted in free groups, alternating with stretches of grassland. Here and there stands a single tree, away from the rest. Narrow, winding paths amble along, as if thought out by dreamers for other dreamers to stroll on. The park is enlivened by a lake with uneven banks. All this "natural" park, with its skilfully chosen picturesque effects, does show clearly the hand of the man who planned it."

Similar to the innovations in garden landscaping, hunting also was given a new look. By the mid–eighteenth century means were sought for getting away from the French–type of hunting. French game reserves with their straight and regular star–shaped paths did not fit into the English park. The mounted hunt and its pack had therefore to adapt to the new shape of the countryside, traversing woodland, meadows and fields. This was not the habitat of the stag, and other species had to be found for coursing. Therefore the hare and the fox, hitherto despised as game for hunting, but both inhabitants of wide open country, became the main objects for hunting in Britain. In fact, foxhunting became the symbol for hunting.

From 1750 onwards foxhunting dominated mounted hunting all over Britain. This kind of hunt was no longer the merciless chase of masses of game, but a genuine race with horses and hounds to catch up with the fleeing hare or fox. As a sport and a pleasure foxhunting developed along with other equestrian sports in Britain. The first obstacle races were run in Ireland, and in 1752 the Earls of Derby instituted races at Epsom, over a course of one and a half mile in length. The raising of thoroughbreds reached a climax in Britain with the famous stallion Eclipse (born in 1764).

In 1766 Lord Oxford founded the first club for the coursing of hare: The Swaffham Coursing Club, in an urban district of the county of Norfolk. Then there was the Altcar Club, founded by Lord Sefton on his estate near Liverpool in 1825. There were others and in 1858 the National Coursing Club was founded, instituting a set of general rules.

The special horse for hunting, the hunter, was bred in Britain mainly by mating a thoroughbred stallion with a half–blood mare. Hunters are bred entirely for foxhunting, and their ability to clear a five–bar gate is essential. Large areas of grass and rough heather in the hilly countryside, particularly in the Midlands and in the North of England, demanded a solid and persevering horse for the hunt. In spite of endurance and toughness, accidents and loss of horses were heavy at times during the annual hunting season. On an average a huntsman required about ten horses during one season, and accidents increased after the fencing of fields with barbed wire.

The season began in November, and ended in May of the following year.

Malton Mowbray was a centre for foxhunting where sportsmen from every part of Britain came for the autumn meets. Some seven hundred hunters stood in the stables, and large packs bayed in the kennels, waiting impatiently for the hunt to begin.

Well known British kennels were the Duke of Rutland's, the Duke of Beaufort's, Earl Charborough's and Earl Fitzwilliam's. Lord Fitzharding's packs at Castle Berkeley, with 114 hounds, are renowned, as are some of the oldest packs, owned by Lord Grey of Wark and the Duke of Monmouth at Charlton near Goodwood.

In 1895 there existed altogether three hundred and twenty-three packs in Britain, and some five million pounds were needed to keep the horses and the 20,835 hounds, surely a noble and costly sport.

In 1971 there were still two hundred and fifty packs in existence, a sign that foxhunting has remained popular in Britain.

The table below lists packs of various kinds of hounds, kept in 1895:

	England	Scotland	Ireland
Stag hounds	16 packs with 790 hounds	–	6 packs with 328 hounds
Foxhounds	153 packs with 11,482 hounds	10 packs with 679 hounds	20 packs with 1,541 hounds
Harriers	110 packs with 3,702 hounds	3 packs with 111 hounds	27 packs with 932 hounds
Beagles	44 packs with 1,170 hounds	–	–
altogether	323 packs with 17,244 hounds	13 packs with 790 hounds	53 packs with 2,801 hounds

Foxhunting is carried out to strict rules which, by and large, have remained unchanged over the years.

The Master of Hounds who arranges the hunt, welcomes his guests, about eighty horsemen and women, at one meet. The pack consists of some sixty hounds, and hunters in hunting pink and white breeches get ready while the whippers–in control the impatient hounds. The whippers–in ride with or behind the pack, keeping an eye on the hounds. The feeders are important hunt servants who take great care of the hounds, also the earth stopper who makes sure that all holes and entrances to foxes' layers are packed with thorny branches and stones. This is done particularly during the night when the fox is out feeding, and assures that the animal will be around to be chased by the pack.

From the meet the hounds are taken to some heath or woodland covert, in quest of a fox. If the fox leaves the covert hounds run it by scent till they either kill the fox or run it to earth, that is it gets into some hole or other hiding place where the hounds cannot get at it. Also, the hounds might loose the scent altogether which could mean the end of the hunt unless another fox is found. Hounds always have to be in advance of riders who must regulate their pace to that of the hounds.

Hounds are of many different breeds. The true hounds, the bloodhound, foxhound and staghound, hunt only by scent, as do the short–legged basset, beagle and harrier. The greyhound and deerhound run by sight alone. A hunt might take four or five hours before a fox is killed. The fox's brush is then taken, and the animal itself thrown to the hounds who greedily devour it. The hunt is usually followed by a formal dinner.

Shooting was always in the main a gentleman's sport, and it consisted in shooting game put up by trained dogs. It was the

49 Bruce Roberts: Foxhunting. Woodcut from: Catfryn-Roberts, *English steel engravings of the 19th century.*

done thing for a sportsman, and it took up such a space of his life that there was an early nineteenth–century sporting print of a shooter so old that he had to be wheeled by a servant in pursuit of his sport.

Foxhunting in Britain has become the model for mounted hunting in many countries. There are hunts where the fox's place is taken by a single huntsman who has a fox's brush attached to his sleeve. This brush has to be snatched from him in a fast ride. Drag–hunting is also popular, when a trail is laid—usually with aniseed—and followed, without the use of a fox.

All kinds of the mounted chase provide exhilerating pleasure.

In the nineteenth century a special kind of hunting on horseback became popular in Eastern Europe: coursing wolves with greyhounds.

Coursing with Greyhounds in the Russian Steppe

"Fifty–four coursing hounds were taken with six mounted horsemen and keepers of hounds. Apart from the Master and his guests, another eight huntsmen took part, with more than forty hounds. In the end there were one hundred and thirty hounds and twenty horsemen in the field."

Lev Tolstoi, War and Peace

What *parforce* hunting was to France, and foxhunting to Britain, coursing with greyhounds was to Russia. No large packs were required here, but a single horseman each led a leash of two or three hounds. The men rode out together, coursing across the vast steppes and grasslands of the Russian South and of Central Asia.

There were different kinds of coursing, some by scent and some by sight. Since the fourteenth century a special kind of greyhound, the "Chart" was bred in Poland and the southern part of Russia. It was a cross between Russian coursing hounds and English greyhounds. These fine–haired, fierce and enduring hounds, crossed with coursing hounds from the Crimea, became the famous Russian greyhounds. These large and quick hounds whose male reached a shoulder height of some 85 centimetres were exceedingly well suited to the coursing of wolves. Charles Darwin described the elegant hounds as an "embodiment of symmetry and beauty". There are several races of these hounds, best known among them, the Borzoi, the Tasy, the Afghan and the Saluki.

Among famous breeders of greyhounds was General J. Lipunov, known through his new breed of Borzoi, with long soft hair which moved with the slightest current of air. The Archduke Nicolai Nikolaevich founded the Perchino kennels in 1887, and in time owned over a hundred Borzois. The duke bred for beauty and for speed and his hunting box was the centre for coursing in tsarist Russia.

Coursing with Russian greyhounds became very popular at the beginning of the nineteenth century, and is still practised in the U.S.S.R. in the regions of Volgograd, Rostov and Tampov. The Borzoi remains important in the Russian economy and its fur trade. It catches foxes without mauling them and spoiling their fur. A skilled practitioner of coursing might have an annual quarry of more than two hundred and fifty foxes.

Coursing in Russia was carried out in several different ways. One way was for huntsmen to ride in a line across the steppe, each one holding two or three greyhounds on a leash. The huntsmen cracked a two to three metre–long whip noisily, so that hares, foxes and even wolves were started. The mounted huntsman closest to the game let loose his greyhounds, so that with a speed of some 70 kilometres per hour the hounds coursed the game and killed it. The quarry belonged to the huntsman whose hounds were first in reaching the game, and holding it at bay. This hunting went on all the year round. While "hunting by sight" for hares was mainly done in the late autumn.

Coursing for hares was described by Sholostov: "The horsemen riding on a broad front, tried to spot the hare, which was probably hiding. As soon as the animal was discovered by a huntsman, he would put the whip to his cap. This meant: "I have spied the hare", and at once the rest got ready, loosening the hounds the moment the hare rose. Once a greyhound was within a few metres of the fleeing hare, the hound began running at such a speed that it became impossible to distinguish single movements. The hound appeared to be a white cloud, catching up with its victim in a flash. All the same, in a series of cunning doublings and jumps the hare often escaped from the hounds, safe and sound."

It was quite different with the coursing of wolves. For a very long time this predator had been relentlessly pursued in Russia, with greyhounds specially trained for the purpose. The inborn keenness of the greyhound to chase wolves, was increased by the systematic training on a captive female wolf. This animal was tied up, so that the coursing hounds instinctively got hold of the wolf crossways. The hound on the righthand side seized the ear of the wolf on the left, while the hound on the left seized the right side of the animal. In that way they held the wolf on the ground, unable to defend itself. The huntsmen galloping up to the spot literally threw themselves on to the wolf's back, to finish it with a well–aimed thrust of the hunting knife, or catch it and tie it up alive. This was done by tying a short, iron–studded, wooden stick between the wolf's jaws.

In the Soviet Republic of Uzbekistan even now 99 per cent of huntsmen keep greyhounds and carry on coursing with two to four greyhounds on a leash. They hunt wolf, fox, wild sheep and the saiga antelope. Only 15 per cent of these huntsmen carry fire-arms, as they prefer coursing with eagle or greyhound in the Asiatic semi–steppes. And actually in their special conditions coursing is the most successful way of hunting.

In Tsarist Russia "combined" coursing was also known, that is using ordinary hounds and greyhounds at one and the same time. Tsar Peter II, for example, kept a pack consisting of 200 coursing hounds and over 420 greyhounds. Prince Somzonov of Smolensk had 1,000 hounds at his hunting box, and he called himself "Russia's Prime Huntsman".

Hunting music was indispensable to the Russian hunting scene. In 1757 the hunting box of Ismailov near Moscow was granted the privilege of having the Imperial hunting music performed on special horns, the so–called Russian horns. Only one full note could be played on each horn, so that thirty–seven musicians were needed for one concert. In 1788 the Imperial hunting music at St Petersburg consisted of eighty–eight musicians. In Germany, too, Russian horns were popular, for example at the fortress of Coburg and at miners' processions in Freiburg in Saxony.

Best known of all was the hunt with Perchino hounds at the hunting box of Perchino, some 32 kilometres from Tula, on the river Upa. The Archduke Nicolai Nikolaevich had established himself here in 1887, and hunting was carried on with two packs of 120 *parforce* hounds, 120 to 150 Borzois and 15 English greyhounds. All hunt servants were mounted, mainly on Kabardine horses, half–bloods from Central Asia, while the hunting party used English half or three quarter thoroughbreds of pale grey colour. All horses and hounds were kept in cold stables to make them hardy for winter wolf hunts.

On an average 20 leashes of Borzois were taken to a hunt, each consisting of two male dogs and a bitch. Sometimes 35 leashes of greyhounds were used. The pack for a *parforce* hunt consisted of 45 coursing hounds with 10 kept in reserve. The hounds were tannish–brown in colour, and were descended from Russian bloodhounds. There were also white flecked hounds, a crossbreed of harriers and French and Russian bloodhounds.

While the pack of ordinary hounds, with a passion for coursing, noisily took up the hot scent by nose the greyhounds coursed silently by sight only.

Combined coursing therefore demanded great skill from the hunt servants if it was to be successful. The Russian hunting laws of 1892 regulated hunting in all its forms and seasons were fixed.

The Perchino Hunt established its seasons, as follows: —
End of May until 6 August: Summer coursing for hare and fox with *parforce* pack and a few leashes of Borzois.

From 1 August onwards: Increased training of Borzois; some 20 kilometres daily walking and trotting next to the hunting horses.

From 1 to 10 September: Autumn coursing for wolves as a try–out for the Borzois.

15 September to the end of October: Coursing the wolf with *parforce* pack and leashes of Borzois.

During winter: According to weather and snow conditions hunting the wolf, from sledges (when greyhounds were taken along in the sledges, while beaters on horseback started the wolves).

To guarantee successful hunting in winter, the wolves were often fed in the late summer to make sure they remained on the ground. After the building of railways across the Russian steppes at the end of the nineteenth century, wolf hunts were carried out in winter mainly along the lines of the railway. By special train hounds, horses and all hunting equipment were conveyed in forty goods wagons, while hunt servants travelled in two second–class carriages, and the master and his guests in two first–class ones. Hunting went on all day, and the train was loaded again in the late afternoon to travel through the night to the next hunting grounds. In that way, between 1887 and 1913 in the Perchino game reserve there were killed: 681 wolves, 743 foxes, 4,630 brown hares *(Lepus europaeus)* and 4,026 white hares (snow hares — *Lepus timidus)*. This was achieved by combined coursing, using the *parforce* pack and leashes of greyhounds. Usually Borzois obtained the biggest part of the quarry.

The October Revolution of 1917 swept away these ostentatious hunting entertainments, to be replaced by the genuine sport of unadorned greyhound coursing. With the end of the tsar's regime court hunts, naturally, became a thing of the past, including the hunt for bison in the Forest of Bialowieźa.

181 W. Perow: Huntsmen, resting. 1871
182 W. Kossak: The Emperor Francis
Joseph I at a hunt in Gödöllö. 1887.
National Museum, Warsaw

183 *Julian Falat: Return from the bear hunt. 1892. National Museum, Warsaw*

184 *W. Leibl: The hunter (Freiherr von Perfall). 1876. Staatliche Museen, National-Galerie, Berlin (lost during war in 1945)*

185 C. Vernet: Fox hunt. Lithograph. Staatliche Museen, Stiftung Preussischer Kulturbesitz, Staatsbibliothek, Berlin (West)

186 "Taunus" pack. Young English foxhounds are trained by the Master of Hounds on the Neuhof estate, south of Frankfort (Main). 1973

187 Mounted hunt in the area of the Hamburg
"Schleppjagdverein", in Wedel-Helm, Holstein. 1957

188 P. F. Frenz: Start of the hunt. 1880

189 J.-B. Oudry: Hounds attacking
a wolf. 1734.
Staatliches Museum, Schwerin

190 P. P. Sokolov: Wolf hunt. 1873

191 Jan Chelminski:
Start of the hunt.
National Museum, Warsaw

192 F. Krüger: Halt
during coursing. 1826.
Staatliches Museum,
Schwerin

193 *Polish huntsmen travelling to the wolf hunt.*

216

194 *Samokish: Grand Duke Vladimir Monomakh hunting. Book illustration to*
N. Kutepov, Die grossfürstliche und Zarenjagd, *St Petersburg, 1896.*

195 *Bison in the Zary Tshelek Reservation in the Kirghiz mountains. 1973*

Hunting the Bison in Bialowieźa Forest

"It has been said for long of the bison that it is ugly, hideous, in fact, thickly covered with hair, with a mane like a horse—and that altogether it looks wild and misshapen."

After Conrad von Gesner, Historia Animalium, 1551/58

During the more than a thousand year history of the Polish people, Poland's large forests have been preserved. Even today a quarter of all Polish territory is woodland, some 8 million hectares of ground. The Forest of Bialowieźa with its herds of bison living in the wild, is known to many huntsmen all over the world, as are the impenetrable forests of the Carpathian mountains. For centuries hunting in Poland has been a much coveted experience.

The name of Bialowieźa is linked to the fate of the European bison. The course of the extinction of the bison in Europe can be traced in detail like that of its counterpart in the American prairie. As late as the end of the nineteenth century great hunts for bison took place in Bialowieźa Forest and these were the very hunts which led to the bison's extermination. The hunts were organised annually by the tsar, and foreign ambassadors to the Imperial Court took part in them. In 1894 there appeared in St Petersburg four richly produced volumes containing the history of these hunts, written by N. Kutepov. Another splendid book with many copperplates on the Forest by G. Karkov appeared in 1903. These writings provide a detailed account of the tsar's hunts, also of the conservation measures taken to preserve enough game for sport. The books are of great importance to the history of hunting in general, and that of the bison in Poland in particular. They treat the settling of the species in the Polish forests, the grand hunts of the Russian tsars—from 1795—1913, and finally the extermination of the bison in the wild. They also tell of the animal's rehabilitation in Poland through deliberate breeding.

As early as the year 800 bisons had become extinct west of the Rhine, and in the tenth century west of the river Elbe. The first written sources, dating from 1107, concern the stock of bisons between Vistula and Niemen. In 1364 the Duke of Pomerania killed the last bison west of the Vistula, so that from the fifteenth century onwards the animal existed only east of that river.

In the fight against the Order of Teutonic Knights (Battle of Grunwald 1410) herds of bison formed a valuable reserve of meat for the Polish and Lithuanian armies.

Under the Polish King, Wladyslaw II (1386—1434) the Forest of Bialowieźa became an important royal hunting ground. Casimir Jagiello (1447—1492) created the office of royal governor of the forest region. There is a report from 1431 stating that for a banquet of the Prince of Witowot in Volhynia one hundred bisons were prepared in the kitchens during one week. Other documents tell of bisons being used as precious diplomatic gifts. The animals were caught alive in Poland, and sent by land or sea to foreign courts. On 8. 1. 1406 the King of Poland presented a bison to the Grand Master of the Order of Teutonic Knights at the Marienburg, while in April 1409 he received another four from the Duke of Lithuania. In 1498 bisons were sent twice to Duke Georg of Saxony, and in 1525 Duke Albrecht sent bisons from East Prussia, "as princes much coveted them because of their being rare". He also sent animals to the Count of the Palatinate of the Rhine, to Duke Wilhelm IV of Bavaria, the Landgrave Philipp of Hesse and the Archbishop of Mayence.

Further reports of 1687, 1724 and 1731 state that bisons, male and female, were sent by "salt boat" to England, Berlin, Dresden and St Petersburg, eighteen animals altogether. Between 1729 and 1742 thirteen animals went to Berlin, and eighteen to England and Russia. Five bisons died while being caught and eight were finished by poachers. All these reports talk about aurochs *(Bos primigenius)* even though bisons were concerned. The last aurochs were killed in the forests of Jaktorov, west of Warsaw in the seventeenth century. What is actually referred to therefore is the bison. In 1564 there were still 38 aurochs, and in 1599 only 24 of them. There were 4 in 1602 with the last killed in 1627. It is not clear whether at that period a strict zoological nomenclature was used, distinguishing between different species of European wild cattle. In fact, the aurochs may have survived longer than is sometimes suggested. It is certain, however, that the true bison in the wild was exterminated in the heart of Europe in the eighteenth century, leaving the Forest of Bialowieźa as the only refuge for the animal. In 1755 two peasants shot the last bison in what was then East Prussia in Germany. In spite of large signs with drawings of the bison, erected in the reserve, a peasant, called Wirulait, killed a semi-tame animal. Possibly done in revenge for his sufferings during a spell of imprisonment, imposed on him by a Prussian court of law for the killing of another bison. This may have been killed by another peasant, and in 1755 both were again sentenced to ten years imprisonment for the killing of the last bison. During the Seven Years' War Russian troops freed both men after having served only three years of their sentence.

A report of 1716 to Tsar Peter I suggests that the last bison in the wild was sighted in the wooded grasslands near the river Don in 1709. In the steppes of Southern Russia single specimens of the animal survived until the mid–nineteenth century.

In Southeast Europe, in Transylvania, now Romania, Count Bethlen killed the last bison in the wild with an axe on 8. 10. 1762.

In the Forest of Bialowieźa, however, the eighteenth century was a time of planned conservation when it was tried systematically to increase the bison population. This was done to render hunting more viable and also for the sake of state representation. As early as the year 1700 a Polish–Saxon commission had taken steps to reform the forest economy. Under the Polish King and Elector of Saxony, Augustus III, grand hunts for bison were organised, when on 27. 9. 1752 forty–two bison were killed. An obelisk, still standing in the castle grounds of Bialowieźa, carries an inscription in Polish and German which states that eleven large, seven small, eighteen young animals and six bison calves were shot.

When Poland was divided in 1795 the Forest of Bialowieźa became a Russian possession. The Empress Catherine of Russia presented parts of the hunting grounds to her favourites, as did her son Tsar Paul. In 1811 a large forest fire ravaged Bialowieźa, and in 1812 French troops further reduced stocks of game, so that only about three hundred bison remained.

By 1830 stocks had risen again to eight hundred animals, so that during the Polish rebellion of 1831 parts of the revolutionary army could feed on the meat of bison. Between 1843 and 1846 hunting grounds in the Forest were newly surveyed and divided into 541 sections with over 122,477 hectares. Stocks of bison under the tsarist regime developed as follows:—

1812	about	300 bison	1889	380 bison
1820		480 bison	1892	491 bison
1832		770 bison	1903	700 bison
1854		1,824 bison	1907	750 bison
1857		1,898 bison	1914	735 bison
1860		1,500 bison	1917	121 bison
1861		1,447 bison	1918	120 bison
1863		874 bison	1919	7 bison
1868/88	about	500—600 bison		

The tsars continued to hold bison hunts annually. After 1888 hunting in the Forest was taken out of state administration and put under the direct administration of the tsar's court. A hunting box was built in 1889—1894 for Tsar Alexander III (1881—1894) which was burnt out in the Second World War.

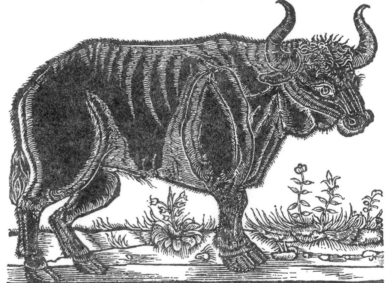

50   Bison and aurochs. From Herberstein's information drawn in 1522 for C. Gesner's *Historia Animalium,* published in 1557 as a marginal drawing on the second map of Russia in *Moskowia.*

During the tsarist regime bison hunts in Bialowieźa Forest counted high among social events of the St Petersburg season. Months before the beginning of the hunt, the animals were driven from the Forest into an enclosed area, some 400 hectares large, which was secured by high palisades. Young animals and calves were taken out, and about one hundred bison kept in readiness for the court hunt. The guests shot from twelve specially built high seats. In 1860, for example, 28 bison were shot in that way, 42 in 1890, 36 in 1897 and 45 in 1900. The last hunt for bison took place in 1913, and at the outbreak of the First World War 727 animals were left in the Forest. Of these 231 were bulls, 347 cows and 149 calves. Stocks of game suffered greatly during the war, so that only 121 bison were left in 1917. After the end of the war in 1919 there were only seven animals. On 21. 2. 1919 (other sources say 12. 4. 1919 or 9. 2. 1921) the last bison in the Forest was killed by a poacher, called Szpakowicz (a former tsarist game-keeper), which meant the end of the bison living in the wild in Europe.

Stocks of bison in Gatchina near St Petersburg and in the Caucasus disappeared in the aftermath of the First World War, about 1919. According to other sources some 500 to 700 bison still lived in the Caucasus in 1890, only 50 in 1920 with the last 3 killed in 1926.

The international congress on the conservation of wildlife, in Paris in 1923 resolved to protect the last bison living in Europe, and use those living in zoological gardens for breeding. The International Society for the Protection of the Bison, in Frankfort on the Main established a stock register in 1924. According to this there are only 66 bison in European zoos.

In the hunting reserve of Jankowice, belonging to Prince Pless in Upper Silesia three pure-blooded animals survived: the bison cow Planta (born 1906, died 1934), the bulls Platan and Plebej. These became the stock for systematic breeding in Poland. In 1929 the first two bison could be sent to Bialowieźa to start a new herd. With the establishment of a Polish National Park in the Forest on 11. 8. 1932 it became possible to build up game stocks, and by 1939 a herd of about 100 animals existed there. In the Second World War bison stocks were again severely reduced, so that it was not until 1951 that there were again 65 animals. On 13. 9. 1952 the first two bison were settled in open ground, and in 1968 there were 186 animals living in herds in the wild. Another 169 were in the reserve.

Also in the Russian part of the Forest stocks have increased. In 1958 there were six conservation areas with altogether 79 pure-blooded bison in the Soviet Union. Soviet and Polish scientists, at a conference for the protection of the bison in 1973 discussed how in future international collaboration might be increased. It is fortunate that through coordinated international collaboration of scientists, foresters and huntsmen the European bison has been saved from extinction, and that the first few bulls have even been set free for shooting. In 1974 six were actually shot in Poland.

Late in 1975 512 animals were counted in the Forest of Bialowieźa, 450 of them in open ground. Considering that a bison in the wild needs some 1,000 hectares of forest to live in, it becomes quite clear that there will soon be no more room in the region, so that controlled shooting of bulls will become necessary. Certain parts of the Forest have been made available to tourists, and during a drive bison may be observed in the best circumstances.

This development is similar to that of the game reservations in the African savannas. Here, too, Big Game hunting at one time dominated the scene, while now the camera–carrying tourist goes on safari.

Safaris of the Elephant Hunters

"Africa, a country known for its Big Game, has been exploited for a long time, and much hunting went on in the regions most easy of access. Some were even emptied of all game. The march of civilisation pushed back the game."
James Dunbar Brunton, Sportsman's Guide to North-West Rhodesia, 1909

Between 1840 and 1890 the African continent became the El Dorado of Big Game hunters from all over the world. The merciless hunt for big trophies, especially ivory, made stocks of game shrink rapidly in the East African savannas and the Transvaal plateaus. Two factors played a considerable part in this development: political differences between the Boers, settled in the Cape, and the advancing British starting a great track of the Boers into the interior, particularly after the abolition of slavery in 1835. On the Orange river and in Natal the Boers forcefully took possession of land from the Zulu tribes, in order to use it for their extensive animal breeding. They founded the provinces of The Orange Free State, Transvaal and Natal, which, in time, together with the Cape of Good Hope were to form the Union of South Africa.

In the rich hunting grounds of the Zulus there was an abundance of antelopes, zebras and elephants, but mass murder began after 1840. The Boers naturally wanted to protect their newly acquired farmland from intruding game, and at the same time mass murder yielded considerable profit. The Boers dried all meat and sold the skins to Europe where prices for skins, ostrich feathers and ivory were very high. This fact kept business with African game going for years. In 1837 a pair of elephant tusks, for example, fetched between sixty and seventy pounds sterling for the hunter. This ivory boom continued, and as early as 1870 the elephant became extinct in Transvaal. Farmers and elephant hunters were both responsible for the extermination of much of the African fauna. In the region of the African coast Arabs, too,

51 Boers track in Griqualand.

carried on a profitable trade in both "black" and white ivory. Negroes, taken by the Arabian slave traders in the interior and put into chains, had to transport heavy loads of elephant tusks to coastal towns on the Indian Ocean which were centres of the ivory trade.

In 1837 Captain William Cornwallis Harris described the many kinds of game in the Transvaal, being particularly impressed by large stocks of elephants. The countryside was full of elephants, he states in his book, *Wild Sports of Southern Africa*. "In a green and narrow valley, two or three miles long, there were clumps of elephants everywhere, and it was easy to get quite close to the animals."

Nearly all books on African travel and hunting of the period tell the very same story, namely of a great abundance of game. Peter Kolb, for example, in his book about the bontebok *(Damaliscus dorcas dorcas)* relates that he came across more than a thousand animals, not afraid of strangers, and not running away. It would have been quite easy to shoot one or even a number of them. George Cumming, a Scotsman, who hunted in South Africa in 1848, observed hundreds and thousands of springboks *(Antidorcas marsupialis)*, roaming in grass and woodlands. This enormous wealth of Big Game attracted hunters from everywhere and contributed to the extermination of game. In the Cape the bontebok, for example, has become practically extinct. Seventeen animals only could be saved and taken to the Bontebok National Park of Bredasdorp. They have increased, and in 1965 there were 750 animals. The blackmaned lion of the Cape, too, became nearly extinct as early as 1850, as high premiums were paid for shooting it. Between 1887 and 1908 in South Africa alone fourteen species of mammals were exterminated, including the quagga and the blaubok. The Boers made sacks for their corn from the skins of the quagga, a dark-coloured zebra with light-coloured legs. The last animal in the wild was shot in 1878, and in 1880 a South African dealer, Kroonstand, exported about two million skins of springbok and other game. To prevent the extermination of more species, President Kruger in 1884 demanded in parliament the establishing of a game reservation. However it took fourteen years for this project to become reality. On 26. 3. 1898 the Sabi Nature Reserve was opened, since 1926 known officially as the Kruger National Park. Here game of the South African grasslands found a refuge. But in the Serengeti steppes the elephant became extinct at the end of the nineteenth century.

There are many tales, reports and statistics about Big Game hunting. One is about Prince Albert, second son of Queen Victoria, who went on a safari on 24. 8. 1860 on the Orange river. It is said that he and his guests opened running fire on 20,000 to 30,000 quaggas, zebras, springboks, blesboks, different kinds of antelopes, gnus and koodooes. More than 5,000 animals appear to have been killed on that day.

52 Hunting for waterbuck.

"This safari," it is reported, which took place on the property of a farmer, called A. H. Blain, was more like butchery, "most hunters looked rather like butchers not sportsmen, spattered all over with blood." All the same, it must have been an exciting day for the prince, and safaris of this kind for African Big Game were often held at the end of the nineteenth century. The "job" of being a Big Game hunter in Africa led to the indiscriminate destruction of game in Southern and Eastern Africa. One, I. A. Hunter, declared that he himself shot more than 1,000 rhinoceroses and over 1,400 elephants. Working as a railway guard in Kenya he shot his quarry, as he recalls in his hunting memoirs, from a moving train. "In 90 days I killed 88 lions and 10 leopards. Hunting elephants was particularly profitable. In Nairobi a dealer would pay twenty-four shillings for every pound of ivory, while a cartridge cost only just over one shilling. On average a good pair of tusks yielded about one hundred and fifty pounds. In fact, a man could make as much money from one elephant as a railway guard earned in two months. Hunter reports that as a Big Game hunter he sometimes earned as much money as the governor of the colony. With more than 1,400 killed elephants this was a profitable job. There are reports of another hunter in the Transvaal who killed 97 elephants in 1866, gaining 2.3 tonnes of ivory, and earning 1,700 pounds sterling. In the same year another ivory hunter, Jan Vilgon, shot 210 elephants in the Transvaal. This list could be continued at random.

About 1850 the annual quarry of elephants in East Africa was about 30,000, even 60,000 to 70,000 in 1880. Between 1880 and 1910 two million elephants were killed according to E. Schulz. Their tusks were sold mainly in Zanzibar.

The annual export figures show some 244,000 kg. of ivory, leaving the traders with a profit of 146,600 pounds sterling. The final sales were made at the ivory auctions in London. Tusks of over 50 kg. were not rare then. In the British Museum is a tusk of an elephant killed in Kenya, some 335 centimetres long, weighing 97.156 kg. It is one of the largest trophies in the world. The world record, however, is held by a tusk 349.25 centimetres long, with a width of 46.91 centimetres, also from an elephant shot in Kenya. Weights of 133.022 kg. are quoted from Haltenorth and Trense. According to E. Schulz (1976) a tusk, 4 metres long, originating from Angola, is in the Smithsonian Institute at Washington.

The heaviest tusks of all are in the Museum of Natural History in Kensington. This elephant was shot with an old muzzleload by a hunter, Tippu Tibs, on the slopes of the Kilimanjaro. The weight of the dry tusks is 101.9 kg. and 96.3 kg., before drying the weight is given as 105.7 kg and 101.7 kg. The trophy was sold in 1900 in Zanzibar to the museum for 5,000 dollars.

At the end of the nineteenth century responsible sportsmen pleaded for the saving of Big Game stocks in Africa and established the first conservation areas (1898 the present Kruger National Park: in 1931 the conservation area of Banagi, and in 1937 a reserve in the Serengeti steppe).

On 8. 11. 1933 all African states signed a convention according to which no gorilla, for example, was to be caught or shot in the African jungle, unless this was important for scientific research and then by special permit only, to be granted by the highest authorities.

Even this enlightened nature conservation policy of several African colonial administrations did not lead to an essential limitation of safari hunting. Well-known biologists concerned with game, hunters and conservationists from everywhere demanded—after 1945—that the conservation of African Big Game should be declared the responsibility of all mankind.

It was not, however, until the formation of the young independent African states that a basis was created for the governments of these states to take full responsibility for the present and future conservation of African fauna within their territories.

Crane Shooting

"Nought moves around him,
save a swarm of cranes who guide him on his way.
Who towards southern regions warm,
have hither come in squadrons grey."

Friedrich Schiller,
"The Cranes of Ibycus", 1797

It may appear strange that a history of hunting devotes a whole chapter to cranes, a bird no longer considered for fowling. Yet, there is much of interest in the lifestyle of this particular species.

This majestic bird which on its annual migration covers thousands of kilometres, has become a symbol of bird migration in general. Indeed, flying or "dancing" cranes stand for the protection of birds and all wildlife. Together with the stork the crane is one of the best–known and most popular of large birds. Many tales and fables have grown about it, maintaining that it is one of the cleverest and "wisest" birds.

It is quite different with the other large birds of Europe. The common heron *(Andea cinerea)* was hated and persecuted for centuries for the harm it did to fish stocks. It was at one time a highly valued delicacy of the dinner table. The great bustard *(Ortis tarda)* is still shot as fair game in many countries and well into the nineteenth century in Germany stork and crane were systematically persecuted under the law. In Mecklenburg, for example, the stork was shot in all pheasant reservations about 1910, and the crane was declared fair game in Mecklenburg until 1934, not protected by firmly laid down close seasons.

In the *Deutsche Jägerzeitung* it was stated in 1911 that in the 1910/11 hunting season 119 storks, among others, had been shot in the principality of Pless, and 33 of them in Count von Thiele–Winkler's hunting grounds. From statistics under the Hapsburg

monarchy of 1895 it appears that 381 eagles, 98,789 hawks and falcon, 1,092 eagle–owls and 24,721 owls were killed. All these birds were shot legally. Hunting for birds was particularly encouraged by the dealers in feathers, who bought considerable quantities during the nineteenth century when feathers were in great demand by fashion houses. Early in this period ostrich feathers were great favourites, and after 1878 many finely coloured feathers were used particularly as ornaments on lady's hats. One firm in Leipzig alone about 1900, used four and a half million lark's wings and one and a half million wings of ptarmigan. Next to Paris and London, Leipzig was the main entrepôt for bird's feathers. According to the writer Schillings the following were auctioned in London about 1910 in only one year: "209,700 white heron; 33,870 bird of paradise; 37,603 humming bird; 18,853 crown pigeon; 34,045 parrot; 1,537 macaw; 17,021 king fisher; 679 rock hen; 2,118 cockatoo; 59,939 sea swallow; 248 emu; 82 lyre–bird; 3,009 toucan; 198 golden cuckoo; 563 condor; 225 red ibis; 166,143 duck; and 307,855 bustard. Also auctioned were the pinions of 69,650 eagles; 9,600 falcons; 29,300 sparrow hawks; 38,751 albatross and Jabiru storks; and 3,222,620 peacocks." "Fashion has brought more distress to the world of birds than anything else," K. R. Hennicke wrote in 1912. In some parts all birds with beautiful or even just useful feathers were ruthlessly exterminated, and dispatched to the dealers in feathers.

53 On their flight across the ocean cranes drop stones they have carried. Drawing from: Münster, *Cosmography.* 1578

At the shores of the Caspian Sea, in India, in Brazil, in Australia, Siberia, New Guinea, North America and Africa, in short, everywhere where there were birds with fine feathers, agents of the Paris and London dealers turned up. The riches they offered meant mass murder for the birds. Among the feathers for ornament were those of the crane, the European as well as varieties from other continents. Some of these feathers were sold as heron feathers. About 1910 there were fewer and fewer breeding places of the crane in Germany, yet in the moorlands and marshes of the Brandenburg–Mecklenburg lake region today 200 pairs of cranes breed, the remains of a species doomed to extinction.

Early in the century (1907) the stock in the same area was about 1,400 pairs. In the eighteenth century the crane was said to be numerous everywhere, and doing much harm to newly sown seeds. By royal decree of 3. 10. 1722 everybody in Prussia was allowed "to shoot or catch cranes", but to take care not to mistake a bustard *(Otis tarda)* for a crane. If at one time the crane was shot with a crossbow this was now done by a nine–barrelled carriage gun. In many countries hunting the crane was considered hunting for large game, and like shooting the eagle or great bustard was a privilege of the monarch.

In Western Europe the crane became almost extinct about 1600, and from the middle of the nineteenth century only few remained in Northwest Germany and Denmark. Only in Lower Saxony and Schleswig–Holstein single breeding pairs have been sighted west of the Elbe. The main breeding places of the bird are now in Norway and the countries bordering on the Baltic.

At the end of August families of crane leave their breeding grounds and fly to gathering places from where in mid–October they migrate to winter quarters in the South of Spain and Northwest Africa. The annual migration of the crane is one of the most spectacular phenomena of bird life. On a stretch, 300 to 400 kilometres wide the birds cross in a southwesterly direction over the German Federal Republic, France and Spain. In certain places they rest a little, for example, in Castile, where some spend the winter. In the spring the same route is followed in the opposite direction when the flight, however, takes only a few days.

For centuries the route of the cranes has remained the same, and for centuries the birds were hunted and shot on their way, being considered fair game in nearly all countries. There were no unified laws nor rulings to protect the bird. In Germany's many principalities certain close seasons were observed.

In Mecklenburg where most cranes of Germany bred, there were no close seasons until 1934, only a ruling of 15. 4. 1904 forbidding the taking of eggs and young birds. Astonishingly too, shot cranes were not accounted for in statistics separately but included with other birds. Shot cranes can, however, be seen in paintings, for example, in a still life by Jean Baptiste Oudry.

In the nineteenth century crane stocks had begun to dwindle rapidly everywhere. There was, as we have seen, no protection on the migration route, with hunting laws varying from country to country. In France, for example, the prefect of every department, according to a law of 3. 5. 1844, decided independently on making rules about hunting which might well differ from year to year. In Spain hunting laws of 1879 regulated the shooting of birds. Also in the first international regulation concerning the protection of birds in Europe, laid down in Paris on 19. 3. 1902 by thirteen countries, the crane is not included in either list of useful or harmful birds.

Where there existed close seasons, they were fixed for May and June which means too late to be effective. We know now that the crane begins breeding during the first ten days of April, and the first eggs have even been observed in the crane's nest at the end of March. With an average breeding time of 29 days a close season between 1. 5. and 30. 6. is quite obviously too late. Birds are attached to their breeding grounds, and shooting near the nests in April means quite a serious disturbance which may well account for the decrease in breeding pairs of crane. This is even more so since we are dealing with a careful and shy bird, threatened at the same time by increasing cultivation and mechanisation of agriculture and forestry. Legal steps for the protection of the crane have now been taken. In Sweden breeding and courting places have been declared reservations. In contrast to single pairs in Northern Germany, cranes in Sweden do their courting in specially reserved areas. Swedish nature lovers each spring wait impatiently for the double pleasure of seeing the cranes return, and then watching their courting.

For centuries the "dance of the cranes" has caught the imagination of naturalists, in fact, early Spanish rock paintings show dancing cranes. The "dance" is not a courting display only, as was assumed at one time, rather is it the expression of the bird's joy of life, and thus may be observed at almost any season. All the fourteen known varieties of the crane show the display, particularly the Japanese variety and that of the Near East.

Sportsmen and conservationists have contributed decisively to measures for the protection of the bird, and there now exist reservations in Japan, Canada and the United States.

In 1811 the ornithologist, Thomas Nutall, observed thousands of whooping cranes on the Mississippi. "The noise of these legions of birds high up in the air was deafening, and the snow–white birds with the red spot on their heads are rightly called whooping crane *(Grus americana)*.

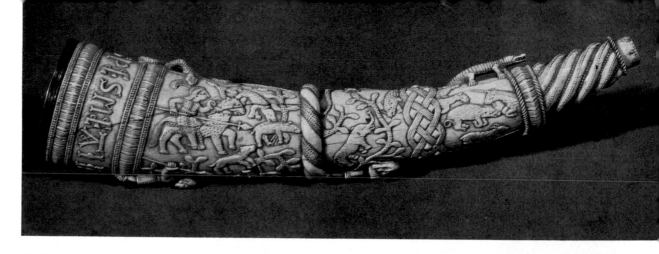

196 *Oliphant. Portuguese colonial work of the 16th century. Hermitage, Leningrad*

197 *Ivory trade in Mombaza.*

198 *In the camp of an ivory dealer in Zanzibar.*

199 *Hall with African trophies and arms. Castle Museum, Opocno (Czechoslovakia)*

200 *J. F. Naumann: Common crane. Copper etching. Museen der Stadt Köthen, Naumann-Museum (German Democratic Republic)*

201 *Manchurian crane in the Crane Reservation at Akune, Northern Japan. 1969*

202 *Shooting buzard and crane with a carriage gun. Sheet 37 from W. Birkner's Jüngeres Jagdbuch. After 1639. Landesbibliothek, Gotha (German Democratic Republic)*

203 *Shooting crane. Miniature from Teatrum Sanitatis. Biblioteca Casanatense, Rome*

204   Cranes flying in the autumn wind.

205   This column marks the frontier of the Akune Reservation. 1969

206   Watching crane with stone in its claw. When he falls asleep, the stone drops
into the water and the birds will wake up. Illustration of the old legend,
concerning the vigilance of cranes. Goblet of cut glass. Staatliche Museen,
Kunstgewerbemuseum, Berlin

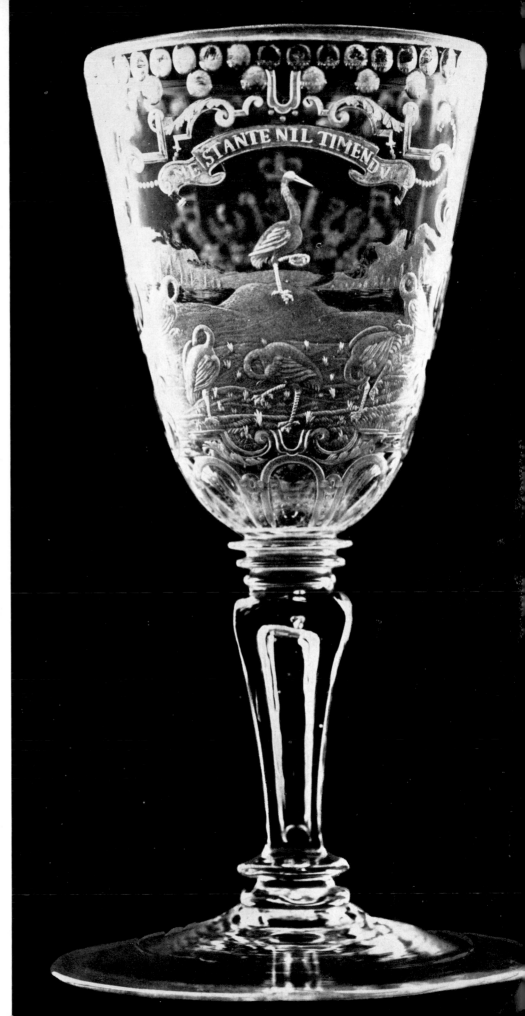

230

207 *Powder flask. Box wood, 18th century. Bayerisches Nationalmuseum, Munich*

208 *Luxury weapons from Suhl are known by their fine arabesques or animal motives, both engraved and embossed. Stocks, too, are ornamented with steel engravings. Drilling, model 30 L*

209 *Suhl double-barrelled gun, model 8, 1972*

232

210   "Bock" double-barrelled gun, model 323
E-Lux. Suhl, 1972

211   Double-barrelled sporting gun with percussion
lock. Made by Moritz August Friese, Dresden,
second half of 19th century. Staatliche
Kunstsammlungen, Historisches Museum, Dresden

Fifty years later on the shores of the Great Slave Lake in Canada only some 700 pairs of crane were breeding, and just 18 birds were counted in 1938. Research by the ornithologist, R. P. Allen, of the United States Fish and Wildlife Service, led to a better knowledge of the life habits of these large birds, and to creating means of saving them from extinction. By systematically alerting the public through the press and television, it became possible to make the protection of the crane a general concern. The two–thousand–mile flight of the whooping crane became a symbol of nature conservation.

In Canada the Wood Buffalo National Park was made a breeding reservation, and in Texas, on the gulf coast, some 4,000 kilometres south a winter reservation came into being (Aransas National Wildlife Refuge). In that way the whooping crane population has gradually increased again during the last decades.

Still more impressive are the measures taken in Japan. Here the great Manchurian crane was of old regarded as a protector and procurer of good fortune. Many legends and stories tell of the bird, and it is often represented in works of art in Japan, China and Korea. In Japan cranes are today concentrated mainly in two regions: in the South is the reservation of Izumi on the island of Kyushu. The dammed lakes of the paddy fields are the winter quarters of the white–necked crane *(Grus vipio)*, the monk crane *(Grus monacha)* and single specimens of the common crane *(Grus grus)*. In the North of Japan on the island of Hokkaido the Japanese Crane Nature Park was established for the Manchurian crane *(Grus japonensis)*. Also a few snow cranes *(Grus leucogeranus)* winter in Japan.

At one time the species was plentiful in Japan, with nobody allowed to kill or disturb it. Under the absolute feudal regime of the Tokugawa Shoguns in the eighteenth and nineteenth centuries cranes were protected solely for the emperor's falconry. It was the special wish of the emperor, the Son of Heaven, as the Japanese rulers liked to be called, to go hawking for heron, crane and duck. In the imperial hunting grounds outside the gates of Tokyo falconry was carried out on a grand scale annually, until 1868. Crane and heron therefore counted as imperial game which nobody was allowed to kill. All nests of crane had to be notified, and whosoever found one, had to guarantee the safety of the nest. Also, according to Buddhist teaching the killing of any animal was forbidden, as was the eating of meat.

When civil war began in Japan in 1868, and the Tokugawa regime was replaced by the Meiji government, a merciless persecution of the crane began, as the bird was considered the lucky symbol of the old regime. Shintoism was re–introduced as a state religion, and these political and religious changes contributed to a change in hunting methods in Japan at the end of the nineteenth

century. This, in turn, led to the complete extermination of the crane all over the country. Similar to European hunting laws, all Japanese owning land could now hunt, which led to indiscriminate hunting and the killing of game, until then protected. Special shoots of crane were arranged and nests were destroyed. Only in the far North, in the Kuccharo Marsh near Kushiro did the last Manchurian cranes find a refuge and began breeding there. The saving of these birds after 1949 makes an interesting story:

Near the village of Akune, cranes were observed in the autumn of 1949. A peasant, Yamasiki fed the birds with maize, and in that way kept them about even during a severe winter when they did not start on their long and precarious migration to the South. In spite of thick snow they gathered annually in the autumn and were fed by the people of the district.

The large Manchurian cranes of Akune became a new symbol for nature conservation in the whole of Japan. Pupils of Akune schools formed a crane–club, and together with sportsmen and conservationists carried out a careful count of cranes every year on 5 December. This supplied exact information about stocks of the Japanese crane *(Grus japonensis)*.

In the Tama zoo in Tokyo an international stock book is kept, showing that in 1952 there were only 23 Manchurian cranes, 93 in 1957 and as many as 123 in 1959. In 1968 there were over 300, a number which possibly included migratory birds. Some from the East Asian mainland may well have settled again in Japan. In 1972 the zoos of the world only kept 32 specimens of the bird in captivity, and 222 were accounted for in other parts of Japan. Nowadays the Manchurian crane is no longer rare in the region of Kushiro. Many nature lovers come every year to watch the beautiful birds in deep snow. Posters and all kinds of pictures represent motives of dancing and flying cranes. There is even a Festival of Cranes held annually in the spring in Akune when the bird is truly honoured, and the mayor ends his speech with this supplication: "May the cranes live here for a thousand years; then they will bring good fortune and contentment."

54 Rock painting of a dancing crane. Northern Sahara

The Development of Hunting Weapons in the Nineteenth and Twentieth Centuries

"Once the bullet is shot from the barrel,
no devil can hold it up."

Traditional huntsman's saying

The invention of fulminate of mercury in 1786 by the Frenchman, Claude Louis Berthollet, followed in 1799 by the Englishman Howard's discoveries, and later by the use of the primer (about 1820) made percussion ignition possible. The first detonating lock was invented in 1807 by a Scottish clergyman, the Rev. Alexander James Forsyth.

The new type of gun was a muzzleloader with the prime set on a nipple, and detonated by the falling of the hammer. This then fired the charge in the barrel. As the interior parts of the percussion gun were similar to that of the flint lock, flint lock guns could be adjusted to percussion from about 1840 onwards. These guns had a higher success rate than the flint lock ones where about every fifteenth shot was a failure. With percussion guns it was only one in three hundred. Loading of the barrel, however, caused some difficulties early on. With the construction of the long–barrel gun the percussion gun became the ideal hunting weapon with a range of some 700 metres and a firing speed of about 1.5 shots a minute.

While black powder was kept in special powder flasks, often richly decorated, lead bullets were carried, together with small shot, in leather pouches. Several moulds, holders and hooks for the casting of bullets and holders for percussion caps belonged to eighteenth and nineteenth–century hunting equipment. Special machines were used for the making of paper cartridges. Each huntsman at that time prepared his own ammunition, and even now in many parts of the world small shot is made by the hunter with powder and lead.

The construction of breechloaders in the nineteenth century greatly improved hunting weapons. Although breechloaders of various types were known since the sixteenth century, it was only the use of cartridges and mercury percussion which made for an essential improvement in their use.

The French gunmaker, LeFaucheux, in 1825 developed a gun with a forward under lever below the fore–end, making for greater safety. After 1832 cartridges became more reliable, and the cartridges of LeFaucheux's gun had pinfire. Pulling of the hammer activated the pinfire and ignited the charge. A safety device avoided the unintentional discharge of the gun. There were single and double–barrelled guns for small shot as well as solid.

A Thuringian gunsmith, Johann Nikolas Dreyse, in 1831 constructed the so–called needle–gun. Used originally as a military weapon (Infantry M/1841 – M/1871) it soon became popular as a hunting weapon because of the high frequency of its shots. It fired 8 to 12 shots a minute, considerably more than the percussion gun. A long needle ignited the charge. The first hammerless double–barrelled gun was made in Germany in Frankfort on the Oder by the firm of Teschner (Collath).

Further improvement in hunting weapons was achieved by the introduction of metal cartridges. In the second half of the nine-teenth century new double–barrelled guns were developed by the English makers of guns, Anson and Deeley and William Greener. With these, metal cartridges were automatically ejected, also small–shot cartridges made of cardboard were used in that way. Greener's guns were very popular about 1880. Also English hunting rifles made by the firms of Lancaster, Dickson, Holland & Holland and Webley and Scott, enjoyed international repute. When in 1873 Henry Winchester had his new rifle made no longer with a gun metal barrel but a steel casing, a prototype for the modern repeater sporting gun had been created. The Win-chester Repeating Arms Company from New Haven, Connecticut had at the turn of the century become known for the making of great numbers of hunting guns and also for the manufacture of a new type of cartridge with central ignition, which led to further developments in multi–loader rifles.

The invention of the revolving cylinder with magazine in the centre shaft by James P. Lee from Ilion in New York State, in 1879 was the start of a new epoch in arms technique. Even though the principle of a cartridge magazine in the central shaft had been known as early as 1645, the patent for "The Lee detachable ma-gazine gun" was taken out only in 1882 by the arms manufac-turers Remington in Ilion. The Remington Arms Company, one of the leading makers of arms in the world, used the system for military weapons and also excellent hunting rifles. Also the Colts Patent Fire Arms Manufacturing Company in Paterson, New

Jersey, world famous for their revolvers, made "Express Arms" until 1895, the Colt hunting rifle with a tube magazine under the barrel.

These firms also manufactured multi–shot guns of which the hammerless one was the most popular and J. Stevens Arms and Troll Company of Chicopee made — since 1872 — five–shot hammerless shot guns. The Higgins models, the well–known Flite–Kung–Trophy multi–loaders were widely distributed in America. The European market was dominated by five–shot multi–loader shot guns with ram–rod made by the Nobel Dynamite Trust Ltd. (Models 50, 60, 65, 70) and hunting rifles made by the Italian Beretta works in the province of Brescia. Industrial production of hunting rifles with interchangeable parts was developed first in 1880 by I. P. Sauer and Sauer of Suhl in Germany.

With the invention of smokeless nitro–cellulose powder in 1886 the calibre of guns was much reduced and lead bullets were covered with a coating of hard metal made of a cupro–nickel alloy or covered with various hard metals. Through it cartridges became longer and more pointed with higher ballistic values.

The barrels of hunting weapons had to stand great pressure (some 4,000 kg per square centimetre) and temperatures of about 2,500 degree Celsius. Special quality steel had therefore to be used in their making. Quality, in fact, was continuously officially controlled in Germany, and the weapons then given a hallmark.

The brothers Paul and Wilhelm Mauser of Obersdorf on the Neckar developed the Prussian needle–gun model 1871. With their model 71/84 they took part in the feverish armament race of the imperial states. The high standard of industrial production of army rifles allowed the Mauser works in 1888/89 to put newly constructed small calibre magazine rifles on the market. They were loaded with a clip of 5 cartridges of 7.65 mm. calibre with coated missile. These rifles supplied to the Belgian army, were again improved in the years to come, and with model 98, as the definite type of infantry rifle, reached high numbers of production. This rifle weighs 4.1 kg. and has a calibre of 7.92 mm. The 740 mm. long barrel has four grooves with righthand turn. It was possible to fire 25 well aimed shots a minute. The 98a for elongated projectiles was developed between 1905 and 1908, and became the main weapon of the German army in the First World War. Calibre K 98k became the standard weapon for the forces of Hitlerite Germany since 1935.

The multi–loader rifle 98, produced by the Mauser works together with the Berlin firm of Ludwig Löwe & Co., was put on the market as a hunting rifle in 1908, as model 98/08. It was lighter, weighing only 3.4 kg., and was supplied in the following calibres 6.5 mm. K (6.5×54); 8 mm. K (8×51); 9 mm. (9×57); 9.3 mm. (9.3×62) and 10.75 mm. (10.75×68). After the Peace Treaty of Versailles of 1918 the Mauser works were limited to producing hunting weapons only. Their model 88 became the prototype for many Mauser hunting guns.

It is impossible here to follow up the development of hunting weapons in different countries, yet it will become clear from the

55 Examples of official proof marks. Suhl, Belgium, Eibar (Spain), Vienna, Paris, Birmingham

56 Official proof marks from Suhl. In the shooting test, shooting and sporting guns of different type are officially tested, and when satisfactory, given the official stamp. Mark of the Suhl Examination Board for small-arms.

few examples shown that the ancient tradition of the gunsmith has not been lost, and that gunmakers now are proud of the long continuity of their craft. In spite of modern techniques the gunsmith's work still demands much personal attention to detail and great precision in finishing the product.

A German rifle, the Suhl three-barrelled gun, with a great tradition behind it, is popular with sportsmen the world over. Also the Suhl gunmakers have carried on producing luxury weapons, finely decorated with precious metal and ivory, and richly decorated stocks, genuine examples of a living tradition of craftsmanship.

Hunting weapons from Austria also enjoy world-wide fame. Ferlach is the most important centre of production, where gunsmiths from the Netherlands laid the foundation for gun manufacturing in 1558. Mention should also be made of Steyr, where up to this day the well-known repetition guns of the firms of Mannlicher and Mannlicher-Schönauer are produced and distributed all over the world.

Hunters and Gamekeepers of Tomorrow

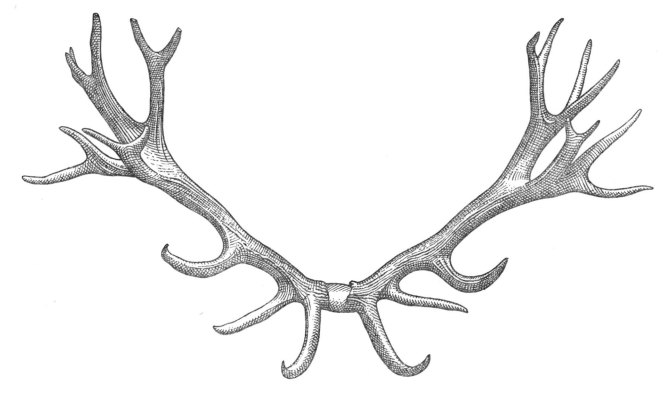

57   The 24-point-head in the Hunting Box Moritzburg near Dresden.

Hunting and Nature Conservation in the Soviet Union

"The protection of Nature is of great significance for all the Republic. It is a question of highest importance, and its solution must not be postponed to the future."

V. I. Lenin

With the rise of the Soviet Union all citizens gained the right to hunt. Many decrees and documents of the Soviet government stress the important function of the hunting economy specially in achieving a rational use of game stocks and the preservation of precious national resources.

On 19 February 1918 nationalisation of the land was confirmed, and in paragraph 1 of a new law it was stated: "private property of land, water and forest as well as the fauna inhabiting it, is abolished, to be now controlled and administered by the state."

Out of this new way of looking at nature, all legislation concerning hunting and fishing and the conservation of wildlife in the Soviet Union must be understood. A decree of 27 May 1918 "About Forests" obliges local administration to keep strict control over forestry, including measures for tree-planting and the protection of natural monuments.

On 27 May 1919 a decree was issued concerning close seasons. According to it, and for the first time, all hunting in the country was prohibited before 1 August. Special close seasons were to be worked out, and among other things the hunting or catching of beavers was forbidden.

In the new decree signed in 1920 "About close hunting seasons and the possession of hunting weapons", the basic principles for socialist hunting economy in the U.S.S.R. were laid down. Every citizen of age, according to this, had the right to join a hunting society, and get a hunting permit after having passed a test in biology, knowledge of hunting and nature conservation.

Lenin who liked hunting himself, and gained recreation and relaxation from it, recognised clearly the practical and ethical potential of it. It is reported that in the winter of 1920 he often went about in his powered sledge, just for pleasure without ever achieving much hunting success. Lenin is said to have been a simple man, modest in his wants. J. E. Rudsutak remembers: "Lenin wakened me by telephone as early as four o'clock in the morning. His whole hunting equipment consisted of felt boots, a black jacket, rifle over his shoulder, some sandwiches in his pocket, a tin with small lumps of sugar and a flask of tea."

The newly formed chief administration for hunting economy with the People's Commissariat for Agriculture organised hunting and issued preservation orders for fowl, prohibiting the hunting of elk and roedeer as well as saiga antelopes, in order to maintain stocks of these animals.

As early as 1919 the first state-owned nature reserve in the U.S.S.R. was established in the delta of the river Volga, the reserve of Astrakhan. On alluvial ground of some 75,630 hectares many water birds have settled. In January 1921 on the north shores of Lake Baikal the reserve of Bargusinsky was created mainly to preserve the valuable Trans-Baikal sable whose habitat is the larch plantations of the Taiga.

On 16 September a decree was issued about the protection of natural monuments, gardens and parks. Through the education authorities many important landscapes could be declared conservation areas by value of this decree. In these reservations working of the soil, extracting material from under it, cutting down trees, hunting or catching animals, birds or fish was prohibited as well as the collecting of eggs and feathers.

In the years to come new reservations and conservation areas were established in all parts of the Soviet Union. In the first years of Soviet power 215 decrees and orders for the protection of nature were made. Lenin himself signed 94 of them.

In 1921, despite civil war in the Ukraine, the government declared the animal paradise of Askania Nova a state nature reserve. This animal park, damaged in the chaos of war, was built up again. In the grasslands of Southern Russia the small German duchy of Anhalt-Köthen had established in 1828 a colony of 480 square kilometres, for the breeding of Merino sheep. In the space of two years 8,000 sheep were driven from Central Germany to the South of Russia, when the herds covered 15 to 20 kilometres daily. Bad management led to Askania Nova becoming the private property of the German-Russian landowner Friedrich Fein. During the following decades he bred herds of 750,000 sheep for wool. His son, Friedrich Falz-Fein in 1887, had deep wells sunk in order to irrigate the steppe country. More than 600 different kinds of trees were planted so that a green paradise developed in the steppes of Southern Russia, and many animals were settled in this oasis. Before the First World War more than 400 different species were accounted for, among them 344 different birds, and more than 50 hooved animals. Predators were not kept in the park. Stocks of the last original wild horses are particularly valuable. They were brought to Askania Nova early this century from the dry steppes of the Transaltai Gobi region. These wild horses are called after the man who discovered them, N. M. Przhevalski, Przhevalski horses *(Equus przhevalskii)*. They were first sighted about 1880 in the steppes of Central Asia, near the Takhinshar-nuru Massif in Southwestern Mongolia, close to the frontier of China. Apart from the wild horses of Askania Nova there were only 28 other specimens caught in the wild in Mongolia, and brought to Europe in 1901 by Carl Hagenbeck of Hamburg–Stellingen, the famous German collector and exhibitor of animals. All wild horses today descend from either strain. In 1956 there were only 36 wild horses left in the zoos of the world. In 1899 a stock register of all wild horses was started which today is being continued in the zoological garden at Prague for the I.U.C.N. According to it there were in 1972 about 200 wild horses in fifty different zoos, but most likely none living in the wild. In spite of careful research no authentic observation of specimens in the wild has been made. There is only one mare in Askania Nova, born in the open steppe. All other horses were born in zoos.

In 1925 Professor M. F. Ivanov took over the management of Askania Nova, and carried out many experiments in acclimatisation and crossbreeding to promote the settling of wild animals. The name of Askania Nova became the symbol of modern zoo management. All kinds of stags and antelopes are the main species kept there, in genuine steppe conditions. They are sent from Askania Nova to be settled in other zoos of the country.

Typical of the conservation of certain wild species is the example of the saiga antelope *(Saiga tatarica)*. Stocks of these animals were much endangered all over the country after the First World War. In Askania Nova systematic studies were carried out, and according to them, means were initiated for the animal's protection. This was necessary, as due to extreme weather conditions there were often severe losses among saigas living in the wild. In the hard winter of 1953/54, with 40 to 60 centimetres thick snow and temperatures of minus 40 degree Celsius in the steppes, 80,000 of the 180,000 saigas living west of the Volga died. Wolves, too, caused much loss among the stocks of saigas. But when in Kazakhstan in the space of ten years more than 210,000 wolves were killed, the saiga rapidly increased.

Meantime there are about two million animals living in the wild in the U.S.S.R. According to a rule of the Ministerial Council of 10 August 1956 measures are to be taken to regulate and make use of the stocks of steppe antelopes, and see to their selection. Recently Soviet zoologists discovered herds of 90,000 to 100,000 animals living even in the "hungry steppe" west of Lake Aral, where the heavy rains of 1972/73 have been favourable to plant growth. It is reported, however, that during the severe winter of 1971/72 in Kazakhstan alone 400,000 saigas died in the extreme cold. The herds moved a long way into the surrounding territories so that they caused damage on agricultural land. In 1974 more than 20,000 hectares of cultivated land are said to have been devastated by saigas.

In Astrakhan the state centre for hunting economy, "Promchos", sees to it that up to 350,000 saigas are shot annually. This game supplies about 6,000 tonnes of meat annually, and over 200,000 square metres of chrome leather. For a region of dry steppes and semi–desert where little animal protein is produced, this is an important economic achievement.

The saigas are an impressive example of the fact that in regions of extreme climates where the usual domestic animals are rare, wild herds can essentially contribute to the population's larder. Hunting economy here returns to one of its oldest functions, namely providing stocks of game as an important source of valuable protein supplies for mankind. Fighting starvation in the world at large stocks of game are essential in filling a gap, provided game is managed in such a way that stocks develop continuously. Results of the Ukrainian research station for animal breeding in Askania Nova where highly productive species of game are bred and acclimatised, may well point the way to experiments on a wider scale.

At one time the saiga was common in regions stretching from the British Isles to Siberia. Fossil finds of the animal have been made as far north as the Arctic, but the saiga cannot easily be bred in captivity. Very few zoos in the world have managed to keep the animal in enclosures for long. The first saiga came to the London zoo in 1864, and ever since it has been tried systematically to improve living conditions for the animals inside zoos. So far, however, only hunting economy and research on game have provided new aspects on the management of saiga stocks. Hunting economy looks at the saiga from a purely practical point of view. From October until 10 November—shortly before rut—the hunt is open. Grzimek (1969) describes this hunt as follows:

"State hunting brigades shoot the animals—not sportsman-like—but with greater consideration, during dark windy nights, lit up only by spotlights. Private people are not allowed to participate in this hunt. A brigade—five men—travels across the steppe in a landrover at a speed of 15 to 20 kilometres per hour. Under spotlights the antelopes can be seen at a distance as their eyes reflect the light. Once the party has approached to a distance of 100 to 200 metres, the landrover stops, and a strong searchlight is switched on. The antelopes stand in the strong light or even slowly approach it, in the same way Thomson antelopes act in East Africa when they are easily caught. Meantime the hunting brigade has climbed down from the landrover, to shoot the animals at a range of only 30 to 40 metres. Contrary to ordinary hunting there are few injured animals which get away to suffer a painful death. Also, from close quarters it is easy to observe age and sex of the animal, and mainly young male animals are shot. One brigade can shoot 100 to 120 animals in five to six hours."

At one time in Kazakhstan hunting the saiga was carried out in a cruel way. Reeds growing along the river beds were cut in winter to a height of 70 centimetres and in addition pointed wooden poles were rammed into the ground. Then the saigas were driven into the prepared area at high speed, when the animals injured their chests or stomachs on the sharp points. In that way 12,000 saigas could be killed in a day, and further thousands were injured and crippled to die later or be eaten by wolves.

The example of the saiga demonstrates how game today under the conditions of an intensive hunting economy may contribute to producing food even for the "hungry" steppe. Methods of hunting have, of course, to be adjusted for the purpose, and they sadly lack the individual satisfying experience of the true sportsman. However, the methods employed guarantee the survival of the species with the continuance of strong and healthy herds.

Stocks of beaver, elk, maral and Sika stag, reindeer, Polar bear, sea otter and wild ass have much increased during the last decades in the Soviet Union. This is due to carefully planned research about game applied in the economy of hunting.

Hunting the Ussuri tiger, the snow leopard and walrus on the Laptev Sea or ringed seals at Lake Baikal is strictly prohibited. In 104 state nature reservations, covering an area of 7.5 million hectares, hunting is altogether prohibited.

More than two and a half million hunters do hunt in regions covering 200 million hectares, according to a report by the Ministerial Council of the U.S.S.R. of 11. 5. 1959. This report deals with state–owned as well as professional hunting, including the hunt for furs in government–owned and co–operative hunting grounds, and the activities of sportsmen and anglers. Huntsmen and anglers are organised in hunting societies in all parts of the Soviet Union.

There are about 300 kinds of game for hunting in the Soviet Union, among them 70 species of fur animals, hunted for their furs. Annually some 50 million skins are obtained for the fur industry, 5 million of these from animals specially bred on fur farms.

The annual quarry of fowl amounts to 50 to 60 millions, among them 50 per cent waterfowl.

Hunting for big trophies is not a main concern in the Soviet Union, even though the country's huntsmen possess several world record trophies, for example, for elk, maral, stag, Marco Polo sheep, Persian gazelle and saiga.

212 *In the steppe region of Askania Nova there are, apart from animals, interesting early sculptures, the so-called "stone women" originating from the time of the Scythians.*

213 Huntsmen at a camp fire in the mountains of Kazakhstan.

214/215 Saiga bucks in Central Kazakhstan. 1964

216 *Curly-headed pelicans in the Astrakhan Nature Reservation. 1971*

217 *Rangers in the Nature Reservation of Kyzyl Agatsh on the Caspian Sea (Azerbaidzhan Soviet Socialist Republic). Many kinds of birds—at least two million migratory birds—spend the winter here.*

218 *Herds in the wild, in the Southern Russian steppes at Askania Nova. More than 36 kinds of wild hooved animals are bred here, for example, wapiti, steppe stag, nilgai, gnu, Cape buffalo and kulan.*

219/220 *Roe deer trophies with world record medals from International Hunting Exhibitions. This buck, killed in Nienadowa (Poland) in 1896, received the Grand Prix in all World Exhibitions. With 196.00 C.I.C. points it still holds second place on a world scale. The medal of the World Exhibition of 1910 in Vienna, being first, is of special interest. Museum of the Polish Hunting Association, Warsaw*

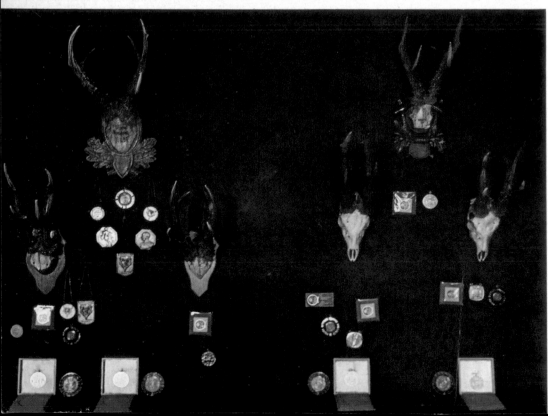

221   *Banquetting hall in Moritzburg Castle with large red deer trophies.*

222   The Hunting Palace of Moritzburg near Dresden

223   Collection of hunting trophies in the castle of Konopiste near Prague.

224 *The Hunting Palace of Moritzburg. Hall of monstrosities with the 66-point-head. Interior from the year 1728.*

225 *Painting of the 66-point-head in the Hunting Palace of Moritzburg.*

250

Diesen Hirsch von 66 Enden
haben
S: Majest: Fridericus I. König in Preußen,
im Ampte Fursten Walde selbst geschoßen
den 18. September. Anno 1696.

Joh. El. Ridinger del. sculps. et excudit Aug. Vind.

227 *J. G. Wolfgang: Silver plate on the sporting gun with which the 66-point-head was killed. Formerly Hohenzollern-Museum, Berlin*

228 *Original trophy of the 66-point-head, the left icetine is badly damaged in fighting. Barockmuseum, Moritzburg*

226 *J. E. Ridinger: 66-point-head. Copperplate, 1768. Staatliche Kunstsammlungen, Kupferstich-Kabinett, Dresden*

229/230/231   D. Männlich the
Elder: Silver-gilt tankard in the shape
of the 66-point-head. About 1700.
Formerly Hohenzollern-Museum,
Berlin

232   *Elands are milked. Animal Park of Askania Nova, 1975*

233   *More than one million gnus were counted in the Serengeti National Park in 1973; assembly of gnus in the Musabi Plains in the western passage of the Serengeti.*

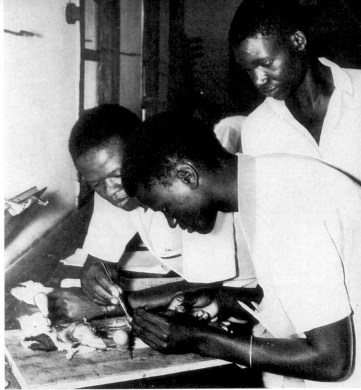

234 Wildlife College, the first training school for gamekeepers in Africa, in Mweka near Moshi. In the background the Kibo surmit of the Kilimanjaro. 1972

235 Gamekeepers at the entrance to the Mikumi National Park in Tanzania. 1971

236 The training of young Tanzanian pupils in the Wildlife Club of a secondary school in Moshi.

237 Poacher with elephant tusks is detained by gamekeepers in Kenya.

238 Tourists' safari in Manyara
Lake National Park. A safari bus in
the background of Gregory Rift Valley.

239 Hunting with a camera in the
Ngorongoro Crater in Northern
Tanzania.

Illustration on the next page:

240 Elephants in the crater of the
Ngorongoro vulcano. 1972

Hunting for Large Trophies alone

"Antlers finely grown with many points are mounted on a wooden stag's head, as a memento, and under the neck a small plaque or piece of parchment carries an inscription as to the year and day, also who has shot the animal and where. The weight is noted, and anything else which has happened during the hunt."

H. F. von Fleming, " Der vollkommene Teutsche Jäger", 1719

This allusion to clearly noting the place of shooting and weight of the quarry, on the base of the trophy, dates from the early eighteenth century. It demands more than the uniform ticketing now applied to trophies which was decided at the congress of the Conseil International de la Chasse (C.I.C.), held in Madrid in 1952.

According to these rules a uniform evaluation of trophies was first achieved at the World Exhibition of Hunting and Shooting in Budapest in 1971. The rules were developed and finalised in collaboration with the Boone and Crockett Club of the United States, at a congress in Copenhagen in 1955.

Apart from measuring skulls, horns, antlers, other appendages and teeth, skins and hides of game are also shown and evaluated at international hunting exhibitions. There is, however, no uniform way of treating hides and skins yet, making it possible to apply general guide lines for evaluation. More importance is bound to be attached to these trophies in future.

Is this cult of trophies, as it is often called by the layman, justified, and is the striving for large trophies still an important part of hunting? Do we hunt only for big trophies to keep them as valuable mementoes on our walls? This surely is a great temptation, the trophies being lasting witnesses to a hunter's skill. Often, however, these customs serve only prestige and the trophy is degraded to a status symbol.

Seen historically, the large trophy has never played the part that some hunters of our day would like to accord it. At one time the skin, the claws of a bear or the teeth of a wolf were the hunter's most valued trophy. As late as the eighteenth century the Master of the Mounted Hunt was presented not with the antlers but the right foreleg of the stag which had been coursed.

Modern research on game and hunting everywhere is devoted to bringing about the natural development of healthy stocks. It aims at guaranteeing good trophies and general perfect quality of the animal.

A good example for the way in which thoughtful keeping and care quickly produced first-rate trophies, may be found in the Hungarian red deer reserves. Here between 1914 and 1945 only 47 gold-medal stags were shot while the numbers rose to 723 between 1946 and 1970. Rewards awarded (gold, silver or bronze for red deer) rose from 529 to 5,651, a convincing proof of the results being achieved by intensive rearing over a comparatively short period.

The question of the largest trophies remains an important topic of discussion. At international hunting exhibitions the finest trophies of our century are on display. Also in recent years publications on game and hunting quote C.I.C. values of gold-medal stags from many countries. All the same, the question as to the largest red deer trophy is still an open one.

At a State Hunting Exhibition in Czechoslovakia, mounted with the participation of socialist countries—from 28.8.—12.9. 1975—in České Budějovice, a ten-year-old red stag from Bulgaria achieved a world record for red deer with 253,62 C.I.C. points. This 18-point stag was shot in the autumn of 1975 in the Hissar mountains by Todor Shiwkow. With a circumference of 35 cm of its buds, it suggests a larger mass of antlers than the 23–point stag shot in Hungary in 1970 by Frau Schuster. At the Budapest exhibition in 1971 this animal was given 251,83 C.I.C. points, and was considered a world record trophy.

These present-day gold-medal stags are surpassed by some older trophies. In the pavilion of Switzerland at the 1971 exhibition antlers were displayed (owned by Dr. René la Roche of Folgensbourg) whose origin was unfortunately unknown. These antlers were evaluated at 286,60 I.P.

In the most important historical hunting collections of different countries there are many trophies whose number of points and conformation of antlers are not inferior to present-day gold-medal stags. Unfortunately data concerning places of origin are often missing, also evaluation according to the C.I.C. point system was not yet in use.

In the Hunting Palace of Moritzburg near Dresden in Germany a twenty-four-point head of a stag is on display and is referred to as the "Great uneven 24–point stag of Moritzburg". In 1969 Dr. R. Bösener and Dr. C. Stubbe of the Institut für Forstschutz und Jagdwesen of the Technical High School in Dresden, evaluated it at 298,60 points. This antler is the largest red deer one known so far all over the world. Under No. 8 of the collection the trophy is shown in the Moritzburg banqueting hall, together with seven other antlers of stags, which also were awarded more than 253 C.I.C. points, and are therefore above the present world record.

The Moritzburg trophies are very rare indeed, hardly ever met in any other collection. The 24–point head with a short skull weighs — even after many years of drying out — 19.865 kg, and is rightly considered a first-rate trophy on a world scale. As established by Bösener in 1969, there is nothing known about the origin of the trophy nor how it came to the collection. Bösener assumed that it was obtained locally. Hunting reports of the *Kursächsische Jagdregister* (Electoral Hunting Register) from the seventeenth and eighteenth centuries (State Archives, Dresden) do not have a record of this particular stag. The heaviest stag mentioned in these records is given as weighing 425.5 kg.

It seems doubtful therefore whether the "Great 24–point stag of Moritzburg" was killed in a hunting ground of Saxony. It is more likely to have come from the forests between the rivers Lawa and Angrapa (north of the Masurian lakes). Research concerned with the history of hunting suggests that the stag was probably shot by Johann Sigismund, Elector of Brandenburg, on 24 August 1617 south of Insterburg (the present Tchernjachovsk) near the village of Siegmuntchova in the Damerau.

The trophy of the "Great 24–point stag of Moritzburg" is beautifully proportioned, with special interest in the centre bud formation, measuring 35.5 cm. The trophy, like all others in the Moritzburg collection, is mounted on the carved head of a stag, fastened by several hand-made nails and wooden screws. The mounting was done in 1728 during a refurnishing of the hunting palace.

Next to No. 24 of the collection, an uneven 24–point head with the note: "Herkunft Preussen" (origin: Prussia), with a weight of antlers of 19.350 kg and 255,038 C.I.C. points, the "Great 24–point stag of Moritzburg" with 298,60 C.I.C. points seems also to have been presented to Moritzburg from Prussia, as was the famous 66–point head. This is most likely the best known red deer antler trophy. It is now kept in the *Monströsensaal* of the palace. The history of the trophy is interesting. The stag was killed some 50 km southeast of Berlin on the Jacobsdorfer Heide near Biegen on 18. 9. 1696. The forester, called Siebenbürger, discovered the stag in 1696 during rut, and reported its presence to his superior who in turn informed his prince. The prince then had the exclusive right of shooting big stags. Three weeks after the Elector Frederick III of Brandenburg (later King Frederick I of Prussia) shot the stag with his heavy hunting weapon.

To shoot a stag of many points was considered great good luck even then, and the elector at once commissioned artists to portray his quarry, and to make copper engravings.

In the collections at the castles of Moritzburg, Grunewald (Berlin–West), Potsdam — Neues Palais (formerly the king's hunting box Wusterhausen) there are still paintings and engravings of the 66–point stag, among them a life-size one of the animal. It is remarkable that in all pictures the left ice tine — battle scarred in the original — is shown as perfect. This is true of paintings and engravings. Apart from these original paintings there exist several copies, for example, a copperplate by Joh. Elias Ridinger, who reproduced the marvellous stag in his hunting book, published in 1768.

A copperplate by Johann Georg Wolfgang has not so far been published in hunting literature, as it was thought lost, although reprinted several times in the early eighteenth century. It has now been found in the Staatliche Kunstsammlungen Dresden, Cabinet of Copperplate Engravings*, and is here published on page 259. The plate goes back to a painting by Merck, and the head is badly drawn. In the original by Merck the antlers were shown in a different position which made Wolfgang sketch an impossible stance. More impressive artistically is a splendid silver-gilt tankard, representing the 66–point stag. This tankard also shows the stag lying down, and its sculptural execution is most excellent. The inscription and hall mark prove it to be the work of the Berlin goldsmith, Daniel Männlich, the Elder. As he died in 1701, the tankard must have been made before 1700. It is likely that the famous sculptur Andreas Schlüter designed the tankard. At the same time he made the design for a monument in sandstone, which was erected in 1707 in the forest near Biegen where the stag was killed. An inscription names the sportsman as well as time and place of the successful hunt together with the weight of the animal. The monument is preserved to this very day while the silver-gilt tankard was lost, probably in 1945.

In the Deutsches Jagdsmuseum at Munich there is also a powder flask showing the 66–point stag. These examples demonstrate the importance of this particular trophy within the history of hunting. The history of the trophy itself becomes more interesting when one considers the fate of the original antlers. During the life of the Elector Frederick III the trophy remained his private property (kept most likely in his hunting box of Wusterhausen). After his

---

* The author wishes to express his gratitude to Herr Friedrich, Dresden for his kind help in tracing the plate.

death in 1713 Frederick William I —the *Soldatenkönig*—became King of Prussia, while the ruler of Saxony was Augustus the Strong. Both princes were hunting enthusiasts and met at state receptions and court hunts when valuable gifts were exchanged.

In Dresden and Moritzburg material was then eagerly collected for the furnishing of the palace of Moritzburg, and in 1727 the court of Saxony was offered precious red deer trophies from Prussia, among them the antlers of the 66–point stag. This was handed to the Elector of Saxony in 1728 on the occasion of a visit to Berlin.*

According to legend the Prussian King is said to have received in exchange a company of soldiers. And even though some authors doubt this, it is, in fact, quite possible.**

In 1727 the interior of the rebuilt palace of Moritzburg was arranged, and the *Monströsensaal* was furnished. The place of honour in this room was given to the 66–point stag trophy. Above the main entrance, surrounded by gilt leather wall hangings, representing the goddess Diana, it is shown at its best set on its artistically carved wooden head. This head was made and gilded by Christian Kirchner in 1728. Also a specially made bracket for the 16–point trophy underlines the importance of the show piece, all in the Baroque style of the period, as it may still be seen today.

In 1969 with the exact measurement and evaluation of the Moritzburg trophies, it was established that the 66–point head by present standards can no longer be regarded as such. It would now be classified as an "uneven 30–point head" with 27 acknowledged points and altogether 185,86 C.I.C. points. The history of this particular trophy is certainly interesting and full of change, considered from the historical aspect of hunting.

Other facts concerning game are in comparison more sober and realistic, as, for example, the fate of other parts of the animal's carcass. Here market values are all important.

* *Journal über den Besuch des Königs Friedrich Wilhelm I. am Königlichen Polnischen Hofe zu Dresden am 13. 1. 1728.* Merseburg, Central State Archives, *Königliches Hausarchiv*, Rep. 46 C2. Akte Jagdsachen Preussen, 1593—1815, *Besuch des Kurfürsten von Sachsen in Berlin*, 1728. Merseburg, Central State Archives, Rep. 41 No. 3.

** *Akte Jagdsachen Preussen*, 1593—1815. "Allerhand über geschickte und verehrte Sachen von und an Kursachsen." Merseburg, Central State Archives, Historische Abteilung II, Rep. 41 No. 8.

58 The 66-point-head. Copperplate by J.G. Wolfgang, from a painting by J.C. Merck, 1707. Staatliche Kunstsammlungen, Kupferstich-Kabinett, Dresden.

Wildlife Management—
the Hunting Economy of the Future

"The protection of and care for stocks of game contributes to the progress of developing countries. This is particularly so when the possibilities of hunting promote tourism. Tourism is an important factor in the economy of many countries ... The experience collected by the F.A.O. during the last decades suggest that in the years to come purposeful use of game stocks will be rapidly developed."

A. Z. Boerma, President of the F. A. O.,
Food and Agriculture Organisation of Uno

There are still many hungry people in this world. Every minute many die of starvation, particularly in regions which at one time were cultivated and fertile. In the Middle East and in Central Asia, in North, East and South Africa, also in South America, Australia, India and the West of the United States there are vast steppes, savannas and deserts. Many of them once yielded crops or were the grazing grounds of herds of cattle, while today they are dried–up, dead land. The intensive keeping of domestic animals is not possible in that kind of countryside without heavy investment. It is not economical either because of lack of fodder and the danger of epidemics. According to present–day knowledge on game, it appears that a planned hunting economy might effectively provide an alternative source of protein for the population. In fact, Soviet experts have had experience of these very methods for years, using and testing them in Askania Nova and also under the auspices of U. N.'s special agency, the Food and Agriculture Organisation, in Central Africa. After 1932 it has been tried in Southern Rhodesia to free the country from the tsetse fly by shooting half a million of wild animals, the tsetse fly being the carrier of the Magana disease which attacks cattle, horses, goats, sheep and other domestic animals. The fly also disseminates the parasite which causes sleeping sickness. The aim of the game–shooting operation was to keep European and Asiatic domestic animals in the fertile countryside. Unfortunately, the massacre, begun by an English veterinary surgeon, called Chorley, proved useless, though carried out with precision by military units with machine guns and quick firing arms. The epidemics could not be fought in that way as the tsetse fly disseminates parasites also from small mammals. Well planned game keeping might have had better results. Through rinderpest breaking out in 1890/91 and again in 1896/97 in East Africa millions of domestic cattle were killed but also 90 per cent of Cape buffalo *(Syncerus caffer)*, greater koodoo *(Tragelaphus strepsiceros)* and roan antelope *(Hippotragus equinus)*. In Kenya experiments are carried out at present with eland antelopes *(Taurotragus oryx)* to be bred and kept in herds. The milk of this antelope has a higher fat content than cow's milk (11 per cent with an annual yield of 330 litres). First successes promise better results than those obtained with the breeding of African cattle.

The example of large herds of Zebu cattle with the Masai tribes in the steppes of Kenya further shows that good veterinary care (protective vaccination against rinderpest) could increase herds substantially. Though there are now over 8 million cattle, the economic situation of the breeders has not been greatly improved. Too large stocks of Zebu cattle may destroy the balance of fodder available over wide areas, and many grazing places are today completely devastated. In contrast the vegetation in the grasslands of the East African game reserves and national parks is hardly endangered, even though stocks of game have much increased here too. In the Serengeti National Park, where stocks have tripled, and in 1972 over 800,000 white–tailed gnus were grazing, also 500,000 steppe zebras and nearly one million gazelles, the meagre vegetation survives as well as watering places in spite of the large game population. Another example is the Ngorongoro Crater where again over 40,000 larger mammals live, with the environment intact. But in the Amboseli–Masai Game Reservation on the frontier of Kenya and Tanzania, an oasis of the square–lipped rhinoceros, the balance between man and animal has been disturbed. The large Zebu herds of the Masai have trampled down the thorn–covered grassland and destroyed it altogether. Similar conditions prevail in the Mara–Masai Game Reserve, north of the Serengeti steppe. There the Masai graze their cattle in the adjoining regions while many species of game keep to the centre of the National Park, migrating only according to seasons.

Every animal lives within an ecological environment, in this case the savanna. If through special circumstances the species increases too much, the natural balance is disturbed, and the animals perish for lack of fodder. According to this biological law the density of game in the reservations and other game areas influenced by man, must be carefully estimated in advance. The prime consideration should be the conservation of a varied wild fauna, guaranteeing biological and ecological balance, a viable denseness of game and proper use of the annual increase in animals.

Only with these principles in mind, can the preservation of wildlife and hunting economy exist side by side successfully. Experiments on the Galana river in Kenya carried out by Jeffrey Lewis, have shown that oryx antelopes are excellently suited for keeping in herds on a grand scale. These animals grow more quickly and gain more weight than Zebu domestic cattle.

Big Game, too, can be an economic asset through proper hunting management, apparent in the example of the hippopotamus and the elephant.

There has been much passionate discussion in recent years about the pros and cons of elephant hunting. In many game reserves and national parks it has been tried to save the animal from destruction. Then herds of elephants grew to such an extent within a few years that they caused much damage in the reservation. In the Tsavo Royal National Park, the biggest African elephant reservation 20,000 elephants transformed the park in a short period of time into a treeless grassy steppe. This large game area of Kenya actually can only maintain some 8,000 elephants. In 1971/72 more than 4,000 elephants died because of a prolonged drought. In a few months this important reservation became the biggest elephant cemetery in the world, and that in quite a natural way. Possibly the heaviest elephant in recent years, Ahmed, a sixty–five–year old bull in the Marsabit National Park in the North of Kenya, became a victim of this natural catastrophe. The animal was under the personal protection of the then President of Kenya, Yomo Kenyatta, yet the elephant met with its death as a result of the long drought, in January 1974. Neither hunter nor poacher but starvation killed the elephant.

The German writer, Harald Lange, in his book, *Hege der Wildnis*, says: "A grown up male elephant needs more than a hundred litres of water daily. Wishing to help the thirsting animals, the administration of the National Park at Tsavo had artificial water holes constructed in the park. Through this measure the elephants did not migrate at the beginning of the drought to other regions, but stayed all the year round in the east of Tsavo where there was plenty of water. However, the vegetation was scanty and did not provide enough fodder to take in extra numbers of elephants for longer periods. The death of so many animals in 1971/72—two specially dry years, with barely a third of the usual rainfall—was not due primarily to lack of water. Rather was it the result of the lack of suitable plants for fodder."

This story shows clearly that any rash human interference with the natural balance of things may have negative results. It is not particularly serious when game is too dense on the ground, and nature itself regulates its own balance, yet this natural balance remains of prime importance. If the principle is violated, nature will work towards its own regulation, and through a process of selection hundreds and thousands of wild animals may perish.

Many scientists consider what has happened in Tsavo an example for nature re–adjusting its balance. A natural and necessary selection within limits is bound to occur to guarantee the survival of fauna and flora, and the natural environment as a whole. This has been scientifically confirmed over and over again. Africa has often witnessed this selection process when, for example, in 1961 during a long drought great numbers of animals died. From the point of view of world nutrition the useless death of so many valuable suppliers of protein is, however, deplorable.

The increase of the elephant population and the damage done by the animals has greatly worried the authorities concerned with hunting and conservation, and planned shooting has again become a necessity. In 1973 about 5,000 elephants were listed to be shot in Africa, another 12,000 became the victims of poachers.

If in 1966 on the Black Continent stocks were estimated at over 300,000 elephants, there were after 1972 165,000 in Kenya and over 945,000 in Tanzania. With an average of five elephants to one square kilometre, the Manyara National Park in Tanzania has the densest elephant population in East Africa.

Should a mass shoot or regulated use of game decide further conservation measures for elephants? To help solving this problem a planned use of the stocks of Big Game was carried out under the direction of Uno's special organisation, the F.A.O., at the Murchison Falls in Uganda and in the Luangwa valley in Zambia. Elephants and hippopotamuses were numbed by shooting them with special bullets, before being humanely killed. The meat was sold cheaply to the local people. In the Kruger National Park, too, it had become necessary to kill some of the elephants, and the salting of meat obtained was arranged in modern installations under supervision of veterinary and health authorities. This meat was then used for the country's population.

Under the direction of experts from the F.A.O. a game cropping scheme was carried out recently at Kirawira on the northwest frontier of the Serengeti plains. Zebra, gnu, topi antelope, impala, Thomson gazelle and other game were shot, using silencers, and the meat processed into 500 gr. tins. According to a report by E. Schulz fifteen tonnes of high quality game were sold in the Nairobi market. The ecological and economic aspects of game farming open out new prospects of animal breeding. The African steppes with their great masses of hooved animals of about 12,000 to 16,000 kg. per square kilometre, allow for natural game keeping and meat production on a scale quite beyond that of domestic animal breeding. Next to the hooved animals of the savanna, the hippopotomus can also be used economically. On the Victoria Nile in the Kabalega Falls National Park in Uganda a quarter of the stock of hippopotamuses had to be shot to secure the animal's future existence in the reserve. The meat of 4,130 hippopotamuses was given to the population, and the hides were sold in aid of wildlife conservation. According to Grzimek the hippopotamuses weighing about 3,200 kg., are most suitable for "farming" away from the reservations. "They are modest feeders, need little room, and many animals can be kept in relatively small enclosures. The weight of the slaughtered body is about 68 per cent of its live weight, much higher than with other wild animals. The extraordinary high content of protein makes the meat of the hippopotamus an extremely valuable source of food." The tusks, too, which may grow to a length of 64 centimetres, are sold at the state auctions of ivory in Dar–es–Salaam, Mombaza, Kampala and Zanzibar.

According to official customs reports from Tanzania, quoted by E. Schulz, 16,000 pairs of elephant tusks were sold in 1969 at state auctions to buyers from abroad.

The weight of tusks is rapidly going down. At present tusks of 10 kg. are the average, and a tusk of 50 kg. is rare nowadays.

Because of the great increase in the smuggling of ivory, caused by rising demand in the world market, several African countries have greatly limited or even stopped the hunt for elephants and rhinoceroses. Kenya has completely prohibited it, and Uganda temporarily stopped all tourist traffic of foreigners, leaving its game reserves and national parks mainly to its own population. The country increased its fight against poachers in national parks, pursuing them relentlessly. In 1974 more than 20,000 elephants were killed in Africa with poisoned arrows or wire slings. For weeks these animals, often injured by six or nine arrows, dragged themselves through the steppe, before their wounds festered, bringing about the giant's slow and agonising death. The vultures then led the poachers to the place where the ivory could be found. The fantastic prices this "white gold from the African savannas" fetched, brought about regular organised campaigns against the game reservations. In 1974 the price on the world market for one kg. of ivory was about £ 44 of which the poacher only received about 10 per cent. If caught by the game-keepers with a tusk in their possession, the poachers were liable to ten years imprisonment, or at least four months detention, should they carry only bow and arrow or slings. Chasing the poacher from bush and savanna has become one of the main concerns of game conservation in Central Africa. Based on the systematic

training of native guards, poaching has been energetically attacked, while the same well trained people effectively cope with an increasing stream of tourists. The College of African Wildlife Management in Mweka near Moshi in Tanzania is the centre for training native gamekeepers.

The college and its training help to create a hunting economy based on scientific knowledge; an economy which organises hunting through large state–owned or co–operative institutions. Here, next to killing the game with expertise, obtaining skins, furs and other hunting products, the export of game is handled as well as undertaking the care of tourist hunters. All this precludes a well–considered keeping of game stocks, aiming at the largest possible number of animals and good quality of game, supplying desirable trophies. To develop this kind of economy, highly qualified professional hunters are required, well versed in hunting techniques and conversant with biological and ecological knowledge concerning all wildlife. This type of economy with the professional use of all products is big business, no longer the mere concern of the sportsman who treats hunting and shooting as a hobby. However, these very sportsmen can hunt in managed areas as tourists, with a licence at a fixed price and for a limited period.

In Texas, too, large game farms, covering over 4,000 hectares, have been established in recent years, and many game animals are kept here. One farm, for example, keeps 2,200 Nubian antelopes and many cervine antelopes which are released for shooting by sportsmen. As this exotic game does not come under the hunting laws of the state of Texas, shooting is permitted according to economic considerations as well as demand and prices to be obtained.

Game farming has also been practised for several years in European countries, and new hunting habits have developed. Old established ways, for example, what kind of shot should be used for which game are being re–considered, and in the African game reservations there are strict rules as to the calibre employed in shooting different kinds of Big Game. Also, the old rule that game must not be shot within 200 metres of its feeding grounds, was changed in Kenya to the extent that in the steppe the hunter has to be at least 300 metres away from his car before he shoots. (Since 1977 in Kenya hunting is prohibited for foreign tourists.)

There are hunting clubs and societies in many countries and for all kinds of hunting. People interested in gun dogs or falconry club together to enjoy their common interests.

In fact, there exists a trend all over the world to specialise in different ways of hunting, and in some countries hunting clubs and societies are run by the state. As hunters and conservationists are drawing closer together everywhere, the outlook for the general protection of wildlife has become much brighter.

Is there a Chance for Game Living in the Wild?

"The I.U.C.N. recommends and promotes national and international measures concerning the conservation of animals living in the wild, and the protection of their natural environment ...
The I.U.C.N. will give particular attention to the preservation of species threatened with extinction."

Article I of the statute of the International Union for Conservation of Nature and Natural Resources (I.U.C.N.), Fontainebleau near Paris, 5 October 1948

The relationship of Man and Nature in the age of the modern industrial society is a problem concerning everybody. This relationship is not limited to either mere material considerations or emotional and ethical thought, the whole development of our society is involved. Hunting, for example, is often regarded as solely an emotional or aesthetic experience.

However, considering our total involvement, modern biological research on game gains in importance as a purposeful use of game stocks and demands their systematic keeping and care.

The contribution of the German Federal Republic to the Hunting Exhibition of 1971 in Budapest developed the theme of game-keeping and shooting in the industrial society.

The desire to hunt, this contribution implied, brings with it the necessity of good gamekeeping, a reality that never can or should be ignored, more so today than ever before, when in densely populated areas game has no chance of survival. Steel and concrete advance further and further into the natural habitat of game. Every day 110 hectares of open countryside are lost, for example, in the German Federal Republic. Technical progress and the density of traffic constantly demand victims among game animals. On the roads of the Federal Republic alone 120,000 hares, 60,000 roedeer and 2,500 red deer, fallow deer and wild boar are run over every year. These big losses do not occur in Germany alone but on all the great roads of Europe. It would need several days of hunting to get these large quarries.

Is there then any protection against such losses? Only the deer fence which stretches for kilometres through the forest, making the woodlands into game reservations. It takes very little to transform animals living in the wild into animals living in enclosures, and depending on the provision of extra fodder. This game also soon looses its natural instinct for flight from man. Behind the fences where game may be watched, herds of game will begin to exhibit some of the attributes of domestic animals. The busy motorroad has an influence similar to that of the fence. The dangers of heavy motor traffic and of railways limit the changeover of game from one district to another.

A noticeable adaptation of game to their new surroundings can be observed. Deer, seen in fields, for example, have quite obviously adapted to the modern world of industrial production. However, it is doubtful whether this type of animal is the prototype of game desired by hunter and nature lover alike, though they may delight the city dweller anxious to escape from his stone desert, to see a piece of what he believes to be true nature.

In reality game has taken over the role of supplier of raw material or the costly object of the sportsman's desire. This is true whether the animal is looked at as a carrier of trophies for an ever increasing swarm of tourists, a protein supplier for hungry mankind or a source of raw material for the fur and leather using trades. The wretched animal may even just become a status symbol for the prestige–seeking hunter.

If during the last hundred years the stock of red deer has multiplied tenfold in Central Europe through careful conservation, too great a density of game has already been observed in some reservations. Heavy investment is required today to guarantee the proper management of game, so that animals living in the wild may continue to do so. In 1972 in the Federal Republic of Germany 500 million D. marks were spent compared to an income of only 93 millions from hunting. Game and hunting have moved, with all their ancient traditions and history, into the field of economics. Next to the gainful lease of hunting grounds which assumes the expensive upkeep of these grounds, hunting equipment is complex and expensive, and the luxury of hunting tourism increasing rapidly.

In some countries travel agencies specialise in safaris and hunting trips which are given great publicity, guaranteeing their clients excellent quarry in many parts of the world.

Modern jets carry these tourists in a few hours close to the hunting grounds of their choice, often in less time than it might have taken to reach game areas at home by horse and carriage. At all seasons this kind of safari offers the wealthy hunter grand opportunities to indulge in his particular sport. Only the wealthy, however, can afford these pleasures which highly commercialised hunting promises even though it does not always pay the entrepreneur.

With the tourist hunter game has little chance of survival unless definite action for its conservation is taken. This is now a universal task for all huntsmen, a responsibility which is shared by many international organisations of hunters and conservationists. It has, in fact, been taken up by the United Nations. The XVII General Conference of Unesco, in Paris in October 1972 set up a convention concerning the protection of nature and man's cultural heritage. According to this convention the protection of nature and the cultural heritage of the world includes cultural monuments and buildings but equally sites of special natural beauty and the endangered rare specimens of flora and fauna. In a "World Heritage" list all endangered objects of international importance are named, and these should, if necessary, be protected and maintained. The Unesco conference resolved unanimously that the natural and cultural heritage is increasingly endangered through the rapid changes in social and economic conditions. Through the conventions and resolutions reached in Paris, the international importance of protection and conservation has been greatly strengthened. In 1948 Unesco sponsored the International Union for the Protection of Nature which, supported by a widening circle, eventually became I.U.C.N., the International Union for Conservation of Nature and Natural Resources. Endangered species were to be protected, both in fauna and flora, and a worldwide list of these species created.

During the last fifty years 79 species of mammals and 139 species of birds have become extinct. At present more than 306 species of mammals and 281 species of birds are in danger of becoming extinct. *The Red Data Book — Wildlife in Danger* lists all threatened species, according to countries. Also the C.I.C. — *Conseil International de la Chasse*, in Paris, and the World Wildlife Fund in Switzerland have over the years contributed to publicising the need for responsible action in re-establishing the biological balance of nature. The W.W.F. promotes in particular the international collaboration of hunters, game biologists and conservationists, to obtain immediate measures and programmes to assist the saving from extinction of endangered species of game.

From 1961 to 1975 the W.W.F. supported more than 1,200 projects with a sum of 17.2 million dollars for the saving of game stocks in every part of the world. In Algeria and Tunisia, for example, the Atlas stag *(Cervus elaphus)* was saved from extinction at the very last minute. With 400 animals left in 1950, there were at most 150 after the Algerian war. On the initiative of the W.W.F.

the home grounds of this stag were investigated, and a protection area of some 500 hectares created, so that stocks increased again.

Also the prong-horned antelope *(Oryx gazella dammah)* in the southern Sahara, and the white oryx *(Oryx gazella leucoryx)* in Arabia, where only some 500 gazelles remained in the desert, had to be protected. The animals were much coveted for their prong-horn trophies, and even shot from a car or low-flying plane.

Another example of excellent international collaboration in the service of conservation is the saving of the sea otter *(Enhydra lutis)* on the northern coasts of the Pacific. In 1880 the world market took up 118,000 skins of otters, while there were only 8,000 in 1885. In 1900 stocks of otters were practically finished.

The countries bordering on the Pacific introduced uniform measures of protection, with the Aleutian Islands about 1911 and the Commander's Islands from 1924 onwards, prohibiting the catching or shooting of otters altogether. By 1973 stocks had recovered, and there were 10,000 animals.

The authority for hunting and fishing in the American state of Alaska reported in the journal, *Das Tier* (No. 6/72), that probably between 300 and 800 otters had perished during the nuclear tests on the island of Anchitka. Thousands of turtles perished miserably during the American H. bomb experiments on the Bikini Islands, and the eggs of millions of seabirds became sterile.

Pesticides, herbicides and other poisons, too, greatly endanger game stocks, particularly fowl and small game.

Mankind carries a heavy responsibility, and should most certainly prevent radioactive rays, poison gases and bombs from continuing to endanger the life of plants, animals and men. A meeting of Uno in October 1974 confirmed a further agreement regarding worldwide prohibition of influencing negatively the natural environment and climate for military or any other purpose.

Measures for the protection of all wildlife and the environment in general, on a national as well as international scale, have gained increasing importance. Every single person is affected, and a peaceful collaboration of all countries and peoples must be a constant aim for everyone who wishes to secure a sane future.

Huntsmen bear the special responsibility for a rational hunting economy and the careful conservation of game stocks. Every true huntsman now is at one and the same time a conservationist, and should more and more become a protecor of all wildlife.

And it is not wildlife only, the whole of our cultural heritage is at stake and in need of active help and guardianship.

Future generations will want to study hunting history, for example, and we must keep in trust for them the special museums and collections, established in former hunting palaces and elsewhere. Their exhibits are witness to a tradition, still alive, to be carried on into the future.

Illustration on page 265:

241 On safari in Masailand, North Tanzania, near Naberera—dead Grant gazelle buck. 1971

242 Camping in the Tarangire National Park; ancient baobab trees provide shade for the tents.

243 Elephant herd at the watering hole.

244 The New Arusha Hotel at the old Cape Cairo Street.

245 *Sika stags, taken against the light.*

246   *Fallow buck killed in the wires of a game enclosure.*

270

247/248/249   *Modern table and coffee set, decorated
with hunting scenes by H. Werner. Meissen, 1976*

250   Herd of 2,000 sika stags in the Soviet animal-breeding co-operative "Silinski" in Primorye (southern part of the Far East; F.R.S.U.).

251   The great morte. Trumpeters of the State Forestry Estate of Mühlhausen in the Christianental near Wernigerode (Harz Mountains).

Bibliography

Game and the Hunt in Prehistoric Society

Bachofen-Echt, A., *Riesenhirsche in der Kunst*. Berlin, 1937

Bandi, H.G.; H. Breul and H. Lhote, *Die Steinzeit. 40,000 Jahre Felsbilder.* Baden-Baden, 1960

Bataille, G., *Die vorgeschichtliche Malerei. Lascaux oder die Geburt der Kunst. Die grossen Jahrhunderte der Malerei.* Geneva, 1955

Behn, F., *Die Jagd der Vorzeit. Kulturgeschichtlicher Wegweiser.* Mainz, 1922

Berger, A., *Die Jagd der Völker im Wandel der Zeiten.* Berlin, 1928

Boe, J., *Felszeichnungen im westlichen Norwegen.* Bergen, 1932

Brentjes, B., *Fels- und Höhlenbilder Afrikas.* Leipzig, 1965

Clark, G., *The Stone Age Hunters.* London, 1972

Cuval, R., *Höhlenmalerei.* Vienna, 1962

Döbler, H.F., *Jäger, Hirten, Bauern.* Gütersloh/Berlin (West)/Munich/Vienna, 1971

Eppel, A., *Stationen der alten Kunst. Im Land der Steinzeithöhlen.* Vienna/Munich, 1963

Kahlke, H.D., *Die Cervidenreste aus den altpleistozänen Ilmkiesen von Süssenborn bei Weimar.* Berlin, 1956

Kühn, H., *Die Felsbilder Europas.* Stuttgart, 1952

Kühn, H., *Eiszeitkunst. Die Geschichte ihrer Erforschungen.* Göttingen, 1965

Lamin, G.A., *Lascaux – Ursprung der Kunst.* Dresden, 1962

Leroi-Gourhan, *Préhistoire de l'art occidental.* Paris, 1965

Leroi-Gourhan, *Prähistorische Kunst. Die Ursprünge der Kunst in Europa.* 1975

Lhote, H., *Die Felsbilder der Sahara.* Würzburg/Vienna, 1958

Lindner, K., *Die Jagd der Vorzeit. Geschichte des deutschen Weidwerks.* Berlin/Leipzig, 1937

Lips, J.E., *Vom Ursprung der Dinge.* Leipzig, 1953

Mania, D., "Altpaläolithische Travertinfundstelle bei Bilzingsleben, Kreis Artern." In: *Ausgrabungen und Funde*, Berlin, 1976

Matthes, H., *Die Verbreitung der Säugetiere in der Vorzeit. Handbuch der Zoologie.* Berlin, 1962

Mirimanow, W.B., *Kunst der Urgesellschaft.* Dresden, 1973

Müller-Karpe, *Handbuch der Vorgeschichte. Die Jagd im Alt-, Mittel- und Jungpaläolithikum.* Munich, 1966

Okladnikow, O.P., *Der Hirsch mit dem goldenen Geweih. Vorgeschichtliche Felsbilder in Sibirien.* Wiesbaden, 1972

Pietsch, E., *Altamira und die Urgeschichte der chemischen Technologie.* Munich, 1963

Schmid, E., "Zur Altersstafflung von Säugetierresten und der Frage paläolithischer Jagdbeute". In: *Eiszeitalter und Gegenwart*, 1959

Sieverking, A.G., *The caves of France and Northern Spain.* London, 1962

Soergel, W., *Das Aussterben diluvialer Säugetiere und die Jagd des diluvialen Menschen*, Jena, 1922

Toepfer, V., *Tierwelt des Eiszeitalters.* Leipzig, 1963

Hunting in Antiquity

Altenmüller, H., *Darstellungen der Jagd im Alten Ägypten.* Hamburg/Berlin (West), 1967

Arrian, Flavius, "Cynegeticus oder 'Das Büchlein von der Jagd'". In: *Langenscheidts-Bibliothek*, 13th series

Bardon, F., *Diane de Poitiers et la mythe de Diane.* Paris, 1963

Bolle, F., "Ein Bild des Davidshirsches von Adloph Menzel". In: *Säugetierkdl. Mitteilungen.* 1957

Böttger, W., *Jagdmagie im alten China.* Leipzig, 1956

Böttger, W., *Die ursprünglichen Jagdmethoden der Chinesen.* Berlin, 1960

Brentjes, B., *Wild und Haustier im Alten Orient.* Berlin, 1962

Brentjes, B., *Die Haustierwerdung im Orient. Neue Brehmbücherei*, No. 344, Wittenberg, 1965

Brentjes, B., *Die Erfindung des Haustieres.* Leipzig/Jena/Berlin, 1975

Caesar, Julius, *De bello gallico.* Lib. V. Munich, 1962

Daltrop, G., *Die Kalydonische Jagd in der Antike.* Hamburg/Berlin (West), 1966

Daltrop, G., *Die Jagdmosaiken der römischen Villa bei Piazza Armerina.* Hamburg/Berlin (West), 1969

Dunkel, U., *Forscher, Fallen, Fabeltiere. David-Hirsche, der Schatz im Garten der "Verbotenen Stadt".* Stuttgart, 1954

Dutoit, J., *Jatakam. Das Buch der Erzählungen aus der frühen Existenz Buddhas.* Leipzig, 1908—1921

Erdmann, K., "Die 'Sasanidischen Jagdschalen'. Untersuchungen zur Entwicklung der Iranischen Edelmetallkunst unter den Sasaniden". In: *Jahrbuch der Preussischen Kunstsammlungen*, Berlin, 1936, Vol. 57

Erdmann, K., *Die Kunst Irans zur Zeit der Sasaniden.* Mainz, 1969

Ereszinski, W., *Löwenjagden im Alten Ägypten.* Leipzig, 1932

Fox, M., *Abbé David's Diary.* New York, 1949

Garrod, D.A.E., "The Natufian Culture: The Life and Economy of a Mesolithic People in the Near East". In: *Proceedings of the British Academy*, London, 1957

Ghirsmann, R., *Iran, Parther und Sasaniden.* Munich, 1962

Godard, A., *Die Kunst des Iran.* Berlin (West), 1964

Grousset, R., *L'Empire de steppes.* Paris, 1970

Helck, W., *Urkunden des Ägyptischen Altertums. Urkunden der 18. Dynastie.* Berlin, 1961

Helck, W., *Jagd und Wild im alten Vorderasien.* Hamburg/Berlin (West), 1968

Heck, H., "Der Milu". In: *Milu*, (Tierpark Berlin), 1970

Jankovich, M., *Pferde, Reiter, Völkerstürmer.* Munich, 1970

Kayser, B., *Jagd und Jagdrecht in Rom.* Göttingen, 1894

Keller, O., *Thiere des classischen Alterthums in culturgeschichtlicher Beziehung.* Innsbruck, 1887

Keller, O., *Die antike Tierwelt*, Leipzig, 1909, 1913

Koch, K. L., *Vom Wildtier zum Haustier*. Darmstadt, 1964

Kühnel, E., *Persische Miniaturmalereien*. Berlin, 1959

Lauchert, F., *Das Weidwerk der Römer*. Rottweil, 1848

Lips, J. E., *Fallensysteme der Naturvölker*. Leipzig, 1927

Laslo, V., *Untersuchungen zur Geschichte der Hirtenkulturen*. Berlin, 1968

Meissner, B., *Der Alte Orient. Assyrische Jagden*. Leipzig, 1911

Mellaart, J., *Chatal Hüyük—a Neolithic Town in Anatolia*. London, 1967

Miller, M., *Das Jagdwesen der alten Griechen und Römer*. Munich, 1883; reprint: Amsterdam, 1970

Overbeck, J., *Antike Jagd*. Munich, 1927

Sälzle, K., *Tier und Mensch, Gottheit und Dämon*. Munich, 1965

Schirmer, K., *Kennen die Römer ein Jagdrecht des Grundeigenthums?* Weimar, 1873

Schumacher, E., *Die letzten Paradiese*. Gütersloh, 1966

Seibert, I., *Hirt—Herde—König. Zur Herausbildung des Königtums in Mesopotamien*. Berlin, 1960

Suleiman, H., *Miniatures of Babur-Nama*. Tashkent, 1970

Trumler, E., "Vom Weidwerk im alten Asien". In: *Österreichisches Weidwerk*, Vienna, 1957

Zänkert, A., "Die Hirsche des Kaisers". In: *Das Tier*, Frankfort on the Main, 1961

Zeuner, F. E., *A History of Domesticated Animals*. London, 1963

Zimmer, H., *Mythen und Symbole in der indischen Kunst und Kultur*. Zurich, 1951

Vandier, J., *Egypte—Peintures des Tombeaux et des Temples. Collection UNESCO de l'Art Mondial*. Paris, 1954

Wiedemann, A., *Der Tierkult der alten Ägypter*. Leipzig, 1912

Wolff, M., and D. Opitz, "Jagd zu Pferde in der altorientalischen und klassischen Kunst". In: *Archiv für Orientforschung*, Berlin, 1935/36

Hunting and Game Conservation in the Middle Ages

Angilbert, *Carolus Magnus et Leo papa*. After: H. Althof, *Angilberts Leben und Dichtung*. Munich, 1888

Arcussia, C., *Falconaria, das ist eigentlicher Bericht und Anleytung, wie man mit Falcken und anderen Weydtvögeln beitzen soll*. Frankfort on the Main, 1617; facsimile edition Leipzig, 1974

Beumann. H., *Karl der Grosse, Lebenswerk und Nachleben*. Düsseldorf, 1968

Beurmann, A., *Der Aberglaube der Jäger*. Hamburg/Berlin (West), 1961

Brander, M., *Hunting and Shooting*. London, 1970; Munich, 1972

Brüll, H., *Die Beizjagd—Ein Leitfaden für die Praxis der Falknerei*. Hamburg/Berlin (West), 1968

Bucher, G., *Das Buch der Jagd*. Lucerne/Frankfort on the Main, 1973

Bujack, J. G., *Geschichte des preussischen Jagdwesens. Falkenfang nach dem Tresslerbuch*. Berlin, 1839

Demarteau, J., *Saint Hubert, sa légende, son histoire*. Liège, 1877

Dombrowski, V., *Geschichte der Beizjagd*. Volume 1: *Altdeutsches Weidwerk*. Vienna, 1886

Finbert, P. E., *La chasse française*. Paris, 1960

Fontaines-Guérin, H. de, *Trésor de Vénerie*. Paris, 1394; Metz, 1856

Fouilloux, J., *La Vénerie*. Paris, 1573; German edition: Dessau, 1727

Friedrich II, *Das Falkenbuch Friedrichs II*. Leipzig 1943, *De Arte Venandi cum Avibus (Über die Kunst mit Vögeln zu jagen)*. Complete facsimile edition. Berlin (West), 1968

Gareis, K., *Die Landgüterordnung Kaiser Karls des Grossen (Capitulare de villis vel curtis imperii)*. Berlin, 1895

Hackmann, G., *Hunting in the old world*. London/Hanover, 1948

Landau, G., *Beiträge zur Geschichte der Jagd und Falknerei in Deutschland. Jagd in Hessen*. Kassel, 1849; reprint, Kassel, 1971

Lindner, K., *Die Jagd im frühen Mittelalter*. Berlin, 1940

Lindner, K., *Bibliographische Veröffentlichungen zur Geschichte der Jagd in deutscher Sprache zwischen 1480 und 1850*. Berlin (West), 1974

Lindner, K., *Quellen und Studien zur Geschichte der Jagd*.
Vol. 2: *Die deutsche Habichtslehre. Das Beizbüchlein und seine Quellen*. Berlin (West), 1955
Vol. 7/8: *Von Falken, Hunden, Pferden. Deutsche Albertus-Magnus-Übersetzung aus der 1. Hälfte des 15. Jh*. Berlin (West), 1962
Vol. 10: *Studien zur mittelalterlichen, arabischen Falknerliteratur*. Berlin (West), 1965
Vol. 11: *Ein Ansbacher Beizbüchlein aus dem 18. Jahrhundert*. Berlin (West), 1967

Lindner, K., *Monumenta Venatoria. Jagdveröffentlichungen des 15.–18. Jahrhunderts*:
– *Das erste buch vahet also an und leret paissen und auch den habich erkennen*. Augsburg, about 1480. Facsimile edition: Hamburg/Berlin (West), 1971
– *Meysterliche stuck von Bayssen und Jagen*. Augsburg, 1531 Facsimile edition: Hamburg/Berlin (West), 1971
– *New Jägerbuch Jacoben von Fouilloux*. Strasbourg, 1590; reprint: 1972
– *Jägerkunst und Waidgeschrey*. Nuremberg, 1590, 1616; reprint: 1973
– *Die ädle Jägerei*. Weimar, 1670; reprint: 1973
Einheimisch- und ausländisch wohlredender Jäger-Rapport derer Holt-, Forst- und Jagd-Kunstwörter nach verschiedener teutscher Mundart. Regensburg, 1779; reprint: 1973
– *Neues und wohl eingerichtetes Forst-, Jagd- und Weidewercks-Lexicon*. Langensalza, 1759; reprint: 1975

Michel, E. B., *The art and practice of Hawking*. London, 1973

Mouchon, P., *Supplément à la bibliographie des ouvrages français sur la chasse de Thiebaud*. Paris, 1953

Niederwolfsgruber, F., *Kaiser Maximilian I. Jagd- und Fischereibücher*. Innsbruck, 1965

Paffrath, A., *Die Legende vom Heiligen Hubertus*. Hamburg/Berlin (West), 1961

Penzoldt, F., *Sankt Hubertus—habe Dank*. Hamburg/Berlin (West), 1961

Phoebus, Gaston, Comte de Foix, *La Chasse*. Paris, 1854

Roth, K., "Zwei Gedichte über Hofjagden aus der Zeit Karls des Grossen und Ludwigs des Frommen". In: *Forstwissenschaftliches Centralblatt*. Berlin, 1881

Röttgen, H., *Das Ambraser Hofjagdspiel*. Leipzig, 1969

Schack, G., *Der Kreis um Maximilian I*. Hamburg/Berlin (West), 1963

Schneider, J. G., *Reliqua librorum Friderici II. imperatoris de arte venandi cum avibus cum Manfredi Regis additionibus*. Vols. 1 and 2. Leipzig, 1788/89

Schwappach, A., *Handbuch der Forst- und Jagdgeschichte Deutschlands*. Berlin, 1886—1888

Schwenk, G.; G. Tilander and C. A. Willemsen, *Et multum et multa. Beiträge zur Literatur, Geschichte und Kultur der Jagd*. Festschrift für K. Lindner. Berlin (West)/New York, 1971

Souhart, R. F., *Bibliographie générale des ouvrages sur la chasse*. Paris, 1896; reprint: Leipzig, 1969

"St. Hubertus—Schutzheiliger der Metzger und Jäger". In: *Das Tier*, 1976, No. 11

Sternber, Z., *Sokolnictivi*. Prague, 1869

Stresemann, E., *Die Entwicklung der Ornithologie*. Berlin (West), 1951

Tardivus, *New Jagd- und Weydwerck-Buch*. Frankfort on the Main, 1582

Thiebaud, J., *Bibliographie des ouvrages français sur la chasse*. Paris, 1934

Uhlenhuth, H., "St. Hubert, der Schutzpatron der Jäger und seine Legende".
In: *Weidwerk in Wort und Bild*. 1905/06

Werth, H., *Altfranzösische Jagdlehrbücher nebst Handschriften. Bibliographien der abendländischen Jagdliteratur*. Halle (Saale), 1889

Wilhelm, P., *Das Jagdbuch des Gaston Phoebus*. Hamburg/Berlin (West), 1965

Wood, C. D. and F. M. Fyfe, *The Art of Falconry of Frederick II of Hohenstaufen*. Stanford University, California, 1943

Vach, M., and J. Kovařík, *Myslivecké zvyky a tradice*. Prague, 1973

Hunting and Gamekeeping under Absolutism

Amman, J., *Künstliche Wolgerissene New Figuren von allerlei Jagd- und Waidwerk*. Franfort on the Main, 1582

Baumann, F. L., *Akten zur Geschichte des deutschen Bauernkrieges aus Oberschwaben*. Freiburg i. B., 1877

Becker, U., "Feudale Jagdanlage auf dem Rieseneck bei Hummelhain".
In: *Unsere Jagd*. Berlin, 1967

Benzel, W., *Wovon Jäger heute nur noch träumen*. Hamburg/Berlin (West), 1973

Bernstein, F., *Der deutsche Schlossbau der Renaissance. 1530—1618*. Strasbourg, 1933

Brütt, E., *Fallenbau und Fallenfang*. Hanover, 1975

Buttlar, W., *Jagdprunk der Vorzeit am sächsischen Hof*. Dresden, 1907

Chenevix-Trench, C., *Schiesskunst einst und jetzt*. Munich, 1974

Colerus, J., *Oeconomia ruralis et domestica*. Nuremberg, 1605

Distel, "Enorme Beute auf den Kursächsischen Sauhatzen 1585".
In: *Der Waidmann—Blätter für Jäger und Jagdfreunde*, Berlin, 1896

Döbel, H. W., *Neueröffnete Jägerpractica oder Der wohlgeübte und erfahrene Jäger*. Leipzig, 1746; new edition: Neudamm, 1912

Dubois, E., *Chasses de France*. Paris, 1970

Duchartre, P. L., *Histoire des Armes de Chasse et de leurs emplois*. Paris, 1955

Eckhardt, K., *Das Allendorfer Jagdbuch 1467—1502*. Witzenhausen, 1968

Feldhaus, F. M., "Die ältesten Darstellungen von Jägern mit Feuergewehren".
In: *Schuss und Waffe*, 1909/10

Flecken, A., *Historische Nachrichten von dem Jagd-Palais Hubertusburg*. Leipzig, 1740

Fleming, H. F., *Der Vollkommene Teutsche Jäger*. Leipzig, 1719, 1749; reprint: Graz, 1971

Frank, H., *Das Fallenbuch. Entwicklung, Verbreitung und Gebrauch jagdlicher Fallen*. Hamburg/Berlin (West), 1975

Franz, G., *Quellen zur Geschichte des Bauernkrieges*. Munich, 1963

Genthe, F., "Die preussischen Oberjägermeister". In: *Hohenzollern-Jahrbücher*. Berlin, 1906

Grund, K., *Jagdliches Schiessen. Mit Büchsen, Flinten und Faustfeuerwaffen*. Hamburg/Berlin (West), 1976

Hagie, C. E., *The American Rifle for Hunting and Target Shooting*. New York, 1944

Hanson, C. F., *The Plains Rifle*. Pennsylvania, 1960

Hasselberg, E., *Parforcejagd im Grunewald vor 100 Jahren*. Berlin, 1933

Hayward, J. F., *Die Kunst der alten Büchsenmacher*. Vol. I: *1500 bis 1660*. Vol. II: *1660 bis 1830*. Hamburg/Berlin (West), 1968/69

Hennicke, R. C., *Handbuch des Vogelschutzes*. Magdeburg, 1912

Herzog zu Mecklenburg, C. G., *Flämische Jagdstilleben von Frans Snyders und Jan Fyt*. Hamburg, 1970

Historische Jagdwaffen aus den Beständen des ehemaligen Schwarberger Zeughauses. Eisenach/Rudolstadt, 1968

Hobusch, E., "In alten Jagdchroniken geblättert. Jagdedikte zum Schutz der Tierwelt in Deutschland". In: *Unsere Jagd*, Berlin, 1971

Holm, E., *Pieter Bruegel und Bernart van Orley*. Hamburg, 1964

Holm, E., *Die Einhornjagd auf den Teppichen der Anne de Bretagne. Spätmittelalterliche Tapisserien*. Hamburg, 1967

Horneck, H., *Jagd in der Zeit*. Graz/Stuttgart, 1975

Hörning, J., *Halali im Rokoko. Rokoko-Museum Schloss Belvedere*. Weimar, 1969

Isermeyer, C. A., *Peter Paul Rubens*. Hamburg, 1965

Jackson, H. J., *European Hand Firearms of the 16th, 17th and 18th Centuries and with a Treatise on Scottish Hand Firearms*. London, 1960

Kalmar, J., *Regi magyar fegyverek*. Budapest, 1971

Keller, E., "Die Reitjagd hinter den Hunden. Parforcejagden".
In: *Zeitschrift für Hundeforschung*, Leipzig, 1939

Knupp, C., *Jagdfriese in Renaissanceschlössern*. Hamburg, 1970

Koepert, O., *Jagdzoologisches aus Altsachsen. Beiträge zur sächsischen Jagdgeschichte*. Dresden, 1914

Kultzen, R., *Jagddarstellungen des Jan van der Straet auf Teppichen und Stichen*. Hamburg, 1970

Kumerloeve, H., "Unterlagen zur 'Schadtiere'-Bekämpfung im Braunschweiger Land. 17./19. Jh.". In: *Festschrift für K. Lindner*. Berlin (West)/New York, 1971

Lauts, J., *Jean-Baptiste Oudry*. Hamburg, 1967

Lenk, T., *Steinschloss-Feuerwaffen. Ursprung und Entwicklung*. Hamburg/Berlin (West), 1973

Lenk, W., *Dokumente aus dem Deutschen Bauernkrieg. Beschwerden, Programme, theoretische Schriften*. Leipzig, 1974

Leverkühn, "Zur Geschichte des Vogelschutzes". In: *Ornithologische Mitteilungen*, 1887

Lindner, K., *Das Jüngere Jagdbuch Wolfgang Birkners*. Leipzig, 1968

Lugs, J., *Handfeuerwaffen. Systematischer Überblick über die Handfeuerwaffen und ihre Geschichte*. Prague, 1956; Berlin, 1970

Luther, M., "Jagdpredigt". In: *Reformatorische Schriften*. Leipzig

Mager, F., *Wildbahn und Jagd Altpreussens im Wandel der geschichtlichen Jahrhunderte*. Neudamm, 1941

Meinz, M., *Jagddarstellungen auf Silbergeräten*. Hamburg, 1965

Meinz, M., *Pulverhörner und Pulverflaschen*. Hamburg/Berlin (West), 1966

Naumann, J. F., *Beleuchtung der Klage über Verminderung der Vögel in der Mitte von Deutschland*. 1849

Negri, F., *Il Fucile da Caccia*. Rome, 1968

Peterson, H. L., and R. Elman, *Berühmte Handfeuerwaffen*. Munich, 1975

Philoparchi, Germani (C. H. Schweser), *Kluger Forst- und Jagdbeamter oder juristische und praktische Anleitung, wie die Forst-, Jagd- und Wildbahngerechtsame aufs beste zu beobachten ... und das Jagd- und Forstwesen überhaupt aufrecht erhalten werden soll*. Nuremberg, 1774

Probst, G. F., *Monumenta Venatoria. Besondere Gespräche von der Par-Force-Jagd zwischen Nimrod Dem Ersten Jäger und dem Weltberühmten Huberto*. Hamburg/Berlin (West), 1973

Puschmann, *Jagd-, Forst- und Vogelschutz in Mecklenburg*. Wismar, 1908

O'Bryn, F. A., *Die Parforcejagd zu Wermsdorf (Hubertusburg) bei Dresden*. Dresden, 1879

Röhrig, F., *Das Weidwerk in Geschichte und Gegenwart*. Potsdam, 1933

Riling, R., *Guns and Shooting. A selected chronological Bibliography.*
New York/Toronto, 1951

Ridinger, J. E., *Vollkommene und gründliche Vorstellungen der vortrefflichen Fürsten-Lust oder der Edlen-Jagtbarkeit.* Augsburg, 1729

Schade, W., *Die Malerfamilie Cranach.* Dresden, 1974

Schedelmann, H., *Die grossen Büchsenmacher. Leben, Werke, Marken 15.—19. Jahrhundert.* Brunswick, 1972

Schinmeyer, K., *Handfeuerwaffen — gestern und heute.* Melsungen, 1975

Schlechtendal, V., "Nachtigallen-Schutzverordnungen von 1698".
In: *Ornithologische Mitteilungen,* 1888

Schmidt, J., *Ist die Kugel aus dem Lauf...* Munich, 1976

Schöbel, J., *Barockes Halali. Jagdwaffen und Jagdgeräte aus dem Historischen Museum der Staatlichen Kunstsammlungen Dresden.* Dresden, 1968

Schöbel, J., *Prunkwaffen und Rüstungen aus dem Historischen Museum zu Dresden.* Leipzig, 1974

Schöbel, J., and J. Karpinski, *Jagdwaffen und Jagdgeräte des Historischen Museums zu Dresden.* Berlin, 1976

Scholze, H. E., *Schloss Hubertusburg.* Leipzig, 1966

Scholz, R., *Jagdlicher Schmuck.* Hamburg, 1970

Schreyer, E., *Historische Jagdwaffen. Staatliches Museum Burg Falkenstein (Harz).* Halle (Saale), 1965

Smoler, F. X., *Historische Blicke auf das Forst- und Jagdwesen, seine Gesetzgebung und Ausbildung von der Urzeit bis zum Ende des 18. Jahrhunderts.* Prague, 1847

Spangenberg, C., *Der Jagdteuffel. Bestendiger und wohlgegründter bericht, wie fern die Jagten rechtmessig und zugelassen.* 1560; reprint: Leipzig, 1977

Sternelle, K., *Lucas Cranach d. Ä.* Hamburg, 1963

Stieglitz, C. L., *Geschichtliche Darstellung der Eigenthumsverhältnisse an Wald und Jagd in Deutschland von den ältesten Zeiten bis zur Ausbildung der Landeshoheit.* Leipzig, 1832

Stisser, F. U., *Forst und Jagdhistorie der Teutschen.* Jena, 1737

Szablowski, J., *Die flämischen Tapisserien im Wawelschloss zu Krakau— der Kunstschatz des Königs Sigismund II. August Jagello.* Antwerp, 1972

Stubbe, W., *Johann Elias Ridinger.* Hamburg, 1966

Täntzer, J., *Der Dianen Hohe und Niedere Jagdgeheimnisse.* Copenhagen, 1682

Thienemann, G. A. W., *Leben und Wirken des unvergleichlichen Thiermalers und Kupferstechers Johann Elias Ridinger mit dem ausführlichen Verzeichnis seiner Kupferstiche, Schwarzkunstblätter usw.* Leipzig, 1856

Thierbach, M., *Die geschichtliche Entwicklung der Handfeuerwaffen.* Dresden, 1886

Thierbach, M., "Die ältesten Radschlösser deutscher Sammlungen".
In: *Zeitschrift für historische Waffenkunde,* Vol. 2, 1900/1902

Waehler, M., "Die Pirschanlage auf dem Rieseneck. Ein Bild aus der thüringischen Kultur- und Jagdgeschichte des 18. Jh.". In: *Thüringen,* 1927/28

Walther, F. L., *Grundlinien der deutschen Forstgeschichte und der Geschichte der Jagd, des Vogelfangs, der wilden Fischerei und der Waldbienenzucht.* Giessen, 1816

Wäschke, H., *Parforce-Jagd in Anhalt.* Zerbst, 1913

Wendt, U., *Kultur und Jagd — ein Birschgang durch die Geschichte.* Berlin, 1907/08

Winckel, A. D., "Über die Hirsch- und Parforcejagden". In: *Handbuch für Jäger, Jagdberechtigte und Jagdliebhaber,* Leipzig, 1820—1822

Traps, Trappers and Leather Hunters

Allen, J. A., *The American Bison. Living and Existence.* New York, 1876

Berg, L. S., *Die Entdeckung von Kamtschatka und die Expedition Berings 1725—1742.* (Russian) Moscow, 1946

Berger, A., *Die Jagd aller Völker im Wandel der Zeiten.* Berlin, 1928

Bondarenko, W., *Jagd in Steppen, Wäldern und Eis. Auf Zobeljagd. Sowjetische Jäger erzählen.* Leipzig, 1969

Boyle, J. A., "An Eurasian hunting ritual". In: *Folklore,* London, 1969

Branch, E. D., *The Hunting of the Buffalo.* New York, 1929

Brass, E., *Aus dem Reich der Pelze.* Vol. I: *Geschichte des Rauchwarenhandels.* Berlin, 1925

Buchholz, E. and G., *Russlands Tierwelt und Jagd im Wandel der Zeit.* Giessen, 1963

Buchholz, E., "Die ältesten russischen und polnischen Jagdbücher".
In: *Festschrift für K. Lindner.* Berlin (West)/New York, 1971

Catlin, G., *Illustrations on the manners and customs and conditions of the North American Indians.* London, 1841

Catlin, G., *Letters and Notes on the North American Indians.* London, 1851

Cooper, J. F., *The Deerslayer.* 1841

Djoshkin, W. W., and W. G. Safonow, *Die Biber der Alten und Neuen Welt. Neue Brehmbücherei,* No. 437, Wittenberg, 1972

Dickason, O. P., Indian Arts in Canada. Ottawa, 1972

Fuller, W. A., *The biology and management of the bison of Wood Buffalo Park. Canadian Wildlife Service,* 1968

Garretson, M. S., *The American Bison.* New York, 1935

Goodwin, G. G., "Buffalo Hunt—1935". In: *Natural History,* New York, 1935

Heck, H., *Der Bison.* (Neue Brehmbücherei), No. 378, Wittenberg, 1968

Herberstein, S. von, *Moskowia.* Vienna, 1557; reprint: Weimar, 1975

Hinze, G., *Der Biber.* Berlin 1950

Jeannin, A., "Les Bisons de la grande prairie". In: *La Vie des Bêtes,* Paris, 1962

Johann, A. E., Pelzjäger, *Prärien und Präsidenten.* Berlin, 1937

Kadisch, H. H., "Der nordamerikanische Bison in Vergangenheit und Gegenwart". In: *Waidwerk in Wort und Bild,* Neudamm, 1900

Klein, J., *Der sibirische Pelzhandel und seine Bedeutung für die Eroberung Sibiriens.* Thesis, Jena, 1906

Kraschennikow, S. T., *Beschreibung des Landes Kamtschatka. Bedeutung des Zobelfanges am Fluss Witim.* (Russian) Petersburg, 1755

Kraus, O., "Hundert Jahre Naturschutz in den Vereinigten Staaten".
In: *Naturschutz und Nationalparks,* Stuttgart, 1965, No. 37

Kraus, O., "Das Beispiel Amerika". In: W. Engelhardt, *Die letzten Oasen der Tierwelt.* Innsbruck, 1977

La Fargue, O., *Die Welt der Indianer.* Berlin, 1975

Lips, E., *Das Indianerbuch.* Leipzig, 1965

Lips, J. E., *Zelte in der Wildnis.* Berlin, 1968

Lips, J. E., *Trap Systems among the Montagnais Naskapi Indians of Labrador Peninsula.* Stockholm, 1936

Mahnzier, A., "Les Bisons canadiens". In: *La Vie des Bêtes,* Paris, 1959

Nowack, E., "Ansiedlung und Ausbreitung des Marderhundes in Europa".
In: *Beiträge zur Jagd- und Wildforschung,* Berlin, 1974

Pallas, P. S., *Reisen durch verschiedene Provinzen des Russischen Reiches in den Jahren 1768—1774.* 3rd vol. St. Petersburg, 1771—1776

Pawlinin, N., *Der Zobel. Neue Brehmbücherei,* No. 363, Wittenberg, 1966

Pedersen, A., *Der Eisfuchs. Neue Brehmbücherei*, No. 235, Wittenberg, 1959

Roe, F. C., *The North American Buffalo*. Toronto, 1951

Sandoz, M., *The Buffalo Hunters. The Story of the Hide Men*. New York, 1959

Schier, B., "Wege und Formen des ältesten Pelzhandels in Europa". In: *Archiv für Pelzkunde*, Frankfort on the Main, 1951

Schleissing, G., *Neu entdecktes Sieweria, worinnen die Zobel gefangen werden, wie es anjetzo angebaut und bewohnt ist*. Danzig, 1692

Seton-Thompson, E., *Lives of game animals*. Boston, 1953

Steller, G. W., *Ausführliche Beschreibung von sonderbaren Meerthieren*. Halle (Saale), 1753

Steller, G. W., *Beschreibung von dem Lande Kamtschatka*. Frankfort on the Main/Leipzig, 1774

Streberg, F. A., *Amerikanische Jagd- und Reiseabenteuer*. Stuttgart/Augsburg, 1858

Suchender, *Neu-entdecktes Sibyria oder Sievveria, worinn die Zobel gefangen werden*. Stettin, 1690

Tanner, J., *Dreissig Jahre unter den Indianern. Nach seinen mündlichen Berichten im Jahre 1830 von Dr. E. James aufgeschrieben*. Weimar, 1968

Wallmeyer, B., *Pelztragende Tiere von A—Z*. Gütersloh/Berlin (West), 1974

Wilsson, L., *Bäver (Biber)*. Stockholm/Wiesbaden, 1966

Wilbur, S. R., *Live-trapping North American upland game birds*. Washington, 1967

Wissler, C., *Indians of the United States. Four Centuries of Their History and Culture*. New York, 1954

Ziswiler, V., *Bedrohte and ausgerottete Tiere*. Berlin (West)/Heidelberg/New York, 1968

Zverovodstvo, *Pelztierjagden in den Kolchosen der RSFSR*. (Russian) Moscow, 1955

Hunting and Game in the Nineteenth Century

Akehurst, A., *Jagdgewehr = Jagdgewehr?* Frankfort on the Main, 1969

Allen R. P., *The Whooping Crane*. New York, 1952

Anofriev, N., *Russische Jagdliteratur*. (Russian), Kiev, 1911

Aragon, L., *Das Beispiel Courbet*. Dresden, 1956

Baldwin, W. C., *African Hunting*. London, 1862

Barthold, W., *Jagdwaffenkunde*. Suhl, 1964

Beard, P. H., *Die letzte Jagd*. Lucerne/Frankfort on the Main, 1965

Bell, W. D. M., *The Wanderings of an Elephant Hunter*. London, 1923

Blackmore, H. L., *Royal Sporting-guns at Windsor*. London, 1968

Blackmore, H. L., *Hunting Weapons*. London, 1971

Bonnet, P., "Histoire et perspectives—Ménagerie et Zoo de Paris". In: *Annales des Zoos*, Paris, 1975, No. 2

Bovill, E. W., *The England of Nimrod and Surtees*. Oxford, 1959

Brunton, D., *Sportman's Guide to North East Rhodesia*. 1909

Bürger, *Wildtiere in Menschenhand*. Berlin, 1972

Calkin, V. J., *Zur Geschichte der Tierzucht und Jagd in Osteuropa*. (Russian) Moscow, 1962

Cholostow, W. G., "Hetzjagden im alten Russland". In: *Unsere Jagd*, Berlin, 1957

Churchill, R., *Das Flintenschiessen*. Hamburg/Berlin (West), 1967

Cikovsky, J., *Zur Geschichte des europäischen Wisents*. Prague, 1968

Coaten, A. W., *British Hunting*. London, 1910

Cook, J., *Observations on Fox Hunting*. London, 1826

Courbet and the Naturalistic Movement. Baltimore, 1938

Craige, J. H., *The Practical Book of American Guns*. Cleveland, 1960

Cumming, R. G. G., *Five Years of a Hunter's Life in the Far Interior of South Africa*. 1850

Deibel, G., *Von Jagden in Russland*. Zurich, 1917

Dementjew, W. J., *Grundlagen der Jagdwirtschaft*. (Russian) Moscow, 1971

Diezel, C. E., *Diezels Niederjagd*. Hamburg, 1970

Ebers, E., "Vom Schicksal der Trompeten-Kraniche". In: *Orion*, 1957

Filipscu, A., "Zimbrul". In: *Salbaticiuni din vremea stramosilor nostri*, Bucharest, 1969

Finbert, E. J., *La Chasse française. Loi du 30 avril 1790 qui abolit le droit exclusif de chasse*. Paris, 1960

Fisher, R. H., *The Russian Fur Trade 1550—1700*. Berkeley, 1943

Floessel, E., "Fürstliche und herrschaftliche Jagdveranstaltungen und deren Einfluss auf die Züchtung und Unterhaltung der Jagdhunde". In: *Der Hund — ein Beitrag zur Geschichte des Hundes*, Vienna/Leipzig, 1906

Fränden, C. A., *Tranor (Kranich)*. Stockholm, 1958

Friess, *Unsere Jagdhunde*. Munich, 1949

Genthe, F., "Das Wisent in der Kulturgeschichte". In: *Wild und Hund*, 1925

Grund, K., *Jagdliches Schiessen*. Hamburg, 1976

Grzimek, B., *Letzte Oasen der Tierwelt*. Frankfort on the Main, 1957

Hackmann, G., *Hunting in the Old World*. Hanover, 1953

Hagen, H., "Geschichte des preussischen Auers". In: *Beiträge zur Kunde Preussens*, Vol. II, 1819

Haltenorth, T., and W. Trense, *Das Grosswild der Erde und seine Trophäen*. Bonn/Munich/Vienna, 1956

Harhoorn, A. M., "Elefanten abschiessen oder nicht: was ist richtig? Elefanten als Landschaftsgärtner schwer ersetzbar". In: *Das Tier*, Frankfort on the Main, 1972

Harris, W. C., *The Wild Sports of Southern Africa*. 1839

Hastings, M., *Einführung in das Flintenschiessen*. Hamburg/Berlin (West), 1969

Hayward, J. F., *The Art of the Gunmakers. 1660—1830*. London, 1963

Heptner, V.; B. Nasimovic and B. Bannikov, *Die Säugetiere der Sowjetunion*. (Russian) Vol. 1: Moscow, 1961. Vol. 2: Moscow, 1974

Hibben, F. G., *Hunting in Africa*. New York, 1962

Hinrichs, J. C., *Entstehung, Fortgang und jetzige Beschaffenheit der russischen Jagdmusik*. Petersburg, 1796

Hippel, C. von, *Die früheren und heutigen Wildbestände der Provinz Ostpreussen*. Königsberg, 1897

Hölzel, W., *Jagdreiten — Geschichten, Vorbereitung, Praxis*. Stuttgart, 1969

Howard, R. W., *The Horse in America*. Follett, 1965

Hubbard, *Working Dogs of the World*. London, 1970

Hugi, L., *Lockende Jagd. Wild, Geschichte, Kunst, Waffen, Hunde*. Berlin (West), 1970

Jaczewski, Z., *Geschützte Wildnis. Der Urwald von Białowieża und seine Wisente*. Wittenberg, 1964

Jahn, H., "Zur Ökologie und Biologie der Vögel Japans". In: *Journal Ornith.*, 1942

Kallmeyer, R., *Die Perchino-Jagd mit Barsoi-Windhunden*. Berlin, 1921

Karcov, G., *Der Urwald von Białowiecża*. (Russian) St. Petersburg, 1903

Karstadt, G., *Lasst lustig die Hörner erschallen. Eine kleine Kulturgeschichte der Jagdmusik*. Hamburg/Berlin (West), 1964

Koch, T., *Zur Geschichte des Pferdes*. Jena, 1961

Koga, T., "On the Cranes of Japan in the Wild and in Captivity". In: *Zoologische Gärten*, New Series, Jena, 1975

Körner, A., and R. Vetter, *Wildnis der Wisente*. Leipzig, 1973

Krysing, G. C., *Bibliotheca Scriptorum Venaticorum*. Altenburg, 1750

Kuorwski, W., *Myslistwo w Polsce i Litwe*. Poznan, 1865

Kutepow, N., *Die grossfürstliche und Zarenjagd in Russland vom 10. bis 16. Jahrhundert*. (Russian) Vol. 4. St. Petersburg, 1894—1900

Lampel, W., and R. Mahrholdt, *Waffenlexikon für Jäger und Schützen*. Munich, 1975

Lampson, *The Observer's Book of Dogs*. London/New York, 1966

Lange, H., *Hege der Wildnis*. Leipzig, 1976

Laurop, C. P., *Handbuch der Forst- und Jagdwissenschaft*. 14 vols., Erfurt/Gotha, 1830

Lenz, H., *Mit dem Pferd durch die Zeiten*. Berlin, 1973

Linders, A., *Afrika aufs Korn genommen*. Hamburg, 1953

Loesch, C., *Die Jagd in Rot. Leitfaden für Reitjagden*. Hamburg, 1963

Lyell, D., *The African Elephant and its Hunters*. 1924

Makatsch, W., *Der Kranich*. Wittenberg, 1970

Makowski, H., "Japan—Land der Blumen und Kraniche". In: *Der Kleine Tierfreund*, Hamburg, 1970

Makowski, H., "Einst Farmland—Heute Nationalparks". In: *Natur und Landschaft*, 1964

Majcherczak, S., *Fünfundzwanzig Jahre sozialistisches Jagdwesen in der Polnischen Volksrepublik*. (Polish, with bibliography) Warsaw, 1969

Mickiewiz, A., "*Pan Tadeusz*" oder die letzte Fehde in Litauen. Diplomatie und Jagd. Translation by H. Buddensieg. Munich, 1963

Moorehead, A., *Was kostet schon ein Elefant?* Munich, 1961

Murray-Smith, T., *Vierzig Jahre unter afrikanischem Wild*. Hamburg/Berlin (West), 1964

Norden, W., *Jagd-Brevier — oder von der Kunst des Weidwerks*. Vienna/Berlin (West), 1970

Nulty, F., *The Whooping Crane*. London, 1966

Orlan, M. P., *Courbet*. Paris, 1951

Ostroroga, H., *Myslictwo z ogary*. Cracow, 1649, edition: Loweczu, 1842

Reille, A., *La législation de la chasse en France*. Ganshoren, 1969

Richter, J., *Jagdliches Schiessen*. Berlin, 1974

Sabaneen, L. P., *Verzeichnis von Büchern und Aufsätzen jagdlichen und zoologischen Inhalts*. (Russian) Moscow, 1883

Schack, H., *Honoré Daumier*. Hamburg, 1965

Schug, A., *Gustave Courbet*. Hamburg, 1967

Schäfer, E., *Auf einsamen Wechseln und Wegen*. Hamburg/Berlin (West), 1962

Schomburgk, H., *Fahrten und Forschungen mit Büchse und Film im unbekannten Afrika*. Berlin, 1925

Schmidt-Breitung, *Die Jagdunruhen von 1790 im Meissener Hochland*. Dresden, 1912

Schmuderer-Maretsch, M., *Jagd- und Sportwaffenkunde*. Berlin, 1928

Schumacher, E., *Die letzten Paradiese*. Gütersloh, 1966

Schulze, *Jagdhunde einst und jetzt*. Hanover, 1965

Singh, K., *Ein Mann und tausend Tiere. Erinnerungen eines indischen Jägermeisters am Hofe des Maharadschas von Gwalior und Jaipur*. Hamburg/Berlin (West), 1963

Suratteau, *La Révolution française, certitudes et controverse*. Paris, 1973

Szalay, B., *100 irrige Wisentbelege*. Neudamm, 1938

Szczepkowski, J. J., "Tysiac lat polskiego lowiectwa". In: *W Krainie lowow*, Warsaw, 1966

Tegetmeier, W. B., *The Natural History of the Cranes*. London, 1881

Thomas, B.; O. Gambert and H. Shedelmann, *Die schönsten Waffen und Rüstungen aus europäischen und amerikanischen Sammlungen*. Heidelberg/Munich, 1963

Trench, Ch. Ch., *A History of Horsemanship*. London, 1970

Ulrich, W., *Afrika einmal nicht über Kimme und Korn gesehen*. Radebeul, 1957

Urk, J. B., *Story of American Foxhunting*. London, 1940

Verschuren, J., *Sterben für die Elefanten*. Frankfort on the Main/Berlin (West)/ Vienna, 1970

Von einem Sachsen, *Schädlichkeit der Jagd*. Dresden/Leipzig, 1799

Voss, R., *Wild und Weidwerk der Welt*. Vienna, 1954

Walzoff, D., *Die Perchino-Jagd*. (Russian) St. Petersburg, 1913

Wawilow, M., *Die Jagd in Russland*. St. Petersburg, 1873

Williams, J. G., *Säugetiere und seltene Vögel in den Nationalparks Ostafrikas*. Hamburg/Berlin (West), 1971

Wurmser, A., *Daumier*. Paris, 1951

Wyler, E., *Demokratie, Freiheit, Jägertum. Schweizer Jagdschriftsteller*. Vienna (no date)

Zwilling, E. A., *Jagd und Wildschutz in Afrika*. Vienna, 1967

Zwilling, E. A., *Seltene Trophäen. Kostbarkeiten aus zwanzig afrikanischen Wanderjahren*. Hamburg/Berlin (West), 1958

Hunters and Gamekeepers of Tomorrow

Akimuschkin, J., *Vom Aussterben bedroht? Tiertragödien, vom Menschen ausgelöst*. Leipzig, 1972

Allgemeine Staatliche Jagdausstellung der ČSSR mit internationaler Beteiligung. Catalogue (Czech) Ceské Budejovice, 1976

Antonoff, G., *Wie behandle ich meine Jagdbeute*. Munich, 1975

Bakkay, L., *Goldmedaillen-Trophäen des letzten Jahrzehntes. 1960—1969*. (Hungarian) Budapest, 1971

Bannikow, A., *Saiga-Antilopen. Neue Brehmbücherei*, No. 320, Wittenberg, 1963

Beck, W. von, *Ein Jäger — zwei Seelen*. Graz/Stuttgart, 1976

Behnke, H., *Jagdbetriebslehre*. Hamburg/Berlin (West), 1975

Behnke, H., and R. Behrendt, *Jagd und Fang des Raubwildes*. Hamburg/Berlin (West), 1974

Behnke, J. and A. Hopp, *Der grosse Pirschgang*. Melsungen, 1975

Bieger, W., *Die formelmässige Bewertung der europäischen Jagdtrophäen*. Hamburg/Berlin (West), 1976

Bösener, R., "Die Geweihsammlung des Jagdschlosses Moritzburg bei Dresden". In: *Sächsische Heimatblätter*, 1972, No. 3

Bösener, R., and C. Stubbe, "Der '66-Ender' von Moritzburg". In: *Unsere Jagd*, Berlin, 1969

Bujack, J. G., Was Johann Sigismund von 1612—1619 an allerlei Wildpret geschlagen hat". In: *Preuss. Prov. Blätter*, 1839

Bulatow, G. and W. Pribitkow, "Die ersten Dekrete über die Natur und Jagd". In: *Ochota i ochtn. chozjajstwo*. (Russian) Moscow, 1967

Carson, R. L., *Der stumme Frühling*, Munich, 1964

Dementjiew, G. P., and V. S. Pokrovskij, "Über den Schutz der Jagdfauna in der SU". In: *Unsere Jagd*, Berlin, 1967

Dröscher, V. B., *Das Tier — ein unbekanntes Wesen*. Munich, 1964
Sketch for a convention for the protection of nature and culture in the world. No. 22 and 23 of the 17th session of the General Conference of UNESCO, Paris, 1972

Frevert, W., *Das jagdliche Brauchtum*. Hamburg/Berlin (West), 1969

Genthe, F., "Der 66-Ender". In: *Wild und Hund*, 1901

Genthe, F., "Jagdliche Beziehungen zwischen Preussen und Sachsen". In: *Deutsche Jäger-Zeitung*, Vol. 33

Gladkow, N. A., "Lenin und der Naturschutz". In: *Naturschutzarbeit in Mecklenburg*, Greifswald, 1970

Gossow, H., *Grundlagen der Wildökologie.* Munich, 1976

Grakov, N. N., *Die Jagd in der UdSSR.* (Russian) Moscow, 1973
  In: *Jagdinformationen des RGW. Die Jagd in den Staaten des Rates für Gegenseitige Wirtschaftshilfe.* Eberswalde, 1975

Grzimek, B., *Wildes Tier, Weisser Mann. Askania Nowa blüht weiter in der Sowjetunion.* Munich, 1965, Leipzig, 1969

Hartlapa, M., and H. III Prince of Reuss, *Wild in Gehegen — Haltung, Ernährung, Pflege, Wildnarkose.* Hamburg/Berlin (West), 1974

Heiss, L., *Askania Nova — Tierparadies in der Ukraine. Der abenteuerliche Weg der Familie Falz-Fein.* Vaduz, 1976

Henning, R., *Die Jagdtrophäe.* Hanover, 1975

Heptner, W. G., *Die Säugetiere in der Schutzwaldzone.* (Russian) Moscow, 1950; Berlin, 1956

Herczeg, A. B., *Das Weidwerk in Bildern.* Berlin, 1975

Hobusch, E., "50 Jahre Schutz der Natur in der Sowjetunion". In: *Unsere Jagd,* Berlin, 1967

Holle/Zimpel, *Das europäische Schalenwild und seine Trophäen.* Leipzig, 1975

IUCN Bulletin — New series. Morges, since 1967

Jung, E., "Jagdgesetz und Jagdwesen in der Sowjetunion". In: *Unsere Jagd,* Berlin, 1967

Köpfermann, R., *Waidwerk ist mehr als Jagd.* Munich, 1960

Krebs, H., *Schiessen oder schonen.* Munich, 1975

Krutyporoch, F. J.; W. D. Treus and P. A. Kramarenko, *Zoopark Askania Nova.* (Russian) Moscow, 1972

Lemke, K., and F. Stoy, *Jagdliches Brauchtum.* Berlin, 1971

Lettow-Vorbeck, G., von, *Das Jagdrevier—wie es sein sollte.* Hamburg/Berlin (West), 1976

Liepmann, H., *Jagen und Hegen—Hegen und Jagen.* Melsungen, 1975

Löther, R., *Zum Verhältnis Mensch und Natur und dem Problem der Umweltgestaltung. Mensch, Natur und Noosphäre.* Berlin, 1969

Mager, F., *Wildbahn und Jagd Altpreussens im Wandel der geschichtlichen Jahrhunderte.* Neudamm, 1941

Meyer, A. B., *Die Hirschgeweih-Sammlung im Königlichen Schlosse zu Moritzburg bei Dresden.* Dresden, 1883

Mirow, G., "Der 66-Ender von Biegen". In: *Heimatkunde für den Kreis Lebus,* 1915

Mohr, E., "Einiges über die Saiga". In: *Der Zoologische Garten* (New Series), Leipzig, 1943

Orban, L., *Die Goldmedaillen-Trophäen des Ungarischen Landwirtschaftsmuseums.* Budapest, 1961

Ormond, C., *The complete Book of Hunting.* New York, 1962

Papperheim, H. E., "Der Lieblingshirsch des Soldatenkönigs". In: *Wild und Hund,* 1935

Red Data Book.
— Mammals listed on the Red Data Book, 1969
— List of Birds. Morges, 1969

Rudsutak, J. E., "Begegnungen mit Lenin". In: *Unsere Jagd,* Berlin, 1971

Rue, L. L., *Sportsman's Guide to Game.* New York, 1968

Schulz, E., *Unter Giraffen und Elefanten. Im Land am Kilimandscharo.* Leipzig/Jena/Berlin, 1977

Schulze, H., *Waidgerecht.* Hanover, 1975

Seidel, P., "Der von Kurfürst Friedrich III. erlegte 66-Ender". In: *Hohenzollern-Jahrbücher,* 1903

Sludski, A. A., *Die Saiga in Kasachstan.* (Russian) Alma-Ata, 1955

Stahl, D., and H. Bibelriether, *Jagd in Deutschland. Wild und Jäger im Industrieland.* Hamburg/Berlin (West), 1971

Szederjei, A. and M., *Geheimnisse des Weltrekordes der Hirsche.* Budapest, 1972

Raesfeld, F. von, *Die Hege in der freien Wildbahn.* Hamburg/Berlin (West), 1976

Treus, W., and P. A. Kramarenkow, *Zoopark Askania Nova.* (Russian) Kiev, 1962

Ueckermann, E., *Die Wildschadenverhütung in Wald und Feld.* Hamburg/Berlin (West), 1970

Ullrich, W., *Tiere—recht verstanden. Ergebnisse und Probleme der Tierpsychologie.* Melsungen, 1975

Wagenknecht, E., *Rehwildhege mit der Büchse.* Leipzig/Radebeul, 1976

Wessel, V., *Grüner geht's nicht.* Melsungen, 1974

Sources of Illustrations

ADN Zentralbild, Berlin 36, 37, 159, 250, 251
Archeologický Ústav, Československá Akademie Ved, Brno 11
Lala Aufsberg, Sonthofen 18, 56, 88
H. Beer, Ansbach 78
Bibliothèque Nationale, Paris 83
CHAT Canada Association Humanity Trap, Toronto 154
Christa Christen, Leipzig 160, 161, 162, p. 171, p. 209, 222
Deutsche Fotothek, Dresden 13, 39, 46, 53, 89, 90, 122, 123, 133, 134, 170, 222, 225, 226, 228, p. 77, p. 122, p. 145, p. 148
Deutsche Staatsbibliothek, Berlin 131
Deutsches Jagdmuseum, Munich 69, 101
DEWAG Dresden 114, 208, 209, 210
DPA, Frankfort on the Main 62, 180, 186, 187
Josef Ehm, Prague 120
Engel, Berlin p. 52
Foto Ewald, Berlin 171, p. 116, p. 170, p. 195
Günter Ewald, Stralsund 151, 152
Giraudon Paris 99, 173
Werner Grundmann, Oberstdorf 12
Claus Hansmann, Munich 7, 20, 25, 27, 28, 32, 33, 44, 59, 60, 67, 68, 82, 84, 85, 108, 118, 126, 130, 141, 156, 168, 169, 174, 207, p. 76, p. 114, p. 168
Joachim Haupt, Berlin 34
Hirmer Fotoarchiv, Munich 45
Information Service, Kenya 237
Jürgen Karpinski, Dresden 50, 51, 96, 97, 109, 110, 115, 116, 117, 119, 211, p. 104
Kunsthistorisches Museum, Vienna 58
Kupferstichkabinett, Basle 107
Harald Lange, Leipzig 242, 243, 244
Mährisches Museum, Brno 9
Henry Makowski, Hamburg 201, 205
Klaus M. Moerl, Berlin 218, 232
Karl-Heinz Moll, Waren 246
Ann Münchow, Aachen 57, 61
Museum für Völkerkunde, Leipzig 38, 149, 150, 164, 165, 166, 167, p. 178, p. 179, p. 180

Museum of the Polish Hunting Association, Warsaw/Ryba 219, 220
National Collection of Fine Arts, Smithsonian Institution, Washington 157
National Museum, Warsaw 182, 183, 191
NOWOSTI, Berlin 4, 73, 158, 181, 195, 212, 213, 216, 217
Pinguin-Verlag, Innsbruck 86, 95
Archives of Edition Leipzig 55, 93, 94, 112, 202, p. 13, 224, 225
Wlodzimierz Puchalski, Cracow 1, 163, 193, 204
Rijksmuseum van Natuurlijke Historie, Leiden 72
Herbert Rost, Darmstadt 138, 142
SCALA, Florence 8, 19, 41, 42, 49, 54, 66, 75, 77, 98, 121, 125, 127, 135, 136, 175, 203
Schatzkammer der Residenz, Munich 64
Horst Schröder, Stralsund 5, 246
Eckhard Schulz, Burg 198, 233, 234, 235, 236, 238, 239, 240, 241
Staatliche Galerie, Dessau 172
Staatliche Kunstsammlungen Greiz, Kupferstichkabinett p. 79
Staatliche Museen, Berlin 14, 15, 16, 17, 21, 22, 23, 24, 26, 30, 31, 35, 47, 48, 52, 70, 71, 76, 81, 102, 103, 104, 105, 111, 132, 139, 140, 176, 177, 178, 179, 184, 196, 206, p. 101
Staatliche Museen, Dessau, Mosigkau Castle 40
Staatliche Museen, Stiftung Preussischer Kulturbesitz (Foto Archives) Berlin (West) 128, 185, p. 196
Staatliche Porzellan-Manufaktur, Meissen 247, 248, 249
Staatliche Schlösser und Gärten, Jagdschloss Grunewald, Berlin (West) 63, 113, 129, 137, 143, 153
Staatliches Museum, Schwerin 124, 189, 192
Státni Ústav Památkové Pece a Ockrany Přírody, Prague 106, 199, 223
Asmus Steuerlein, Dresden 2, 80, 91, 92, 144, 145, 146, 147, 221, 224
Tierbilder Okapia, Frankfort on the Main 214, 215
United States Department of the Interior, National Park Service, Washington 155
Verlag der Kunst, Dresden 3, 10, 43, 65, 79, 100
Weidenfeld & Nicolson, London 87
World Wildlife Fund, Morges/Peter Balley 197
Zentrales Haus der Deutsch-Sowjetischen Freundschaft, Berlin 148